RUSSIA IN THE TWENTIETH CENTURY:

The View of a Soviet Historian

RUSSIA

Translated from the Russian by David Windheim

N THE TWENTIETH CENTURY:

The View of a Soviet Historian

by

ALBERT P. NENAROKOV

With Forewords by Cosmonaut Herman Titov *and*
Georgi Isachenko, *Editor of* SOVIET LIFE

William Morrow & Company, Inc. *New York* 1968

Foreword

With this brief introduction, I should like to express my opinion about the publication of a work by a Soviet historian in the U.S.A.

Today not a single nation striving for progress can fence itself off from the rest of the world and take no interest in how other nations live or what they strive for. Contacts between countries promote mutual understanding and trust so necessary for a normal, peaceful and happy life on earth. I am deeply convinced that no matter how great the differences in political outlook or religious beliefs may be, all disputes between states, near and far, in this age of rocketry and atomic energy, must be settled by peaceful means. For we are all living on the same planet.

What I have just said doubly applies to the Soviet Union and the United States on whose relations the destiny of the world largely depends.

Soviet people have always been interested in learning more about the United States. I am sure that this interest, the desire to know and understand the other, is mutual. At least, that is the impression I got during my visit to America in the spring of 1962. That is why I warmly approve the undertaking of William Morrow Publishers.

Although the book spans a considerable period of time (from the early twentieth century up to last summer's events), it is actually devoted to one event: to the revolution that took place, or rather began, on the night of October 25 (November 7, old calendar), 1917, in one of the world's most beautiful cities now called Leningrad after Lenin, the great leader of the Revolution. The book explains what prompted the Russians and other peoples who inhabited the Russian Empire to make a revolution, known in history as the Great October Socialist Revolution. The book also tells how half a century ago the Soviet peoples, in the face of tremendous difficulties and with selfless, dedicated effort, pulled their country out of the mire of age-old backwardness and are now marching confidently along the road of progress towards a new society, a society of social justice and happiness for all.

I am certain that after reading the history of the Soviet land you will understand better the genuine aims and aspirations of our people; you will see that they sincerely desire peace and friendship with other nations. And so from the bottom of my heart I wish all success to the book and recommend it to the American reader.

Herman Titov

Foreword

Albert Nenarokov's *Russia in the 20th Century* is very rich in factual material and the reader, who would wish to understand the historical events in Russia in all their diversity will find much useful information in this book.

Hardly anyone today would undertake to question the achievements of the Soviet people in the fields of economy, culture, science and technology.

In many respects Russian people were and still are treading unknown paths; they are discoverers in the full sense of the word. The Americans, who were also pioneers in many fields of human endeavor, know full well how hard it is to be "the first."

The difficulties which Soviet people had to overcome were tremendous, indeed. Even those whose attitude towards the Soviet people was most loyal, sincerely believed that it was beyond human power to surmount all those difficulties.

Interesting evidence of the impression Soviet Russia of the twenties produced on foreigners was left by the great English science-fiction writer H. G. Wells.

Those were very trying years for the Soviet country. Russia, weakened as it was, had barely managed to scramble out of the trenches of World War I, when it found itself in the clutches of a more cruel and devastating Civil War, followed by the intervention of fourteen states. The country lacked the most vital things—food, clothes, transportation facilities, equipment and raw materials. Unheard-of economic dislocation reigned supreme. Factories and plants stood idle; there was no fuel for locomotives and rails turned rusty.

The population of big cities got their meager *osmushka* of bread (one-eighth of a pound). This situation was worsened by an all-time low in the yield of bread in the Volga area. The soldiers lacked clothes and rifles, not to mention tanks or planes, for those were non-existent in the army.

Such was, in short, the situation when H. G. Wells came to Russia in the twenties. His visit resulted in a book, *Russia in the Shadows,* an excerpt from which is cited by Albert Nenarokov. H. G. Wells gave a vivid and quite accurate picture of Russia. However if you re-read *Russia in the Shadows* you will not find an answer to the question which any thinking person is sure to pose: how could a poverty-stricken, hungry and illiterate country, with soldiers barefoot and unarmed, emerge victorious from the death struggle and create, in the shortest possible time, a new, powerful state and manage to advance to one of the world's first places in the fields of economy, culture and science?

The fact is that H. G. Wells failed to notice one of the major features of the Soviet people: their revolutionary enthusiasm and their creative powers. The author of *The Time-Machine* and *The Invisible Man,* the man with the boldest of imaginations, the one who predicted the A-bomb, failed to believe in quite earthly things—Lenin's daring plan of electrification of Russia. Wells called Lenin "the dreamer in the Kremlin," and the plan itself—"superfantasy." It might be the result of a depressing image of Russia at the time.

Lenin was looking far ahead into the future and there is no need to mention that his daring plan has long since become a reality and has been fulfilled many times over. It is precisely the Soviet people's revolutionary enthusiasm and their tremendous creative powers that are a pledge of the Soviet country's further progress.

I sincerely hope that American readers will find this book interesting and useful, and that they will learn many new things about the Soviet Union and its people. I believe it will help the American people to understand us better. If it does, then the author of *Russia in the Twentieth Century* has accomplished his goal.

Georgi Isachenko, EDITOR, *Soviet Life*

CONTENTS

ILLUSTRATIONS APPEAR BETWEEN PAGES 86–87; 150–151; 214–215

PART I

RUSSIA:

PARIS 1900

1 OFFICIAL RUSSIA

On April 15, 1900, a Sunday, the Eleventh World Exposition opened in Paris and its purpose, as proclaimed by the French government in a Presidential Decree dated July 13, 1892, was to show culture and progress as they stood at the end of the nineteenth century.

Although the official opening of the Exposition had been set for two o'clock, lines of carriages from all parts of the large city began converging in the early morning on the area in which it was to be held. All public buildings and most private homes were decked out with flags. The fine weather and the colorful spectacle brought large crowds into the streets of the city. Towards one o'clock in the afternoon, the congestion of carriages was so great, even at a considerable distance from the main entrance, that most of the arrivals had to make their way on foot through the dense crowd.

President of the French Republic Loubet emerged from the Elysée Palace at 1:45 P.M., in a state carriage followed by four coaches conveying members of the government. The procession was escorted by an impressive body of cuirassiers. Loubet was in tails and decorated with the ribbon of the Legion of Honor.

At the entrance to the Festival Hall in the *Champs de Mars* he was met by the Minister of Commerce and Industry, Alexandre Millerand, the Commissioner-General of the Exposition, Alfred Picard, and the higher officials of the administration of the Exposition. Loubet was greeted by the officials, the ambassadors and commissioners of foreign countries, and the representatives of the press. The orchestra struck up the *Marseillaise*.

Millerand and Loubet delivered brief speeches. Then the President of the French Republic announced that the World Exposition was officially open.

At the invitation of France, a total of fifty states participated in the Paris World Exposition of 1900. It included the arts, industry and agriculture. Russia, with her 2,500 exhibits, was hardly at the tail end of it all.

The Russian Section of the Paris Exposition. The Russian, or rather the Siberian pavilion, as it was dubbed by the French, was situated near the Trocadero Palace. The structure that housed it was designed to resemble the Kremlin. Situated as it was to good advantage on the rise of the Trocadero Palace, it loomed larger than it was in actual fact.

Through the pavilion's main entrance the public poured into the hallway. Visitors were not allowed into the room that opened from it. This room, an enormous hall with a vaulted ceiling, reminiscent of the Granite Chamber of the Kremlin in Moscow, was the so-called Chamber of the Tsar, set aside for the imperial family and for the reception of guests of honor. One's first acquaintance with Russia was made here.

Next, visitors came upon a vast courtyard. In the left corner loomed a rotunda that served as a stage for concerts, and standing close by were small tables of the tavern variety decked with white tablecloths. In this "restaurant of the Siberian Railroad" as the French chose to call it, the waiters were dressed in white, *à la* Moscow. The restaurant's *spécialités de la maison* were a pink kvass* and a golden-hued beer.

On the right side of the courtyard a teahouse *à la* Tashkent snuggled cozily swathed in a mound of carpets and rugs.

Situated between the crenellated wall of the main pavilion and a wing of the Trocadero Palace, the other buildings of the Russian section formed a miniature town or a so-called Russian village.

In a simple, crude lean-to of a very coarse and unfinished variety, one could see a display of handicraft wares, such as an assortment of harnesses, blinkers, bits, stirrups, spurs, saddles, wheels of bare iron or shod with wood, sleighs and many other objects tooled with artistic skill by outstanding Russian craftsmen. There was also what the French tagged an *isba russe*, that is, a Russian peasant hut; but in fact it did not come anywhere near the original. One could also find there a large collection of feminine handicrafts, particularly embroideries, along with every sort of household utensil and furniture as well as a profusion of trifles produced by craftsmen, such as tooled chests, carved objects made of a single piece of wood, candlesticks, cups, and the like.

One also could not help noticing a small wooden church constructed in the style of the ancient Russian churches, a miniature of the churches typically found in the Russian far north. All of the church plates were patterned after the ancient originals and the icons were uncommonly deft replicas of the ancient images which are so greatly prized by devotees of antiquity.

A replica of a tower chamber of the type common in the sixteenth or seventeenth century on boyar estates could be seen nearer to the principal avenue. Here one could also find a collection of the carved wooden furniture and opulent appointments of the affluent gentry of old Moscow. The attire of

---

*Kvass: A beverage made of fermented cereals, raisins, etc.

two feminine wax figures reproduced with a high regard to authenticity the manner of dress of the wives of the Moscow nobility in old Russia. One of the figures represented a lady who had settled herself behind an embroidery frame, and was getting down to work in earnest. Also to be found here was a large collection of women's headdresses, sent to Paris by Natalya Shabelskaya.

Separate accommodations were made available for the collections of the Land Curatorship* and holding the center of this exhibit was a stuffed European bison of the Belovezhsk Forest in full splendor. Farther along in the principal building were housed the exhibits of Central Asia, the Caucasus and the Far North.

What exhibits, one might ask, represented the Far North, which was at the time unknown and incomprehensible to many? Hanging all around the room were furs—one of the principal gifts of the North. Here, of course, were on display the finer specimens of sable, beaver and sealskins from the Komandorskie Islands. An enormous canvas by Konstantin Korovin on one of the walls of the chamber depicted a colony of wild animals. Stuffed white bears, wolves and Eskimo huskies completed the motley décor of this set of exhibits, which transported viewers into a mysterious land of eternal ice and frost that would remain unattainable to them.

In the central hall of the pavilion, two figures dressed in the national costume of mountaineers were posted at the entrance to the Caucasian section. These mannequins invited visitors to examine photos and paintings by Korovin and Baron Klodt, who depicted the people and nature of the Caucasus. The entire collection of exhibits representing the Caucasus, which was allotted quarters entirely too small, had been assembled by Professor Gustav Radde, curator of the Caucasian Museum and the Tiflis Public Library.

---

* The Land Curatorship managed the land that belonged to the tsar's family.

French periodicals spoke with high praise of the expertness of the professor's selection, and referred to it as "a sheer marvel of method and classification." There was a great deal here that afforded knowledge of this most interesting territory, its dwellings, clothes, household utensils, fabrics, musical instruments, ornaments, weapons, stuffed birds and animals, varieties of fruit, wines and vegetation.

Hanging on the wall in the Central Asian exhibit was another painting by Konstantin Korovin. "Korovin and the Emir of Bukhara," noted a reviewer of *Illustration*, "are the principal heroes of that chamber." Korovin depicted Asia in his enormous canvas, while the Emir furnished the most interesting exhibits for the Exposition; he even dispatched to Paris two of his representatives, Colonel Zyunnetdin Toksabi and Captain Mirza-Malek-Karaul-Bek. The Emir's personal collection was in a large showcase. It comprised beautiful clothes in fabrics finely woven of golden yarn, sumptuous horse trappings, ornaments and embroideries, with which one of the French reviewers was so taken that, overwhelmed by their meticulous refinement, he gasped out a compliment, calling them "stupendous." Flanking the showcase was an ottoman, which the aforementioned representatives of the Emir frequently preempted with their own stateliness as they draped about them their oriental robes.

Mindful of the fact that the purpose of the Exposition was to show how far man had progressed in the nineteenth century, the reviewers sought to take advantage of the stay in Paris of the emissaries of the Bukhara Emir. The following story made the rounds in this connection: It appeared that some twenty years prior to the Exposition, someone answering to the name of Mozer (Commissioner for Bosnia and Herzegovina at the Paris Exposition of 1900) had been traveling through Central Asia. While on his journey, he visited Bukhara, met the Emir and had the honor of a chat with him. As they were conversing, the Emir unrolled before him a map, and wonder of wonders, right there in the middle, believe it or not, lay Bukhara, the hub and helm of the world! Sweeping around it was an utter wilderness, fringed by China, the Land of the White Tsar, India belonging to the Inglizi (the English) and skirting the map, Frengistan, which is to say the land of the French. The point of the story was as follows: The Bukharans knew nothing of this country a few decades ago, and now they had sent over here to the capital of this same France the priceless gems of their Emir, along with their emissaries. "How much water has flowed over the dam during these decades!" exclaimed the journalists and a pall of silence fell as they considered what it actually cost the Asian khanates to "join the progress of tsarist Russia."

The Russian pavilion, dubbed the "Trocadero Kremlin," contained everything related to the construction of the Trans-Siberian railroad line running across Central Asia. Besides a profusion of maps, charts and photos there was a panoramic view, by P. Y. Piasetsky, showing the Siberian railroad track on a long paper streamer. The International Steel Car Company exhibited the cars in which the long and weary journey was then made over the Moscow-Tomsk line, and from there on to Irkutsk. It was so arranged that if a person took a seat in one of the railway cars there on display, he was able to view through the window the shifting scenes along the route as though he were actually making the trip.

Many of the official Russian pavilions at the Paris Exposition could be identified by their distinctive style and by the double-headed eagles mounted on their roofs and turrets. The Russian Empire had a separate pavilion devoted to forestry and hunting, and one for military affairs and the liquor monopoly; there was also a pavilion showing the institutions sponsored by the Empress Maria (state charitable organizations), a pavilion given over to meteorology, another to flour milling, and lastly a pavilion for Finland, which was then part of Russia.

A huge pavilion devoted to the Russian-American rubber industry received from the French the sobriquet, "The Galoshes Pavilion." It stood behind the building that housed the section devoted to the building arts, alongside the pavilion touting Bavarian beer. Off in the distance an enormous heap of galoshes rose in the very center of the pavilion, standing out boldly as a black patch against the bright background of the structures ranging across the *Champs de Mars*. This veritable mountain of galoshes, 35,000 pairs in all, represented the output of a twenty-four-hour day's work at the Russian-American plant. There was nothing like it in the world, in terms of output. At the Paris Exposition the diversity of the plant's exhibits was quite considerable. It gave a dioramic view of the different steps in the cultivation of rubber trees, the technique employed in the extraction of rubber and the manner in which it was processed. A special scale model afforded visitors to the pavilion a view of the entire little urban community in Petrograd, on the Obvodnoy Canal, which sheltered the factory complex. Figures accompanying the exhibit disclosed the fact that it had 253 management personnel, 2,500 male workers and a nearly equal number of women workers; that to run the machinery the factory required five thousand horsepower, and that if the buildings of the little urban community were all to be reduced to a single story and strung out in a single line, they would stretch over a distance of some seven versts.* However, these were mere figures, which indicated nothing about those who produced this mound of 35,000 pairs of galoshes in the course of a twenty-four-hour day, or about those who went about shod in them.

Of the different exhibits, according to the official reports, the work of the Bureau of State Documents drew the most enthusiastic attention. The Bureau had an enormous showcase built for the Exposition, in which it presented its history from its inception, commencing with the earliest decrees of 1762 ordering the replacement of copper coin with banknotes. Also on display was a collection of actual documents that the Bu-

---

* Verst: A measure of length equal to about two-thirds of a mile.

reau had issued, and here one could find specimens of securities, such as stock certificates or debentures, along with specimens of artistic duplication, which the Bureau produced by all conceivable techniques in its graphic shops, custom-produced illustrated editions and galvanoplastic reproductions of examples of the fine and industrial arts.

In the exhibit devoted to railroads equipment used in dealing with snowdrifts drew particular attention. In the manufacturing section one was struck by the dimensions of Russia's cotton textile industry and its output, which was valued at some 250-million rubles annually.

Platinum stood out in the empire's mining and metallurgical displays. Russia produced 97 per cent of the world's output of this metal. Richly represented at the Exposition were the mineral treasures and the coal of the Donets region.

The pavilion devoted to military subjects displayed the aerostat "Vive la France," which had made its first flight at Krasnoye Selo when President Felix Faure was on a visit to Russia in 1897.

The effort that was being expended here to stress the ties of friendship and sympathy between the Russian Empire and the French Republic was evident everywhere. On the occasion of the opening of the Exposition, Millerand received a cable from Witte, Russian Minister of Finance. It spoke of the mutual esteem and support that prevailed between Russia and France, and expressed gratitude to the French Minister for his cooperation in the establishment of the Russian section of the Exposition. On the day of the official opening of the Exposition, French President Loubet congratulated the Commissioner-General of the Russian section, Prince Vyacheslav Tenishchev, Vice-Chairman of the Commission on Russian Participation in the Paris World Exposition established by his Imperial Majesty, a member of the Chamber of Commerce and Manufacture and a Councillor of State. The President announced that he would personally visit all of the Russian pavilions at the Exposition.

In one of the buildings of the Place des Invalides, the Russian Ambassador, Prince Urusov, presented President Loubet with a personal gift from Emperor Nicholas II. It was a map of France made at Ekaterinburg of precious stones from the Urals. The map was in the form of a square with sides of forty-two inches, framed in gray jasper. The waters surrounding France were an inlay of bright-hued marble, and each of the departments of the country was represented by jasper of a different color. The map showed 105 cities; Paris itself was marked by a large ruby, while Le Havre was studded with an emerald, Rouen with a sapphire, Lille with flakite, Rheims with chrysolite, Lyon with tourmaline, Nantes with beryl, Bordeaux with aquamarine, Marseilles with emerald, Nice with hyacinth, Cherbourg with alexandrite and Toulon with chrysoberyl. The other cities were studded with amethysts, tourmalines and rock crystal. The names of the cities were in gold and the rivers shown by platinum lines flowing through jasper.

The French press paid a good deal of attention to the Russian section of the Exposition, and so did the officialdom of France. *L'Evénement* compared Russia as it appeared at the Exposition with the Russia that had participated in the 1867 Exposition, and called attention to its enormous progress. *La Liberté* gave a detailed description of the Russian section, declaring that a close scrutiny of the wealth assembled in it afforded visitors an accurate picture of the new industrial power, and of the empire which but a few years earlier had been unable to make a show of anything save its raw materials. Today, however, insisted the newspaper, it was on a par with the most civilized nations. All of these exchanges of presents and praises were no mere matter of chance.

The sharpening of international tensions at the end of the nineteenth and the beginning of the twentieth centuries had led to the emergence in Europe of two military and political camps facing each other. Germany, whose influence in Europe after the defeat of France in 1871 had advanced considerably, concluded an alliance in 1879 with the Austro-Hungarian monarchy, which was joined in 1882 by Italy, giving a start to the establishment of the Triple Alliance. The earliest response to the establishment of the aggressive bloc headed by Germany was the Franco-Russian Alliance of 1891–1893. This is in fact what accounted for the mutual courtesies and the round of festivities scheduled for the inauguration of the Paris Exposition, as well as the praise showered by the French press on the Russian exhibit, whose object first and foremost was to highlight the strength and unshakable stability of the Russian autocracy.

Autocracy plus Orthodoxy. The beginning of the Exposition coincided with the opening of two landmarks named after Russian emperors; a new street starting at the Champs Elysées, which was christened Nicholas II Street, and a new bridge across the Seine, which was to bear the name of Emperor Alexander III.

The solemn cornerstone ceremony, as the French and Russian papers of the day reminisced, had taken place in October 1896 in the presence of Emperor Nicholas II and Empress Alexandra Fyodorovna. The name of the new street was officially adopted in a decree issued by the President of France dated October 5, 1896.

The cornerstone of the bridge was laid in a grandiose ceremony. A piece of French granite of a bluish hue had been prepared for the occasion. Noted French jewellers fashioned the shovels and hammers called for as part of the ceremony. The shovel and hammer intended for Nicholas II were the handiwork of the great French master Falise. The gold shovel weighed 750 grams and consisted of three parts—a rectangular board, a rod and a handle. Engraved on the handle was the emblem of Paris, the symbolic ship and the lily skirted at the lower end by an olive branch with the inscription *Sequana*, which was in ancient times the name of the Seine. Engraved on the face of the shovel was the following inscription: "On 7 October 1896, His Majesty, Nicholas II, the Emperor of All the Russias, Her Majesty, the Empress Alexandra Fyodorovna and Felix Faure, President of the French Republic, laid the cornerstone of the Alexander III Bridge, in the presence of Méline, Chairman of the Council of Ministers, Henri Boucher, Minister of Commerce and Industry, and Alfred Picard, Commissioner-General of the 1900 World Exposition."

The hefts of the hammers were of ivory and just over one foot in length. The hammers proper, which were of polished steel, had damascened on the sides the words *Pax* (peace) and *Robur* (strength). The hammers were joined to the hefts by means of golden chased fish-plates with the initials *RF* (*République Française*). The hammer that was to be used by the Russian Emperor displayed the initial *N* and the other hammer displayed the initial *F* designating the name of the President of France, Faure.

A gold penholder in the form of a stalk of sugarcane with foliage was also at hand for the solemn act of signing the protocol of the occasion. The protocol, when signed, was placed in a special case, which was in turn sealed up in a niche hollowed out in the cornerstone. Russian and French coins minted in 1896 also went into the case.

A mere few months separated this celebration held amidst such pomp from an even more gala celebration, the coronation of the Russian tsar. It took place in May 1896 and revealed the true relationship between the autocrat and the people.

As a general rule, following the coronation the tsar gave an enormous outdoor fête where presents of all kinds were distributed, the people being fed and entertained on behalf of the emperor.

Dressed in their Sunday best, people began gathering on the Khodynskoye Field at noon on May 17 although the fête was scheduled for the 18th. By nine o'clock in the evening the crowd "had grown to considerable proportions" and by one o'clock in the morning of May 18 it numbered from 400,000 to 500,000.*

---

* The description of the Khodynskoye catastrophe has been taken from

By five o'clock in the morning "a thick mist floated above the people, making it impossible to distinguish one face from another at close range. Even those in the front rows were drenched in perspiration, and looked fatigued." From the crowd "came continuously agonized screams and wailing while the atmosphere was so heavily charged with fumes that people were gasping for lack of air and suffocating with the stench." The crush of the crowd grew more menacing and people began to faint. "They pushed such people out of the crowd and they were hurtled down around the buffets, whereupon the soldiers yanked them out and brought them to. . . . Moreover, the crowd lifted the unconscious individuals above their heads and rolled them with upraised hands to the buffets where the soldiers could reach them." Children as well "were tumbled about the heads of the crowd to reach an open space." Even before the handing out of the presents had gotten under way, many people who had grown faint and become unconscious were trampled to death and tossed overhead by the crowd, but because of the crush of the crowd, they continued to be swept along in an upright position until it was possible to pull them out. Aghast with horror, people tried to shy away from the corpses, but all in vain and the stampede grew further. As a result, when the doling out of presents began and the crowd veered to the aisles between the buffets, the corpses caught in the vise of the crowd veered along with it until they tumbled onto the grounds of the fête. One of the eyewitnesses counted some twenty of these corpses.

The distribution of the presents began towards six o'clock. They consisted of a loaf of bread and a small parcel made up of sausage, cake, candy, an enameled mug and a program of the entertainment. A terrible stampede was unleashed. "Those who managed to reach the square leaped out of the aisles tattered, drenched and wild-eyed. Many of them

---

a special report by the Minister of Justice, N. V. Muravyov, who was in charge of the investigation of these tragic events. Everything in quotes is the actual testimony given by Muravyov.

dropped with a groan, while others stretched out on the ground, propping their heads on the parcels handed them, and died." The crowd stepped over the corpses. "One of the victims who managed to survive was found to be resting on fifteen corpses, and ten bodies were on top of him." The first batch of the tsar's presents had been distributed and the crush was somewhat relieved. Then the second round of handouts began, and again the same thing happened.

"According to the facts uncovered by the investigation, the number of people who suffered injury on May 18 on the occasion of the festivities on the Khodynskoye Field came to 2,690, and the number of fatalities was 1,389."

Notwithstanding this immense catastrophe, the coronation celebrations were not called off. This was mentioned in the memoirs of Count S. Witte, who reported that in the evening of the same day a ball was held at the quarters of the French Ambassador, Count Montebello. The young tsar danced the first dance with Countess Montebello and the young Empress danced with the French Ambassador. "Many urged the sovereign not to go to the ball and to put off the festivities," writes Witte, "but he would not listen: in his opinion 'what happened was a great calamity but a calamity which must not be allowed to cast a pall over the coronation festival; one must put out of one's mind the Khodynskoye catastrophe on that account.'"

And they did in fact put it out of mind. They also put out of mind "the flimsy fantasies and the contemptible liberalism" of the bourgeois reforms of the sixties and seventies, and bolstered the rights of the government, ensuring financial support to the estates of the nobles; placing all police and judicial powers over the peasants and their self-government in the hands of the Zemstvo or District Council heads, who were from among the landowners; decreeing that "the children of coachmen, valets, cooks, laundresses and petty officials" should not be admitted into secondary schools. They put it so much out of mind that four years later hardly anyone had the audacity to mention it. In 1900, the coronation robes of the imperial couple were among the exhibits at the World Exposition in Paris.

It was not by mere chance that Nicholas II Street in Paris, which was opened in solemn ceremony by the President of France on the first day of the World Exposition, ran beyond the Alexander III Bridge. It symbolized continuity and attested to the undeviating course of both the domestic and the foreign policy of the new tsar.

When receiving a delegation of members of the local elective district councils, or Zemstvos, established after the reforms of the sixties, Nicholas II declared: "Some members of the district assemblies have allowed themselves to be deluded by irrational fantasies concerning the participation of representatives of the Zemstvos in the government of the country. Let them all know that I will uphold the principles of autocracy just as steadfastly as they were upheld by my father of blessed and unforgettable memory." The Emperor of All the Russias, Nicholas II, was an ardent advocate of the inalienability of autocracy and orthodoxy. Is there any wonder that when, after his round of viewing the Russian sections of the Exposition, the President of France attended services held on the inner grounds at the "Trocadero Kremlin," the Dean of the embassy church, Archpriest Iakov Smirnov, addressed the assemblage as follows:

. . . The Kremlin and the Tsar's pavilion and the cross in their foundation, put in with the firm hope that blessings will descend from above on the work which has just been completed, are in fact the central theme of our celebration today. Scattered throughout this vast emporium of worldwide competition that has been inaugurated here [in Paris], in this center of the world's life, in this country of a people so dedicated to us in friendship, in a new World Exposition, among exhibits manifesting the attainments of man's labor, talents and energies, are the products of Russia, which wherever they appear can be understood only if associated in our minds with the invisible but indissoluble sponsorship of the Kremlin and the double-headed Russian eagle.

"Orthodoxy, autocracy and the spirit of nationalism," these are what the tsarist government would have the people accept as an antidote to revolutionary and progressive ideas and theories. This theory of official nationalism had been formulated by Prince S. Uvarov in those distant days when he held office as Minister of Education under Nicholas I. It rested on the contention that the people of Russia were religious, faithful to the tsar from time immemorial and that they found nothing abnormal in their position.

Dispensing his patronage to the church in every way, Nicholas could rely on it as a faithful buttress of the autocracy. Stressing the firm roots of his unlimited powers at the time of the first Russian census of 1897, he furnished the following information on the census form:

FAMILY NAME: *Romanov, N. A.*
ESTATE: *Emperor of All the Russias*
CHIEF OCCUPATION: *Proprietor of the Russian land*
SECONDARY OCCUPATION: *Landowner*

His spouse, who was a German princess, wrote in a similar vein:

FAMILY NAME: *Romanova, Alexandra Fyodorovna*
NATIVE LANGUAGE: *German*
CHIEF OCCUPATION: *Proprietor of the Russian land*

So far as the third ingredient of the Uvarov formula is concerned, the tsar promptly laid to rest all misgivings of those who entertained any doubts as to the stability of his position. He demanded that any revolutionary movement be met with suppression by torture and the firing squad. When a suppressor of one of the uprisings reported to the tsar that only a few people had been killed, the tsar replied with a show of dissatisfaction: "Not enough blood, General!"

In Russia one had to have peace and quiet.

The Chief Exhibitors. One might ask, who actually represented Russia at the Paris Exposition? Who were its principal exhibitors? It would be difficult to make the account comprehensive and we will confine ourselves to no more than a few of the exhibitors, taking them at random, although undoubtedly the biographies and activities of all whose merchandise, products, shops, factories and stores were displayed at the Paris Exposition could furnish us the image of a quiet and peaceful Russia so fondly entertained by the autocracy.

We shall take as an example the owner of the well-known sugar refining and sugar-beet processing plants, Pavel Kharitonenko (doing business under the name of I. G. Kharitonenko & Son), a gentleman by birth. He owned land in fee simple and under leaseholds in the following provinces:

1. In Kharkov province: 25,448 desyatins* in direct ownership and 6,183 desyatins under lease.

2. In Kursk province: 12,064 desyatins of land in direct ownership and 10,605 desyatins under lease.

3. In Chernigov province: 4,700 desyatins.

4. In Poltava province: 4,570 desyatins.

The composition of his land holdings in the four provinces was as follows: arable and meadowlands—35,535 desyatins directly owned and 17,193 desyatins leased; and 10,842 desyatins of forest in direct ownership. His overall land holdings came to 63,570 desyatins.

P. I. Kharitonenko owned one refining plant and seven granulated sugar plants, of which he owned six directly and leased the seventh.

The aggregate production of his plants was as follows: 38,830 tons of lump and loaf sugar, and 36,447 tons of granulated sugar.

Kharitonenko employed 4,054 people in his plants.

His companies had been awarded the following prizes prior to the Paris Exposition of 1900:

1. A silver medal at the All-Russian Exposition of 1870 in Petersburg.

2. An achievement medal at the Vienna International Exposition of 1873.

---

* *Desyatina*—measure of ground equal to approximately 2.7 acres.

3. A First-Class medal at the World Exposition of 1876 in Finland.

4. A gold medal at the Paris World Exposition of 1878.

5. A print of the state emblem at the World Exposition of Arts and Trades in Moscow, 1882.

6. A certificate of merit at the 1884 World Exposition in Nice.

7. A gold medal at the 1885 World Exposition in Antwerp.

8. The highest award at the World Exposition in Paris, 1889.

9. Again a print of the state emblem at the All-Russian Exposition in Nizhny Novgorod, 1896.

In recognition of the services rendered "in the sphere of public and industrial activity" by the founder of the company, acting State Councillor Ivan Kharitonenko, who had died on November 30, 1891, a monument to his memory was constructed with government sanction in the city of Suma, in Kharkov province.

The company worthily represented Russia's sugar-refinery owners at the Paris Exposition of 1900. P. I. Kharitonenko was honored with the highest award while his company received a gold medal.

The only other Russian company to receive a gold medal was the plant of the Saatchi and Mangubi Company, which supplied provisions for the palace of His Imperial Highness. The company's fixed capital came to one million rubles. The Chairman of the Board of Directors was Baron Pavel Fyodorovich von der Osten-Driesen, and its Board members included S. F. Kefeli and P. I. Taneyev. The plant processed up to 4.4 tons of tobacco daily and it produced cigarettes only of a higher quality, among them such brands as Palma, Babochka, Golubka. The products of the plant had been honored with the following awards: Honorable Mention at the Russian Exposition of 1870 in Petersburg; a silver medal at the Vienna Exposition of 1873; silver medals in 1876 in Philadelphia, and in 1878 and 1889 in Paris, and in 1894 in Borovici, followed in

1894 by the title of Caterer to the Palace of the Crown Prince of Sweden and Norway, and in 1895, in Petersburg, the title of Caterer to the Household of His Imperial Highness, followed again by two gold medals, in 1896, in Nizhny Novgorod, and in 1897, in Stockholm.

The Grand Prix had been bestowed on the coal-mine owners of the Donets Basin. They brought with them to the Exposition a geological map that had been compiled on the basis of the most recent findings, showing the location of the anthracite deposits, separate from the so-called smoky coals, as well as all railways and railway spur lines, and the distribution of ores according to different groupings. They also displayed specimens of the different varieties of coal, with a chemical analysis of each. To give an idea of the appearance of the mines, a display of fifty-three colored photographs was set up, showing various mine facilities and buildings, residential quarters, schools, churches, groups of workers and the like. The organizer of this section, mining engineer and acting State Councillor Yevgeny Taskin, was given a gold medal, as were other engineers of the coal companies of the Donets region.

The Grand Prix was also conferred at the Paris Exposition on the Caterer to the Palace of His Imperial Highness, V. A. Stritter, for the products of his liquor and vodka distillery and mineral water plants.

A third gold medal (following those received at the expositions in Nizhny Novgorod in 1896 and Stockholm in 1897) was awarded at the World Exposition of 1900 to the cloth and table linen plant of the Yakovlev Manufacturing Company, operated by the sons of Vasily Dorodnov. Like many of the large manufacturers (the Morozovs, Prokhorovs, Garelins and some others), Vasily Dorodnov was born into a milieu of peasant-craftsmen. He, like all the others, grew rich exploiting the ruined and impoverished peasants. The company had been founded by Vasily Dorodnov in the year 1860. At the outset cloth was woven for him at the homes of residents of Yakovlev, a village in the Nerekhty District in the Province of Kostroma. Subsequently, in 1864, a bleaching and finishing factory was erected, operated manually at first but converted in 1880 to mechanical operation. Still later, in 1886, a steam-driven mill and a bleaching and finishing plant were built. In 1895 Alexander and Mefody Dorodnov (sons of V. F. Dorodnov) founded a company known as Yakovlev Manufacturing Company Vasily Dorodnov Sons. At the time the plant had a total of 260 mechanical looms and 55 manually operated looms.

A gold medal was awarded to the master shoemaker, Caterer to the Household of His Imperial Highness, G. F. Sitnov & Sons. The awards bestowed on the company are characteristic: in 1865—the National Emblem; in 1881—the National Emblem; in 1888—the National Emblem, on the occasion of the All-Russian Exposition in Moscow; in 1895—the National Emblem and title of Caterer to the Palace of His Imperial Majesty Emperor Nicholas II; in 1896—the National Emblem, on the occasion of the All-Russian Exposition in Nizhny Novgorod; in 1874—the Emblem of His Imperial Highness Prince Vladimir Alexandrovich; in 1896—the Emblem of Chernogorye Count Nicholas I and title of Caterer; in 1897— the State Emblem of Franz Joseph, Emperor of Austria and King of Hungary, and title of Caterer to the Palace. Medals were received at the following expositions: in 1862—London (First Class); 1865—Moscow (Silver medal); 1867—Paris (First Class); 1870—St. Petersburg (Gold); 1873—Vienna (Silver, Honorable Mention); 1876—Philadelphia (First Class); 1878—Paris (First Class); 1883—Amsterdam (Gold); 1885—Antwerp (Gold). The proprietors of the company received the following awards on the recommendation of the Ministry of Finance, Department of Commerce and Manufacture, in 1897: Grigory Sitnov—the Order of St. Stanislaus, Second Class; and Konstantin Sitnov—Order of St. Stanislaus, Third Class.

The total number of exhibitors from Russia was 2,500. The number of awards for exhibits was 1,589, and included in that number were 212 higher awards, 370 gold medals, 436 silver medals, 347 bronze medals and 224 honorable mentions. A very large number of awards went to collective exhibitors; that is to say, government and public institutions and large industrial companies, which presented large and diversified exhibits.

This was Russia of the autocracy, Russia of large industrialists and the richest landowners. Here everything fell under the rules of the Table of Ranks, promulgated by Peter I in 1722, which regulated the steps through which one had to ascend the ladder of government service. No one was eligible to receive an elevated rank bypassing lower ranks. All wore uniforms and strictly observed the rules of subordination and hierarchy. In an empire where lawlessness received the sanction of the laws, the Table of Ranks was intended to fix things in an eternal order, protocol and regimentation, with everything established once and for all. Looking at it all from the sidelines, one gained the impression that nothing had changed, that the machine was performing with precision and that the gears were meshing smoothly.

The Country of Uniforms. Official Russia, it appeared, was a country where commands from anyone in uniform were obeyed without question. The uniform made the man and fixed his place in society. The earliest statutes prescribing the wearing of uniforms by officials of municipal departments go back to Peter I. Legislative enactments in this connection were confined at the time to the assignment of different categories of uniforms to officials of the different departments. The cut and style of dress underwent frequent changes.

In 1834 Emperor Nicholas I issued Mandatory Imperial Regulations concerning Civil Uniforms. These regulations served as a foundation for all subsequent legislation on uniforms. Some amendments were introduced by the Decree of March 8, 1856. At the same time regulations were issued on the wearing of uniforms by officials and civil servants.

In 1894, with the intent of establishing a new code on uniforms for civil officials, a special commission was set up under the chairmanship of the director of the tsar's Chancellery, and on May 6, 1894, the Emperor ratified The Code of Rules on the Wearing of Uniforms by Officials. These regulations, which were compiled in the Addendum to Article 531 of the

"Regulations of the Civil Service" (*Code of Laws*, Vol. 3, 1896 Edition), became mandatory.

The uniforms of the different official ranks identified the place of employment, as well as rank and the position held. There was the full-dress uniform, the holiday uniform and the standard, everyday uniform, as well as special, travel and summer uniforms.

The full-dress half-tunic was laid down as obligatory only for the first three ranks, while the others wore an ordinary half-tunic. Parade dress called for white trousers, vest and tie, a three-cornered hat, a sword and sword-knot on the sword belt and white gloves. The first three ranks also donned a special half-tunic for holidays and another for everyday wear.

The everyday uniform consisted of a dress coat or a double-breasted frock coat, trousers matching the color of the dress coat and the like. The prescribed headgear when wearing a frock coat was a peaked cap with a cockade.

Retired officials were allowed to wear only full-dress uniforms of the holiday and everyday type.

The full-dress uniform was worn by civil servants for gala events at the palace, at important balls and for solemn religious services.

The holiday uniform was obligatory at religious services and on the occasions when the official was being presented to their majesties or to personages of the imperial household.

In the summer, uniform dress coats and double-breasted frock coats could be replaced with double-breasted frock coats tailored of bleached or unbleached linen.

A special uniform was prescribed for making special reports to senior officials, at imperial dinners, at dinners in private homes honored by the presence of their majesties, and on occasions for which no other uniform had been prescribed.

One type of sword was prescribed for all departments and posts, with a silver sword-knot and tassel. It was suspended from a shoulder strap which was worn under the half-tunic.

Subordination of ranks among the civil servants was rigid and brutally enforced.

In the army, Nicholas II did not introduce any changes whatsoever in the uniforms that had been prescribed during the reign of his father. By gradual steps the uniform of the Guards of the Cavalry Regiments of the period of Alexander II (early nineteenth century) emerged. The officers of the entire army received gallooned shoulder straps in lieu of the plain leather strap introduced by Alexander III. The headgear of the armies of the southern regions was found to be too heavy and replaced by a simple cap with a metal shield.

The only substantial changes were those introduced in the uniforms of the mounted troops, for which Nicholas II had a special weakness.

Special attention was always paid to uniforms during the reign of the autocrats. Even as far back as the reign of Paul I (1796–1801), as one Soviet literary critic, A. Belenkov, justly observes, "it was for the first time realized with full clarity that it is much easier to command people constricted into uniforms of the different departments, and lined up in keeping with rank, subject to systematic punishments and receiving methodical rewards, than it would be to lord it over individuals who take off in all directions, are unaccustomed to jump to at the blast of a whistle, who refuse to think when bidden to, or obey orders implicitly and are prone to start arguments.

"It appeared to people in uniform that they were the key figures in a well-functioning mechanism set into operation by the autocratic state, where despotic rulership was customary, universal and unvarying and where man fulfilled his mission only if he responded to the demands of the mechanism, which called for constituent parts of a strictly defined shape and function. Hence the ideal man for the mechanism called state is one who may not actually be a man, but only called one." *

And in fact, such were the people in uniform who, submitting without cavil to the regulations, lived strictly in subservience to them.

---

* A quote from A. Belenkov's book *Yury Tynyanov*, Moscow, 1965.

2 THE TRUE FACE OF RUSSIA

However, neither the full-dress uniforms of the aristocracy and the officialdom nor the military uniforms that one encountered in every corner of Russia represented the true face of Russia. That became apparent on many an occasion.

It happened for the first time in 1606, when the arbitrary rule of oppressors of the people had brought it about that most of the peasantry were regarded as the chattels of the ruling class.* This was the year in which for the first time in the history of Russia the discontent of the people brimmed over into a real peasant war. The movement started in the remote southern regions of Russia where Ivan Bolotnikov rose up at

---

* Serfdom was that condition of the peasantry under which they had no right to leave the landowner's soil on which they worked and to which they were bound. Its emergence in Russia goes back to the eleventh century. First to be turned into the landowner's chattels were the menials of the palace. The Synodal Code of Tsar Alexis in 1649 laid the legal foundation for the serfdom of all categories of peasants.

the head of an insurgent army of thousands. Although the uprising was crushed it did nevertheless postpone the official introduction of serfdom in Russia by some decades.

The second occasion was in 1670. A new, even more menacing peasant war under the leadership of Stepan Razin spread
over a vast territory, from the Don and Astrakhan to Simbirsk
and Nizhny Novgorod. Though defeated, it also bore its fruit,
since the peasant wars of the seventeenth century, forcing the
tsarist government to introduce reforms, helped to overcome
the vestiges of the country's economic and political fragmen-
tation and blazed a trail for the development of the towns. In
the course of the uprising the friendship between equally
abandoned and forgotten peoples of the vast empire also grew
a step.

The third and last peasant war in the history of feudal Russia was the war of 1773, led by Emelian Pugachev. This rebellion staggered tsarism and serfdom and showed just what Russia was in actual fact.

The peasant movements failed because they were the expression of a spontaneous protest on the part of the oppressed
masses unilluminated by any political consciousness or clear
program. The beginning of the revolutionary movement
against the autocracy came from the more progressive representatives of the nobility, who took up the cudgels for the
people's liberation from the yoke of serfdom. It was they in
fact who, surging into St. Petersburg's Senate Square in December 1825 (hence their name—Decembrists), and making
a bid for the overthrow of the autocracy, lit the spark that later
blazed into a flame of revolution in Russia. There is good reason why Lenin, in characterizing the fundamental stages in
the struggle waged by the Russian people, described the first
period (from 1825 to 1861) as the period of "the revolution-
ism of the nobles." The second period (1861 to 1895) saw
broader circles of the intelligentsia, who were closer to the
people than the Decembrists, enter into the struggle. This second phase was defined by Lenin as the revolutionary-

democratic period. Although in this stage a broader program of revolutionary reorganization of society was put forward, it still failed to develop a mass revolutionary movement. As Lenin used to say, this was not yet the real storm. The storm comes when the broad masses take part in the movement. Its earliest fury was vented in 1905. Lenin spoke of this historical period of the revolutionary movement in Russia as the proletarian period. It was consummated in 1917 by the victory of the Great October Socialist Revolution.

The peasantry, the revolutionary nobility, the representatives of the revolutionary intelligentsia, and the working class of Russia: these are the strata that determined the historical destinies of the country and the paths it pursued in its development; these constituted the true face of Russia.

The Peasantry. At the Paris World Exposition of 1900 one was able to form a judgment of the peasantry, who numbered 97 million out of a total population of 125.6 million (77 per cent), from the exhibits of the special groups of the Russian section. There were firstly some one hundred exhibits in Agricultural Group number seven, which covered vegetables, fruit and hothouse vegetation. Group number eight showed the products of horticulture and truck farming. Group number nine had sixty exhibits on forestry, hunting, fishing. In addition, there was a collection of natural products, and exhibits of Russian handicrafts.

Displayed in the agricultural pavilion were agricultural implements, products of agriculture and farming, specimens of fertilizers and instruments employed in agricultural meteorology and specialized literature. Among the exhibits there was the interesting soil collection of the famous Russian scientist and naturalist V. V. Dokuchayev. However, none of these things conveyed the slightest idea about the life of the Russian peasantry, any more than did the two hundred wax models of rare varieties of apples, the canned fish and fishing equipment (A. K. Dubinin, Sapozhnikov Brothers), the furs of the P. Grinwald Company, and the diminutive Russian village built from the drawings of the artist K. Korovin. No one took the trouble to tell the peasants' story because, in fact, it was all quite unpleasant.

The Reform of 1861, which was to free the peasantry from the bonds of serfdom, not only failed to give them true freedom but, on the contrary, led to the ruin of millions of peasants. Although they were granted personal freedom, they nevertheless continued over a period of many years to pay special taxes to the government and continued to bear a burden of assessments in kind for the benefit of the former owners. Moreover, they had no political rights and were subject to corporal punishment by sentence of the courts.

The peasants were obliged to pay a redemption fee if they were to receive land on emancipation. The redemption law called for compensation to the landowners, to be paid as the price of the land allotted to the peasant. This also included non-agricultural earnings, which previously had gone into the pocket of the landowner. In addition, the redemption price was so high that it amounted not only to an obviously augmented compensation for the soil and other illicitly inflated forfeitures, but also to payment for emancipation itself. The peasant thus paid for his own person. In the course of the forty-nine years following 1861 peasants were forced to part with some two billion rubles. Consequently, the destitute Russian village was in bondage both to the landowner and to the government.

Numerous survivals of serfdom continued for a long time to beset the village and impede its development.

The retention of landlord property left the heaviest imprint on the entire economy of Russia. "At one pole of Russian land ownership," wrote Lenin, "we have 10.5 million peasant households (some fifty million persons) with seventy-five million desyatins of land, and at the other pole 30,000 families (about 150,000 persons) with seventy million desyatins of land." An average of 2,333 desyatins fell to the share of each manor, while the share accruing to every peasant household was about seven desyatins of land.

One thousand large landowners had as much land as two million peasants, in European Russia alone the tsar's family owned seven million desyatins, and the Russian peasantry was perishing of land hunger. They were incapable of feeding even their own families by working the small patches of land that came into their ownership after they had paid out enormous sums for redemption. " 'There's no room to turn a chicken out;' this is bitter peasant truth, this grim 'humor of the gallow-bird,' " wrote Lenin, "it describes better than any long quotation the peculiar feature of peasant land ownership which is beyond the power of statistics to express."

In carrying out the Reforms of 1861 landowners dispossessed 720,000 manor serfs without any soil. Then 600,000 former serfs were turned into land-poor "endowees." Relieved of paying the bondman's redemption fee, they received so-called endowed allotments of land, constituting in all one-fourth of the allotment lands of the rest of the peasants. Moreover, the landowners cut off from peasant holdings a part of their allotment lands. The total land area thus cut off represented on the average 20 per cent of all peasant allotment land, and this, as a rule, was the best land. In some of the provinces these *otrezki* or strips represented more than 30 per cent of their land holdings.

The peasants were frequently deprived of reservoirs, common pastures, and droving paths for cattle. Moreover, they were left without forests, and responded by illegally felling trees in the forests of the landowners. The landowners' lands frequently cut a wedge into the peasant allotments, and furnished the landowners with convenient pretexts for claiming damages, or afforded them an income from renting these wedges at excessive prices.

Forced to lease manorial land, the peasants found themselves surrendering a considerable part of their income to the landowners, who preferred to exploit the peasants by methods which traced back to the period of serfdom. Among the means of exploitation were a system of paying off with labor (in former days this was simply known as *corvée*) and the system of *métayage* (under which the landowner received part of the peasant's crop). In the second half of the nineteenth and the beginning of the twentieth centuries the payment of rent took on extensive proportions. From 1861 to the end of the nineteenth century it increased on the average three-fold, and in some regions particularly land poor, and where the incidence of the village poor was considerable, it increased by as much as five or ten times. Frequently landowners did not find it worthwhile to run any independent enterprise since profits could not possibly compare with the enormous rents collected from the hire of the land.

The peasants suffered ruin and impoverishment. Some of them fell into bondage to the proprietors of the land, while others preferred to leave for the towns and swell the ranks of the working class. Town life was indeed the more difficult way out, but not only because work was hard to get. Because the Reform of 1861 was introduced in the interest of the ruling class, the tsarist government did everything in its power to retain the communal organization of the Russian village. The entire peasant community was made responsible for every single peasant's payment of taxes, for the payment of land rent and for the fulfillment of all obligations. Unless the community gave its permission, there was no leaving the village for the town. In this way the landowners were assured of a cheap labor source and the backwardness of the patriarchal Russian village was safeguarded. How great was the toll of impoverishment can be observed from the increase in farm holdings without a horse or with but one horse from 5.6 million in 1900 to 8.4 million in 1912. The situation of the peasants with even one horse underwent continual decline, and the holdings of small areas of allotment lands were frequently surrendered for the purchase of seed or implements. The peasant received no more than pitiable crumbs from leasing or purchasing land. He was condemned to live a life of destitution.

Technologically, the agricultural economy of Russia was in a stage of extreme backwardness. There was a scarcity of machinery. The land was worked by the most archaic means, and the most widely used implements were the wooden plow and the harrow. One could not possibly speak of any scientific management of the economy.

The upshot of this situation was that almost every year a partial famine broke out in some locality. Every three years a famine of middle proportions was experienced and every ten years a famine of epidemic proportions raged in the country. Particularly serious crop failures and famines occurred in 1873, 1880, 1883, 1891, 1902 and 1905.

Famine, attended by typhus and scurvy, which invariably followed in its wake, more than once descended on the impoverished Russian villages. From earliest times Russia held first place among the countries of Europe in terms of its population mortality rate and child mortality rate. Over a period of twenty-five to thirty years this rate declined in the empire by only two to three units, while in Germany, Austria, Belgium and other countries, where it was low to begin with, it dropped by six and more units (that is, six persons per thousand).

In 1909 the mortality rate (persons per thousand) of different countries was recorded as follows:

Great Britain	14.5
Belgium	15.7
Germany	17.1
Denmark	13.1
Norway	13.5
Sweden	13.7
Russia	28.9

Hence, according to official data, the mortality rate in Russia clearly was double the rate of mortality in most European countries.

All of this was brought about by the impoverished condition of the population, by the uncommonly poor sanitary conditions and by very frequent epidemics. It is significant that out of every hundred infants born in the Russian village, no more than thirty-seven survived to the draft age. There is good reason why, in their writings, even the liberals referred to the villages of tsarist Russia as the dying villages. By poverty and social inequality, the village in Russia was forced into an extremely low cultural level, and almost staggering illiteracy.

The 1897 census laid bare a shocking picture of the country's cultural backwardness. Of a total registered population of 126 million the number of those able to read and write added up to no more than 21.1 per cent. Some 100 million people were unable either to read or write. However, even these statistics were obviously short of the actual figures.

Most of the illiterates were to be found in the rural population. Among peasants in the age bracket of twenty-five to forty the literacy rate came only to 22.4 per cent while the rate in urban centers was 55.5 per cent.

The situation of the non-Russian peoples was particularly grave: Illiteracy among the Tadzhiks came to 99.5 per cent; among the Kirghiz population, it was 99.4 per cent; among the Yakuts, 99.3 per cent; among the Turkmens, 99.3 per cent, and among the Uzbeks, 98.4 per cent. No disclosures were made at all concerning illiteracy in the Far North. The liberal newspaper *Nedelya* wrote in one of its 1893 editorials that even if an all-out effort were made, such as the building of 3,250 new schools every year, it would take approximately twenty years to bring into the educational system all the children of school age.

The reduced pace of development of the productive forces in the village and an inadequate flow of population into the urban centers led to an enormous surplus of manpower in the village and to the accumulation of a huge labor reserve. In 1900 this surplus numbered 23 million, which represented more than half of the entire adult peasant population. This was one of the reasons why wages were low, not only in the village but in town as well.

As a consequence of these conditions, the revolutionary situation speedily gained impetus. To a certain extent even the tsarist government and the representatives of the ruling classes began to acknowledge this. Police reports and letters from landowners were ever more frequently punctuated by reports of "a growing destructive mood among the peasantry."

The greatest panic seized landowners in regions that were ravaged by famine. One of the landowners wrote in August 1901 from Voronezh province: "Something ominous is in the air here; every day the glow of fires lights up the horizon; a blood-soaked mist creeps along the ground, smothering and making life difficult, like the precursor of a storm. The peasants stand sullenly mute, but if they say something it makes your flesh creep."

The stratification of the peasantry, the emergence of a class of agricultural workers—or as Lenin used to refer to them a class of "wage workers with an allotment of land"—farmhands, day laborers, unskilled laborers and the like, precipitated a new social war in the village between the poor peasantry and the affluent peasants (*kulaks*). However, the basic contradiction, as before, was that between the peasantry and the landowners. The peasantry sought to erase all vestiges of serfdom, especially land holding by the landowners. This was the basis of the revolutionary alliance of the working class with the peasantry in their struggle against autocracy.

The Workers. It was only natural that the story concerning the growth of industry and the position of the working class in Russia was told at the World Exposition of 1900 by the representatives of the larger firms, joint-stock companies, state enterprises and plants, as well as the principal curatorship administration.

Quite a complete representation of the sugar industry (sugar manufacturers Tereshchenko, Kharitonenko, Balashov) participated. The K. & S. Popov Company exhibited tea from their own plantations in Russia in a separate pavilion on the *Place des Invalides*. The collection of alcoholic and various other beverages displayed for the benefit of the visitors was highly diversified and far-ranging. The central liquor sales administration displayed a complete chart of the production of wines sold by the state monopoly which showed all accessory materials employed in the processing and preparation of wine before it was sent out to be sold. Mining and metallurgy were represented by larger enterprises such as Auerbach & Co., Guta-Bankov, Demidov, Prince San-Donato & Heirs, the coal operators of Dombrov and the Donets, the Donets railway and metallurgical plants, the Sosnovitskoy Coal, Ore and Processing Company, the Bryansk, Kashtym and Ural state monopoly mining plants, and others. The metalworking industry was represented by the samovar output of Batashev, by standard as well as artistically executed castings (the Kyshtym Mining Works, the Ural Mining Monopoly Works and others), zinc and lead products (The Russian-American Company, a lead rolling mill and pipe producer), specimens of gold leaf and silver (Puchugin Matveyev), and the bell-making works of Mamgin Brothers. Oil was on display by courtesy of the Nobel Brothers Company (in a special pavilion of the Trocadero), as well as the Baku and the Caspian-Black Sea Companies. The Russian-American Rubber Manufacturing Company, as already stated, displayed the products of its plant in a separate pavilion. Products of the textile, paper and leather industries, of chemical and pharmaceutical plants, and of perfumeries were also exhibited. The exhibits in the section devoted to civil engineering, transportation, railways and other forms of conveyance and navigation were less impressive. In the electrical section, all references to it were inevitably accompanied by remarks such as "it is a young business" and "it has not been adequately developed in Russia."

The situation of the working class was reflected in the exhibits of Group sixteen, the section dealing with social economics, hygiene and social welfare. It was a complex section under the management of academician Prince Ivan Tarkhanov, acting State Councillor. The prince was a medical doctor and as part of his special mission he visited nearly all of the physiological laboratories in Europe and was engaged in research at the Hoppe-Zeiler Laboratories, as well as the Holtz and Rechlinghausen Laboratories at the University of Strasbourg and in the Laboratories of Claude Bernard, Ranvier and Vullipan in Paris. His name was well-known in scientific circles and this fact was of itself sufficient to lend a good name to the displays in the section, and to confirm their authenticity.

The numerous cartograms, diagrams, statistical tables, models and photos unfolded a magnificent but unreal canvas of workers' living conditions, of the medical and charitable organizations available to them, and of measures adopted for the protection of the life and limb of the working people. Not without reason was this section treated with particular solicitude and a very large area set aside for it. The exhibits were in part displayed in a 391-square-meter area in a building on the *Champs de Mars,* and in part in a 150-square-meter area at the Palace of Social Economics and Congresses near the Alma Bridge. Along with it was an exhibit of the Trusteeship for National Sobriety. The only section larger than this was the one devoted to the land and maritime armed forces (886 square meters and 390 square meters). However, not its magnitude, nor the splendidly executed models of non-existent schools, hospitals and clinics, nor the retouched photos of workers' barracks, nor the overly precious and tidy spit-and-polish houses allegedly sold to the workers were able to win any plaudits for this section. It was apparent to all that the truth was not to be found there and that there was no purpose in trying to track it down elsewhere at the Exposition.

The growth of industry that came in the wake of the Reform of 1861 led to an increase in the numbers of the Russian working class. Even early in the century the number of workers in factories and workshops and in the mining industry, including those working in railway transportation, had reached a level of three million, which was quite impressive for that period. At the beginning of the First World War the number of industrial and railroad workers increased to 4.2 million. These were the cadres of a hereditary proletariat.

The bulk of this stratum was concentrated in the largest enterprises. Lenin showed the growth of this concentration of production in Russian industry, with its consequent concentration of the working class, by citing the following figures:

As far back as 1890, 71.1 per cent of all workers were employed in large plants and factories employing one hundred or more workers. In 1894–1895 large enterprises constituted 10.1 per cent of all plants and factories, embracing 74 per cent of all plant and factory workers and more than 70 per cent of the total output. In 1903 large factories employing in excess of one hundred workers represented 17 per cent of the total number of plants and factories in European Russia, and employed 76.6 per cent of the total number of plant and factory workers.

Lenin observed that the large Russian factories were of greater proportions than the German factories. The ever-growing concentration of workers in large plants and factories, in large cities and industrial centers aided the consolidation and organization of the working class, augmenting its strength and enhancing its political role in the life of the country.

The position of the proletariat in Russia was uncommonly difficult. The working day, wages, working and living conditions were not regulated by any laws and were completely subject to the will of the owners of the enterprises.

The average length of the working day in the 1880s throughout Russia was no less than 12.5 hours, and in the textile industry it reached 14 to 15 hours. In wadding and matting factories, in canvas-making plants and distilleries workers labored as much as 16 to 18 hours per day and in some cases even longer without any change of shift. Even the matting manufacturers themselves used to say about these workers that after having worked the winter through, by summer they "reel with the breeze." In the 1880s, according to the facts unearthed by a well-known investigator, who looked into the situation of the workers of the Dementyev factories in three districts of the Moscow province, the working day was of the following duration:

Less than 12 hours	10	per cent of all factories
12–12.5 hours	29	per cent
13–13.5 hours	44	per cent
14–14.5 hours	11.6	per cent
15 hours and more	5.4	per cent

Later, when the working day was reduced to 11.5 hours by legislative enactment under the tsars, it actually ran from 12 to 13 hours.

There was widespread employment of women and children for low wages. There was no legislation for the protection of labor. Children and adolescents worked equally with adults: 33.9 per cent of the workers came into the factory before the age of twelve and 63.6 per cent before they were fourteen. Pregnant women worked to the last minute, leaving the factory only a few hours before delivery, and occasionally delivering their children at the machine. For the same kind of work as performed by men, women and children received appreciably lower wages.

Vasily Gerasimov,* a worker who was sentenced in 1875 to nine years of hard labor for his participation in revolutionary activities, had the following things to say concerning this state of affairs: ". . . When we entered the factory the manager assigned us wages of four rubles each, and of that amount they gave us only eight kopecks a month, that is two kopecks out of each ruble. On such wages I lived all four years. Until I reached the age of sixteen my boss deducted 6.50 rubles for my upkeep. That is how it came about that I remained owing him every month the sum of 2.50 rubles and even more at times, particularly since they frequently collected from us fines for all kinds of offences, and these fines became part of our debt."

Fines were imposed on the slightest pretext, such as late-

---

* V. Gerasimov was brought up in the St. Petersburg Orphanage and at the age of eleven he was placed with the Krengolm Plant (in the vicinity of Narva). Having served his sentence at hard labor, he was deported to the Yakut Region where he died in 1892.

ness, breakage of an instrument, inebriation, rudeness, smoking, singing, noise, whistling, trespassing into the office, bad treatment of animals or failure to attend church. At the Morozov Textile Plant (at the workers' settlement of Nikolskoye, Vladimir province) the fines brought in as much as twenty thousand rubles in income annually. Not infrequently the fines consumed 30 to 40 per cent of the wages. In addition there were countless deductions: For the pay-books, medical aid, passport registration, maintenance of the yardkeeper, cleaning of lavatories, for the bath, for boiler water, coal for the samovar, or church donation. All of this cut down the worker's pay, which was already paltry enough, even further.

The payment of wages took place entirely at the will of the factory owner and a perfectly arbitrary regime prevailed in this respect. This also applied to the term of hire: The worker could not leave his job ahead of the stipulated term but the employer had the right to drive out the worker whenever it pleased him. The taunts and demands of the factory owners and foremen humiliated and tore down the dignity of the worker.

V. Gerasimov described the punishments administered to children in the factories:

". . . Punishment in the factory was meted out by lashing. The butcher Golyanishchev was always posted at the door of the office. He administered beatings at the behest of the superiors. I am citing only a few facts which deal with my own lashings. Once I accidentally broke a broom, which earned me twenty-five lashes, and another time I received fifty lashes for riding the elevator from the fourth to the third floor: they beat me with such force that not a white spot remained on my back; it turned all black. I was sent into the punitive cell on several occasions; in fact, I landed there because I was late for inspection. I will not even bother to talk about the many beatings I received from the foremen and others. . . . All I can say is that at the factory the foremen and assistant foremen were killing children in broad daylight. I was myself witness of a beating which a certain assistant foreman administered to a girl, who died the very following day in the hospital. Children were ordered down on their knees for about two hours where they had to kneel on splinters of old bricks and on rock salt, or were dragged by their hair, whipped with leather straps. . . . In a word, they dealt with them any way they wished."

The working conditions were horrible: Complete lack of ventilation, poor lighting, grime and overcrowding. No safety precautions of any kind were taken for the prevention of accidents; machines were arranged without regard to comfort and safety, and no shields were provided to prevent access to dangerous areas, causing innumerable multilations and fatal accidents. In Vladimir province 325 accidents occurred in one of the factories over a period of two years (1881 and 1882). At the Putilov Works there were 148 accidents in 1880, and a total of some 2,000 serious accidents occurred at the Morozov Plant from 1869 to 1892.

In 1882 a decree was promulgated creating the Institute of Factory Inspection. Its purpose was presumably to ensure the observance of the provisions of the labor laws. However, the Institute of Factory Inspection soon fell into disuse. Upright men of good will, such as I. Yanzhul, Professor of Financial Law at Moscow University, and formerly Inspector of the Moscow Factory Area from 1882 to 1887, and Doctor P. Peskov, Inspector of the Vladimir Area, were removed from their posts. Men of lesser endurance failed to notice what they considered best left unnoticed.

The reports of Yanzhul and Peskov for the year 1885, which were published in separate books, drew public attention to the grave situation of the workers and enjoyed great success. The Russian Geographical Society awarded a large gold medal to Yanzhul for his book. Lenin wrote about these reports as follows: "Only the earliest reports of the factory inspectors got into print, and the government immediately stopped their publication. The factory conditions turned out to be so bad that they were afraid to make them public."

Here is what Yanzhul had to say about the conditions under which the workers labored:

. . . At mill No. 48, as in many other cloth mills, the air in the dye-works was so saturated with steam that when the inspection was conducted nothing could be seen, and I groped my way through the dyeworks as though they had put blinders over my eyes. Obviously no ventilation had been provided on these premises. Moreover, the machines were highly crowded and the belts crisscrossed in all directions. It was extremely difficult to make one's way between them and the machines were highly prone to cause accidents for which the workers were in no way responsible.

In chemical plant No. 44 the noxious gases in the department where the lead salts were prepared were so strong that people who were unaccustomed to it could not endure it even for a few minutes. In the department where mercury was prepared, masks over the workers' mouths constituted the only precaution taken in this terribly toxic operation. . . .

At textile mill No. 131 there was in actual fact only a single staircase in the principal section, the other staircase threatening to cave in, so dilapidated was its condition. All the machines were improperly partitioned and the gears were for the most part exposed. . . .

I. Yanzhul was echoed by P. Peskov:

". . . The conditions of the production of linen at a vast majority of flax mills which I inspected . . . represented a violation of all hygienic rules."

And from the Donbass came the following:

". . . The mine shafts proper . . . are in a state of disrepair; cave-ins are not infrequent and as a consequence ventilation of the subterranean passages, inadequate as it is, becomes even more difficult and the air inside them grows so heavy that the lamps are extinguished, or as the workers usually say, 'the lights do not burn.' One can imagine what it is like to breathe this 'air.' "

The living conditions of the workers were also intolerable. They huddled in factory barracks which, according to the statement of a contemporary, represented "something in the nature of a cattle yard where every worker, regardless of sex and age lies down to sleep wherever and however he is able to manage."

Here is what I. Yanzhul wrote:

The sleeping quarters in Moscow factories are of two kinds: Dormitories, or barracks and closets. In a few comparatively small factories

one finds exclusively the first kind of sleeping quarters. For the most
part, however, the quarters are of the mixed type, which is to say that
both barracks and closets are to be found in the same factory; the former generally accommodate unmarried workers, and married men as
well where there is a shortage of space. Closets are occupied by married
workers only. Moreover, this division is not strictly observed in a considerable number of factories, and while in some of them one finds single men, unmarried women, and married men separated from each
other, there is an indiscriminate mingling of sex and age in most of
them and all of them quite frequently sleep in one and the same closet
or barrack. . . . The furnishings of workers' sleeping quarters, be it
barrack or closet, are invariably identical and consist generally of row
after row of wooden trundle beds, for the most part without any bedding whatsoever, and very seldom does one find iron bedsteads. . . .
Bedding is the workers' own concern and for the most part they sleep
on their sheepskin coats or caftans. . . .

The back-breaking conditions under which the workers
lived and labored mercilessly impaired their health and
strength, and there was neither insurance nor compensation in
case of disability. The factory owners did nothing to provide
medical aid for the workers and any care administered had to
be paid for.

All of this was happening in almost the only European country where large-scale industry and the working class were developing under a regime of autocracy and police rule.

The workers were forbidden to hold meetings, to establish
unions or to declare strikes. A weaver, Pyotr Alexeyev, drew a
shocking picture of the deprivation of political rights in a
speech that he delivered in court on March 10, 1877.

". . . When we, I regret to say, are forced occasionally to
ask for a raise in wages, which the capitalists have kept low, we
are accused of striking and they deport us to Siberia, which
means that we are serfs. When we are forced to leave the factory due to all kinds of fines and unbearable conditions created by the capitalist himself, and when we demand final pay
they accuse us of mutiny and use soldiers against us; they force
us to continue working for the capitalist, while some of us,
branded as instigators, are deported to distant parts, and that
also means that we are serfs! If none of us is able to bring a

complaint against a capitalist and if any common policeman can pound us in the face with his fists and boot us out of the place, this means that we are serfs."

Notwithstanding arrests and armed reprisals the workers not only persisted in their struggles and strikes, but continued them with greater fervor. For example, while in the first years following the abolition of serfdom sixty-three strikes took place, involving thirty thousand participants, in the period from 1880 to 1889 their numbers gained so that 322,000 people were involved in a total of 322 strikes.

The most conscientious workers began to feel the necessity for joining hands and striking back collectively. The first revolutionary workers' organization in Russia was the South Russian Workers' Union founded in 1875 in Odessa by Evegeny Zaslavsky. The Union declared its aim to "propagate the idea of the workers' liberation from the yoke of oppression by capital and by the privileged classes," but it lasted no longer than about a year and was crushed by the police. Zaslavsky was sentenced to ten years at hard labor and soon died in prison.

In St. Petersburg, in the year 1878, Victor Obnorsky and Stepan Khalturin founded the Northern Union of Russian Workers. It had a membership of about two hundred and as many sympathizers. The Union even tried to organize an underground press but failed in the attempt. In 1880 the Union was crushed and Victor Obnorsky was deported under a ten-year sentence of hard labor. Stepan Khalturin, who resorted to terrorism, participated in an attempt on the life of Alexander II and subsequently, in 1882, died on the gallows.

An enormous strike took place in the 1880s, showing the power the workers were able to summon when joined in a common cause. This strike, known as the Morozov strike, broke out on January 7, 1885. It bears the name of the factory owner, Morozov, in whose plant Russian workers demanded for the first time in Russian history the abolition of exorbitant fines. At the governor's orders the army spent two days dispersing the demonstrating workers. About eight hundred of the most active participants were arrested. However, in court such abuses were uncovered and so terrifying a picture emerged of the life of the workers of the Morozov factory that even the special blue-ribbon jury sitting on the case rejected all 101 counts of the indictment. The leaders of the strike were deported by administrative order.

The Morozov strike, according to the formulation given it by the reactionary M. N. Katkov, who described himself as the "faithful watchdog of the autocracy," showed the tsarist government that "it is dangerous to trifle with the populace."

Notwithstanding the high surge of the workers' movement of the 1880s, it still remained spontaneous. ". . . There could not have been any social democratic consciousness among the workers," wrote Lenin. "It could only be brought in from the outside. The history of all countries shows that the working class exclusively by its own efforts is able to develop only a trade union consciousness, *i.e.* the conviction that it is necessary to form unions, fight the employers, and strive to compel the government to pass necessary legislation. The theory of socialism, on the other hand, emerged from the philosophical, historical and economic theories elaborated by educated representatives of the propertied classes and the intelligentsia. By their social status, the founders of modern scientific socialism, Marx and Engels, themselves belonged to the bourgeois intelligentsia. In the very same way in Russia, the theoretical doctrine of social democracy arose altogether independently of the spontaneous growth of the working-class movement. It arose as a natural and inevitable outcome of the development of thought among the revolutionary socialist intelligentsia."

The Revolutionary Socialist Intelligentsia. The Russian revolutionary-democratic movement advanced many famous names, such as: Alexander Herzen and Nikolai Ogaryov, Vissarion Belinsky and Nikolai Nekrasov, Mikhail Petrashevsky, Nikolai Chernishevsky and Nikolai Dobrolyubov. They sought answers to the question of the paths and perspectives to be followed in Russia's development. Each of them understood the absolute necessity for change and they were convinced that in Russia the struggle against the survivals of the old and decayed order could be waged only by revolutionary means. They called for a break with abstract philosophy and political activity in favor of the propagation of socialist ideas. These were the objectives they pursued.

The famous periodical *Kolokol*, published by Herzen and Ogaryov with the motto "I call on the living," summoned all progressive people in Russia to join in the struggle.

The periodical *Sovremennik*, which had been founded by Russia's great national poet Alexander Pushkin, was transformed by Belinsky, Nekrasov, Chernishevsky and Dobrolyubov into an organ of revolutionary democracy that called for a struggle in behalf of a better life for the people.

When in the 1870s the peasantry, entirely dissatisfied with the Reform of 1861, demanded *Cherny Peredel* (general redistribution, that is to say the abolition of landlord property ownership and the transfer of all land to the peasants), the representatives of the non-gentry intelligentsia* laid the foundations of the revolutionary democratic movement known as "Narodism" or Populism.

Members of the movement came to be known as *Narodniki* or Populists for the reason that, changing into the dress of the peasantry, they went among the people throughout the villages to spread revolutionary propaganda. Among their theoreticians were M. Bakunin, P. Lavrov and P. Tkachev, whose views were incorporated into the program of the *Narodniki* as its theoretical foundation.

In 1876, those among the *Narodniki* who had escaped arrest (which was nearly always the outcome of "going among the people") formed an underground organization called Land and Freedom. Among its founders were George Plekhanov, Vera Figner, Mark Natanson, Sofia Perovskaya and others.

---

* Non-gentry intelligentsia was the term used to designate members of the intelligentsia of the 1860s and 1870s who were not of noble descent but belonged to other social strata and circles.

Land and Freedom (*Zemlya i Volya*) continued in existence until 1879, when wrangling over further paths to be followed (the choice being between the old positions and transition to a campaign of terrorism against the ruling classes) brought about its split into two independent groups.

In the autumn of 1879, those of the *Narodniki* who sponsored the former views of Populism founded a party known as *Cherny Peredel*, or General Redistribution, but it soon ceased to exist because of its inability to continue the struggle in its previous form.

The advocates of terrorism organized in St. Petersburg a party called *Narodnaya Volya* (The Will of the People), headed by Zhelyabov, Perovskaya and Figner. On March 1, 1881, members of *Narodnaya Volya* assassinated Alexander II. The terror failed to attract a mass movement and no action was undertaken either by the peasantry or the working class. This clearly demonstrated to most of the *Narodniki* that the tactic of individual terror was seriously deceptive and harmful. Four young members of *Narodnaya Volya* went to the gallows in 1887 for an attempted assassination plot against Alexander III, among them Alexander Ulyanov, the elder brother of Vladimir Lenin, but in actual fact these young men had already embarked on the road leading from Populism to Marxism.

The Marxist group called The Liberation of Labor (*Ozvobozhdenie Truda*), was the wellspring of Russian social democracy. It was founded in 1883, in Geneva, Switzerland, by George Plekhanov. The group included P. Axelrod, V. Zasulich, L. Deutsch and V. Ignatov. They earned great merit for their contributions to the spread of Marxism in Russia. The members of the group not only translated and clandestinely distributed the works of K. Marx and F. Engels among the Russian revolutionary intelligentsia and the vanguard workers, but even published their own brochures and books shedding light on the most important questions of the social life of Russia from the standpoint of Marxism.

The Liberation of Labor group was not alone. Almost simultaneously with it appeared the earliest Marxist circles and groups inside Russia proper.

In 1883 a social democratic group was founded in the capital of the Russian Empire under the leadership of Dimitri Blagoyev, a student at Petersburg University, who eventually became the founder of the Communist Party of Bulgaria. The followers of Blagoyev established links with the group known as The Liberation of Labor. They drew the workers into these circles to study Marxist literature and they succeeded in publishing two issues of the social democratic newspaper *Rabochy* (*The Worker*).

Within three years the tsar's minions crushed the Blagoyev group. However, this did not put an end to the social democratic movement in St. Petersburg. The group of Pavel Tochisky continued the work of the Blagoyev group. It called itself the Society of St. Petersburg Artisans. This group propagated the ideas of Marxism at the Alexandrov, Obukhov, Baltisky, and other larger plants. They also succeeded in establishing contact with the workers of some other plants.

When many members of the Society of St. Petersburg Artisans were arrested, a new Marxist group came into being. This group was headed by Mikhail Brusnev, a student of the St. Petersburg Technological Institute. It became one of the major Marxist organizations in Russia during the late 1880s and early 1890s. The group formed a Central Workmen's Circle, which controlled the lower workmen's circles.

Under Russia's autocratic regime, the activity of young social democratic circles, as yet without experience in conspiratorial work, was of short duration. Most of them managed to survive for no more than two or three years. However, no sooner was one circle put out of existence than new circles sprang into life, establishing closer ties with the proletariat and intensifying their revolutionary propaganda. Such was the case in St. Petersburg and in other cities and workers' centers of Russia.

But still, the social democratic circles and groups spread

Marxism only among a narrow circle of workers. The broad masses remained beyond the sphere of influence of Marxist ideas. The weakness of social democracy stemmed from the fact that it did not rest on a mass movement of the workers and did not direct it. The immediate task was to link up the workers' movement with socialism. The preliminary conditions for this had been prepared by the preceding development of the working class of Russia.

The transformation of the social democratic movement from an ideological current into a Marxist party, into a militant political leader of the Russian proletariat, is associated with the name of Vladimir Ilyich Ulyanov (Lenin).

Lenin learned about the struggle being waged against tsarism by the Russian revolutionaries in the same year that his older brother, Alexander Ulyanov, was executed. His brother's death made an indelible impression on the seventeen-year-old Vladimir. The young man felt the full impact of the evil effects of terror, which snatched out of the revolutionary struggle some of the best people and did nothing to develop a mass movement. "No, we will not follow such a road. This is not the way to go," he said, speaking of his brother's death.

Vladimir Ulyanov was arrested for the first time during his first year at the Kazan University. He was expelled from the university and deported to a village.

"Why are you inciting to rebellion, young man?" he was asked by the police officer after the arrest. "Don't you see you are facing a wall?"

"A wall, to be sure, but rotten; touch it and it will cave in," was Lenin's reply.

Having reached St. Petersburg in the autumn of 1893, Lenin immediately assumed a leading position among the St. Petersburg Marxists. In 1894 he delivered a series of lectures that were compiled into a famous work later published under the title *What the "Friends of the People" Are and How They Fight the Social Democrats*. In it Lenin showed that the liberal *Narodniki* of the 1890s had abandoned the revolutionary struggle against the autocracy that had been waged by the

Narodnik revolutionaries of the 1870s. The pseudo-*Narodniki* had reconciled themselves to the tsarist regime and "they were willing to vegetate under the cover of humane landowners and liberal administrators." Lenin showed that the program of the liberal *Narodniki* of the 1890s was basically hostile to socialism.

Lenin's struggle against the *Narodniki* and other groups that blocked an accord between the social democratic trends and the workers' movement prepared the ground for the establishment of a proletarian revolutionary party in Russia. A considerable achievement along this road was the founding in St. Petersburg in 1895 of the League of Struggle for the Emancipation of the Working Class. It was associated with the workers of seventy enterprises, among them twenty-two of the largest plants in St. Petersburg employing more than one thousand workers. In the summer of 1896 the League headed a three-week strike of textile workers which Lenin referred to as the famous St. Petersburg industrial war of 1896.

At the outset three people constituted the leadership— Lenin, Krzhizhanovsky and Starkov. Subsequently they were joined by Vaneyev and Martov. This group acted as a city-wide social democratic committee and three regional groups served as its liaison with the lower cells of the League of Struggle, or workmen's circles. This was more or less the structure that a few years later was adopted by all large city-wide organizations in Russia when the social democratic committees made their appearance.

The League decided to publish an underground newspaper, *Rabocheye Delo* (*The Workers' Cause*), but on the night of December 9, 1895, Lenin, Vaneyev, Krzhizhanovsky and Starkov were arrested. In 1897 the tsarist government deported Lenin to Eastern Siberia for a period of three years. He remained in exile in the village of Shushenskoye, District of Minusinsk, from 1897 to 1900.

Before his deportation Lenin undertook the task of uniting the separate social democratic organizations into the Russian Social Democratic Labor Party (R.S.D.R.P.), but the arrest prevented him from completing this task. In March 1898 the First Congress of the R.S.D.R.P. took place in Minsk with Lenin absent. The congress proclaimed the formation of the Russian Social Democratic Labor Party. However, this congress did not actually witness the founding of the party. Its Central Committee and most of the congress participants were soon arrested, but no manner of persecution was able to halt the spreading revolutionary movement in Russia.

In January 1900, the term of Lenin's exile ended. On January 29 he left the village of Shushenskoye accompanied by his wife, Nadezhda Konstantinovna Krupskaya. Krupskaya, who had been arrested after Vladimir Ilyich, remained in Ufa to continue serving the term of her sentence.

On account of the law that forbade his living in capitals, university towns or large workers' centers, Lenin chose the town of Pskov, which was most conveniently situated for contact with St. Petersburg. However, even while in exile and on his return journey from exile, in Ufa and Moscow (where he made illegal trips), Pskov, Smolensk, Riga and St. Petersburg (where he also made illegal trips), Podolsk, Samara, Syzran and subsequently while abroad (where he went in 1900), everywhere in fact, Vladimir Ilyich was preparing the ground for the founding of the first all-Russian newspaper, *Iskra* (*The Spark*), which was to play a decisive part in the establishment of a proletarian party of Russia's revolutionary Marxists.

"Before us," wrote Lenin in the editorial of the first number of *Iskra,* which appeared in December 1900, "in all its strength, towers the enemy fortress which is raining lead shot and shells upon us, mowing down our best fighters. We must capture this fortress and we will capture it, if we unite all the forces of the awakening proletariat with all the forces of the Russian revolutionaries into one party which will attract all that is vital and honest in Russia. Only then will the great prophecy of the Russian worker-revolutionary, Pyotr Alexeyev, be fulfilled: 'The muscular arm of the working millions will be uplifted, and the yoke of despotism, guarded by soldiers' bayonets, will be smashed to dust.' "

3 WHAT BROUGHT ABOUT THE RUSSIAN REVOLUTION?

Autocracy prized the services of the people in uniform highly, and especially those whose function it was to check the advance of the revolutionary movement. It never spared its generosity when it came to matters of this sort.

It was on January 1, 1900, at the most humble solicitation of the Director of the Ministry of Home Affairs that His Royal Highness, the Emperor, most graciously deigned to confer medals with the inscription "For assiduousness" with a Vladimir ribbon, silver medals on a St. Anne ribbon, silver chest medals on an Alexander, and silver chest medals on a St. Stanislaus ribbon on a group of police inspectors, policemen, guards, senior and junior inspectors of reformatories and hard-labor camps, and others. Awards went to a total of 250 men.

But what could these people in uniform possibly do, even if their number had not been 250 but ten times or hundreds and thousands of times that much? The revolutionary movement was developing according to its own laws, in a reflection of the political and economic development of Russia in those years, and there was no way of halting it.

The Decay of the Regime. One hears frequently that one of the fundamental reasons for the revolution was the vacillating nature, the weakness and the imperceptive mind of the last Russian emperor. Such a contention is, in fact, put forward in the television film *Leningrad* made by the ABC television network in the U.S.A. Regretfully I did not commit to memory either the name of the writer of the scenario or that of the consultant, as it did not occur to me that I might have to take issue with them.

Throughout the film the authors referred to Leningrad, one of the largest and most beautiful of European cities, as a creation of the Russian autocrats, and speaking of the autocratic regime proper, they made it appear as though it were something immemorially inherent in Russian society. Only in one sequence showing a profusion of spectacular magnificence and the dazzling brilliance of cut glass on the tables in the reception halls of the Russian Empress Catherine II do they make an obscure reference to the peasant wars, and only while showing the Senate Square as it appeared in 1825 do they say something about the Decembrist uprising as the last attempt of the Russian aristocracy to save the monarchy. They forget that the principal group of Decembrists, headed by Colonel Pavel Pestel, called not only for the overthrow, but for the actual physical extermination of the imperial family. The camera then goes on to show an endless array of bedrooms, reception rooms, portraits, monuments (all of it, it must be said, very pleasingly executed from the cinematic standpoint and in point of the accompanying commentary), churches, exotic apparel of the Russian tsars, and in short, everything that in the opinion of the authors bears eloquent testimony to the fact that the will and wish of the autocrats was the main driving force in the development of Russia and that only the degradation of the mind and character of the last representatives of the autocracy brought about the outbreak of the Russian revolution.

Indeed, the city might have, and did in fact, come into being at the will of the emperor but, one might ask, did this determine the place and role of Leningrad in shaping the destinies of the country? Were not the true and authentic creators of the great city those who built the remarkable urban complexes of Northern Palmyra, who cut canals into the land and lined them with granite, who constructed the Admiralty, who built the Putilov, Nevsky, Baltiisky and other plants and factories? Was it not created by the will that found expression in the working people's actions in 1725, in the agitation which spread among the people during the ensuing years, in the remarkable book of the revolutionary republican Alexander Radishchev *A Journey from St. Petersburg to Moscow*, in the secret societies of the revolutionary nobility, in their uprising on Senate Square on a December day in 1825, in the cholera mutiny of 1831, in the revolutionary democratic activity of the intelligentsia and the early Marxists? Are not these the events that transformed St. Petersburg (Leningrad) into a center of the revolutionary democratic movement in the empire, determining its role and position in the shaping of the country's destinies?

True enough, over a period of more than three hundred years the Romanovs stood at the helm of Russia, degenerating as political leaders with the ascent of every new tsar. But who can possibly assert that the lack of foresight and lack of political ingenuity of Tsar Nicholas II constituted a more important cause of the revolution than the psychopathological rule of Paul I, the hypocrisy, mendaciousness and the dominance of personal motives in the political course pursued by Alexander I, the execution of the Decembrists and the police regime of Nicholas I, the vulgar oversimplification of the political course of Alexander II and the colonial political inertia of Alexander III? The crux of the matter was not the weak character of the last autocrat (during the days of the February

Revolution of 1917, he alone sought to organize an armed assault on the insurgent capital) and not the baneful influence brought to bear on him by Grigory Rasputin, an illiterate Siberian peasant who wielded such unlimited power that he was called the "Chancellor of the Russian Empire," "the uncrowned monarch" and the like.* The root cause was elsewhere, in a more complex set of circumstances reflecting the total collapse of the regime—the degenerate state of the autocratic system. The activities of Nicholas II and the political maneuvers of the court coterie enhanced the isolation of the autocracy and hastened its downfall, but any other activities, any other political course and any other ruler could not have done a thing to save tsarism.

Russia of the autocracy was a land of lawlessness and arbitrary rule where, according to Herzen's graphic description, every police inspector was "an uncrowned monarch" and the tsar was "a crowned policeman." The omnipotence of the police and the unlimited despotism of the bureaucratic apparatus hampered any further development of the country.

The retention of almost 100 per cent of the political power in the hands of absolutism and the landowners hindered more than anything else the economic development of the country. This was evidenced particularly by the retarded development of whole branches of industry and of entire regions and by the deliberate obstruction of technological progress. The rapid growth of capitalism in Russia did not end the country's age-long backwardness. Although towards the end of the nineteenth century Russia was overtaking other capitalist states in terms of the rate of growth, it was nevertheless retrograde in terms of its level of development. From the standpoint of per

---

* Playing on the attachment of the Empress to her son, who suffered from hemophilia (prolonged bleeding due to non-coagulation of the blood), Rasputin convinced her that his "prayers" would be able to save the life of the heir apparent. Exerting a boundless influence on the Empress, Rasputin influenced Nicholas II through her. The "Old Man" interfered in all matters of domestic and foreign policy, removing and appointing ministers.

capita production of iron on the eve of the First World War, Britain surpassed Russia four times, Germany five times and the United States ten times. To cite another example: Over a period of fifteen years (1885–1900) Russia's railway network had doubled. The mean annual increment of roadways during that period was more than 2,000 kilometers. Nevertheless in terms of density of the railway network Russia continued to remain far behind Western Europe. In 1895, so far as European Russia is concerned, the count was 9.7 kilometers of railways per one thousand square kilometers of territory, while the respective figures for an equal territory in Britain were 106 kilometers, and in Germany 80 kilometers.

The development of industry in the country was brought about by the intensified flow of foreign capital attracted by the prospects of high profits through the exploitation of cheap and abundant manpower. During the years of industrial growth, the foreign capital invested in Russian industry increased fourfold, attaining the level of one billion rubles in 1900. The annual payment of interest by the empire came to 275 million rubles, or 20 per cent of Russia's entire budget expenditures. From 1896 to 1900 a total of 190 joint-stock companies were set up, of which one-fourth were foreign companies. These investments of foreign capital in Russian industry, along with the increased state indebtedness to foreign capitalists (4,265,-000,000 rubles in 1899), brought about the subjection of the Russian economy to the capital of Western Europe, especially French capital.

In the 1890s monopolistic organizations began to emerge in Russia, along with a mingling of industrial and bank capital. In 1899 eight of the largest banks in the country owned more than half of all bank capital, which they invested in new enterprises and in the organization of trusts and syndicates. By the end of the nineteenth century syndicates had been established in the oil, mining and metallurgical and coal-mining industries. Summing up the development of capitalism in the 1890s, Lenin pointed out that although the development of capitalism in Russia had to be regarded as rapid when compared with the rate of development during the pre-reform period,* one also had to acknowledge that its progress was slow when viewed from the level of culture and technology then available. "And it cannot but be slow," concluded Lenin, "for in no other capitalist country has there been such an abundant survival of ancient institutions that are incompatible with capitalism, retarding its development and immeasurably worsening the condition of the producers, who suffer not only from the development of capitalist production, but also from the incompleteness of that development."

The general backwardness of the country could not be overcome by half-measures or reforms of any kind. It was a reflection of the crisis of the whole system and called for its reorganization.

The same could also be said about Russia's political development at the time. Stagnation, routine and bureaucratism in state institutions blocked all the steps which might have affected the omnipotence of officialdom. With rare exceptions, none of the ministers and people who were close to the Russian emperor ventured to pose, or sought to resolve independently, any of the important state problems. The only man who (on the testimony of his associates) was a tough-minded politician, and in many respects contributed to the development of capitalist industry and the consolidation of the state's financial position, was Count S. Witte.† Nicholas II, as many of his contemporaries remarked, was elated at Witte's death and did not find it necessary to mask his feelings. He favored ministers of a different type, such as Minister of the Interior I. L. Goremykin who, his colleagues reported, devoted so many hours to his dress that he lacked sufficient

---

* *I.e.,* Up to the abolition of serfdom in 1861.
† Among other things, S. Y. Witte introduced a monetary reform, established a fixed rate of exchange for the gold ruble, set up a vodka monopoly which brought in an enormous income.

time to receive the governors. However, when the Governor of
Tula finally managed to get an appointment and told the
Minister that the peasants were suffering hunger, Goremykin
replied: "To think that you are inclined to bother your head
about feeding these cattle."

The decay of the tsarist regime was most apparent in the
Rasputin cult. The living quarters of Rasputin, who made himself quite at home at the court, were perpetually crowded with
all sorts of swindlers and shady characters. The apportionment
of ministerial posts was conditioned on a recommendation of
the "star chamber," as the Rasputin clique was called. Over a
period of two years during the First World War, four Chair-
men of the Council of Ministers passed through the political
arena—I. L. Goremykin, B. V. Styurmer, A. F. Trepov and
N. D. Golitsyn, as well as six Ministers of the Interior, three
Ministers of War, and three Ministers of Foreign Affairs. The
illiterate notes scribbled by Rasputin held the answer to many
questions. He even went so far as to permit himself to dispatch the following memorandum to A. Khvostov, the Minister of the Interior:

"To the Minister Khvostov. My dear fellow I am sending
you a pretty little damsel; poor soul she needs something, so
talk to her. Grigory." And the minister had to receive the
"pretty damsel" like a good and obedient fellow, since he was
beholden for his appointment to the "Old Man."

The murder of Rasputin by a group of aristocrats, among
whom were members of the tsar's family, in December 1916,
did not change anything at all in the conduct of state policy by
the tsarist government. Venality and corruption had pene-
trated deep down, as had the unscrupulousness and indiffer-
ence of the ruling circles. The system of provocations became
very widespread. The tsar's administration made an attempt
to employ that unscrupulousness in its struggle against the
revolutionary movement.

On the initiative of the chief of the Moscow Secret Political
Police Department, S. V. Zubatov, the government began or-

ganizing spurious "workers' unions." It tried by this means to stifle the workers' movement from the inside, to split it and bring it under its own control. The epithet the "Great Provocateur" clings to the name of Evno Azef, whose life and acts represented above anything else the spiritual decay and dishonor of the autocratic system as a whole.

For a period of sixteen years Azef was in the pay of the police. For nearly ten years he worked within the Socialist-Revolutionary Party (S. R.s or Essars) and during a considerable portion of that time he was active in the Fighting Organization of the Party of the Socialist-Revolutionaries which engaged in the principal acts of terrorism at the instruction of the Party. He was even a member of the Central Committee of the S.R. Party. It was he in fact who organized the assassination of Grand Duke Sergei and Plehve, Minister of Foreign Affairs. Azef denounced revolutionaries to the secret police by the hundreds, causing them to be deported, jailed, sentenced to hard labor or executed on the gallows. This was the man who received from the Party vast sums of money to do with as he saw fit without any accountability on his part; he also received monthly commissions from the Secret Political Police, amounting to 12,000 rubles annually and nearly an identical amount in the form of special monetary bonuses. Evno Azef, the son of a lower-middle-class couple in Grodno, Fishel and Sara Azef, became the embodiment of the corruption and deceit of the officialdom in all of Imperial Russia. Is there any wonder then, the regime of Russia being what it was, that all social and political progress in the life of the country was entirely out of the question?

It was extremely difficult for public opinion to have any influence in Russia's autocratic police state. The press was in a precarious position. There wasn't a single more or less important event in the life of the empire that was not marked with a rash of fines levied on the newspapers and periodicals. On the basis of incomplete data, the number of fines imposed for the period 1906–1912 was as follows:

YEAR	NUMBER OF FINES	AMOUNT (*rubles*)
1906	16	15,525
1907	148	65,000
1908	120	82,200
1909	182	87,315
1910	243	60,150
1911	268	73,450
1912	317	96,800
TOTAL: 1,294		480,440

The most glaring example of lawlessness, which stirred all progressive opinion in Russia, was the first ritual case of the nineteenth century, the so-called Multan Affair (1892–1896). It involved a group of Udmurt peasants living in the village of Staryi Multan, in the Malmyzhsky District of Vyatka province, who were falsely accused of practicing human sacrifice to heathen gods, as a pretext for instigating bloodshed between nationalities.

On May 15 1892, the body of a pauper was found in the vicinity of the village of Staryi Multan. Inflating the matter out of all proportion by conducting the inquest in a manner which played havoc even with the tsarist laws (intimidating people rounded up as suspects, resorting to torture and taking advantage of ignorance of the Russian language, hurling charges, etc.), the local authorities trumped up a trial incriminating the entire Udmurt population of the village of Staryi Multan, and the Udmurt nation as a whole, on a charge of practicing human sacrifice.

The writer and journalist Vladimir Korolenko took a heartfelt interest in the predicament of the Udmurts. In one of his articles, he wrote as follows:

"If it seems to you . . . that only a single resident of Multan is being accused of continuing this horrible custom and survival, you are . . . mistaken indeed. . . . This sentence of the court amounts to a judgment condemning an entire nationality consisting of some hundreds of thousands of people residing in the Vyatka Territory, shoulder to shoulder with the Russian nationality, and eking out their livelihood in an identical manner, namely, by farming. . . . Try to picture yourself as clearly as you possibly can in the position of the V*otyak** peasant, your neighbor in a Russian village, in the role of a V*otyak* teacher, and lastly, in the role of a priest of the Vyatka Territory, and you will immediately grasp the full, horrible implications of this sentence . . ." The Multan trial clearly confirmed the truth of the old Russian saying: "The law is a carriage shaft, it will follow your turns and twists:" This was perfectly true of what went by the name of justice in the realm of the empire.

The growth of the revolutionary movement was also attended by a growth in the number of death sentences meted out. During only the period of 1906 to 1912 the newspapers recorded 3,203 death sentences. Taken by single years, the distribution was as follows:

1906	1,010
1907	627
1908	728
1909	543
1910	129
1911	58
1912	108

It should be noted that the upsurge of the working-class movement after the news spread concerning the bloody carnage in the Lena gold fields, which occurred on April 3, 1912, during a workers' demonstration, sharply boosted the ratio of executions to the total number of those who were actually arrested. Thus, for example, in 1908, the percentage of people executed out of the total number of those sentenced came to 39.9 per cent; in 1909, 37.8 per cent; in 1910, 29.7 per cent; in 1911, 24.5 per cent; and in 1912 it grew to 47.1 per cent.

---

* V*otyaki*: An obsolete and incorrect name applied to the Udmurts.

Of the different towns in Russia, the largest number of death sentences during the period from 1906 to 1912 was imposed in Ekaterinoslavl, a large working-class center in the south of Russia. More than 225 people were sentenced to death in this city. More than 150 death sentences were imposed in Kiev and Warsaw and some 100 death sentences in Odessa, Moscow, Riga, Kherson and in other cities. More than 50 death sentences were issued in Kharkov and Elisavetgrad, more than 40 in St. Petersburg, upward of 25 in Perm, Vilna, Ekaterinburg, Tiflis, Sevastopol, Kremenchug and other towns. In answer to an inquiry made by the Social Democratic deputies in the Duma* concerning the Lena shooting, the Minister of the Interior, Alexander Makarov, declared cynically: "That is the way it was and the way it is going to be." This reply concentrated everything in itself: The decay of the regime that produced the conditions making such a reply possible, and the inevitability of a revolutionary conflagration that was to reduce the hateful autocracy to ashes.

The Flame Fanned from the Spark. The nucleus of professional revolutionaries who grouped themselves around Lenin's newspaper *Iskra* formed the foundation of Russia's future Marxist party, which led the revolutionary struggle of the country.

Replete with dangers and anxiety, the underground work to create a revolutionary party was conducted under the most severe conditions of an autocratic police state, and demanded not only boldness but also a selfless devotion to the cause. It gave birth to real heroes. Legends grew up about the names of some of these people. Ivan Babushkin and Nikolai Bauman, who laid down their lives in the first Russian Revolution of 1905; Yakov Sverdlov and Mikhail Kalinin, the future presidents of the first Soviet Republic in the world; Felix Dzerzhinsky, who sacrificed everything for the revolution until his very

---

* The State Duma was established by the tsar's proclamation of October 17, 1905. It was an elective body of the legislature. It was one of the principal concessions wrung from tsarism during the first Russian Revolution.

last breath; the heroic Stepan Shaumyan, basely executed by interventionists on the sands of Central Asia; Gleb Krzhizhanovsky, a friend of Lenin and one of the first to undertake to make Lenin's dream of Russia's total electrification come true; the fiery pamphleteer Watslaw Vorovsky—these and many other names of *Iskra* fame have earned for themselves an everlasting place in the history of the Soviet land. It was they who carried the burden of delivering *Iskra* from abroad, reprinting it in secret printing shops, and distributing it among the social democratic worker-activists who were not affiliated with the party.

We shall give here a detailed account of one of the rank and file agents of *Iskra*, Elena Stasova. This will not only give us an opportunity to understand the kind of work they were doing but also, though only in part, to unfold the entire depth and treasure of their minds and characters.

The Stasovs belonged to a well-known noble Russian family. Elena's grandfather Vasily Stasov was a famous architect. It was he who built the Smolny and the Ismailovsky (Troitsky) cathedrals in Leningrad, along with a number of other large structures. Her uncle, Vladimir Stasov, an outstanding art critic and archaeologist, was the founder of the movement of young painters who broke with the official style of the Academy of the Arts. The group assumed the name Itinerants and was led by N. I. Kramskoy. In its number were counted I. E. Repin, V. E. Makovsky, V. G. Perov, V. V. Vereshchagin, N. N. Ge, I. I. Shishkin, A. I. Kuindzhi and the sculptors M. M. Antokolsky and I. Y. Ginzburg. Vladimir Stasov was also the heart and center of the musical circle that came to be known as the Mighty Group and had among its members M. A. Balakirev, N. A. Rimsky-Korsakov, A. P. Borodin, T. A. Kyui and M. P. Moussorgsky. These people were the pride of Russia and, as Elena Stasova writes, they had a great influence on her: "I recall my feeling of indebtedness towards the 'people,' towards the workers and peasants who made it possible for us, the intelligentsia, to live as we lived."

She had before her the inspiring example of her father,

Dmitry Stasov, who was dismissed from his post at the age of thirty-three for collecting signatures opposing an attempt to compile a dossier on every student to enable the authorities to maintain permanent surveillance over them. He subsequently participated in the compilation of the Judicial Code in the 1860s, serving thereafter as the first Chairman of the Council of the Russian Bar in St. Petersburg. There was not a single public enterprise in which Dmitry Stasov did not participate. That was why, when ordering him to be banished from St. Petersburg in 1880, Tsar Alexander II remarked irascibly: "You can't spit anywhere without hitting Stasov." It was from the father that the daughter learned not to barter her convictions.

In 1898 she entered firmly on the revolutionary path. From the moment that *Iskra* appeared and began waging its struggle for the establishment of the party, she was an agent for it. She had charge of the technical phase of the St. Petersburg Committee and in her hands rested all matters relating to addresses, quarters, passports, codes, and literature. Getting *Iskra* into Russia was likewise one of her tasks.

In those instances where the literature was shipped in under the guise of baggage, a special technique was devised to clear the shipments. There existed in St. Petersburg a group of porters, so-called redcaps. One of the comrades would be handed a bill of lading. It was his assignment to hire a porter who would go down to the railroad station, while he kept an eye on the man. He had to observe whether he was followed by anyone upon leaving the railway station. Once he made sure that everything was in order, he went ahead to the residence where Stasova was waiting for him.

The literature was always removed from the apartment by hiding it on some person, since packages, which might arouse the suspicion of some spy of the secret police, could not be carried by hand. The distributors of literature acquired a rather odd appearance of obesity. The resident of one of the apartments from which illegal literature was frequently transported, Dr. K. A. Kresnikov, joked that he had a most amazing therapeutic system which made his patients put on weight in a matter of minutes.

Secret correspondence between the members of the party was also a difficult and intricate matter. *Iskra* and Lenin received a vast amount of correspondence from every corner of Russia. As many as three hundred letters a month came to the home of Lenin's wife, Nadezhda Krupskaya.

Elena Stasova recalls:

The code used in our correspondence with Nadezhda Krupskaya was the Krylov fable *The Oak and the Cane*, for the simple reason that this fable contains all the letters of the alphabet. Since we frequently employed this code we had memorized the position of the different letters in any given line. This was important because no matter how clean our hands were, if we continued every day running our finger across the lines, it would always leave some traces. Nadezhda and myself took the precaution of copying the fable down on a separate piece of paper and used it for encoding.

There were also other methods of coding. When some of our comrades would call at the secret address and bring various addresses with them, I was unable to receive them in a written form, since I could not be certain of not being stopped by the police somewhere along the way. For this reason I had to encode it. For this purpose, as was also the case with the other comrades, I had my own code. It consisted of seven words which comprised all letters of the alphabet.

    1. *Telefonia*
    2. *Privychka*
    3. *Khitryuga*
    4. *Budushcheye*
    5. *Mezdra*
    6. *Stsepshchik*
    7. *Zhenshen*

In the code each letter was denoted by two digits, consisting of the ordinal number of the line and of the position which the letter occupied in the word. Thus, for example, the letter L was denoted in my code by 1–3 (line 1, 3rd letter). Moreover, I was also able to modify the code, say by numbering the first line as the eighth, then as the fifteenth, then as the twenty-second. The letter F might bear the code numbers 1–5, then 8–5 and then 22–5.

I coded in digits at the same speed I used in spelling out, since I had committed to memory the position occupied by the letter. Here, for example, is an encoded word which spells *provocator:* 213462416675633,

15622. As you can see, the continuous line of digits is broken only once by a comma. Its purpose was to indicate that the number 15 does not denote line 1, fifth letter but line 15, sixth letter.

This is the way the letters were handled. To begin with, an addressee was selected abroad from among those who would not arouse the suspicion of the police. He was then to forward the letters to *Iskra*. Letters had to be phrased circumspectly so that they would not draw the attention of the inspectors. The encoded text was inserted by chemical means between the lines of the simulated letter.

Illegal work called for presence of mind, attentiveness, nimble reflexes, vigilance and the exercise of self-control.

"What traits of character must the party worker cultivate in a period of illegality?" asked Elena Stasova. And her answer was:

First of all punctuality. It was not always possible to meet comrades in the apartment, and there were times when one had to meet in the street on some corner, and on such occasions the important thing was punctuality. Should you come late, your comrade was forced to stroll up and down. This drew the attention of the policeman and what you actually did was place yourself and your comrade under surveillance. The occasion demanded that you meet within a minute and continue walking. Only then had your meeting passed unobserved.

Secret gatherings frequently took place at the homes of physicians and lawyers. Their office hours were also limited. This meant arriving on time and leaving on time.

Also needed was keenness of observation and attentiveness to surroundings. These traits of character were cultivated in the following manner: Say that I came into a room and my comrade said to me: "Turn the other way and tell me what you have seen." I then had to enumerate all things I had observed on entering the room.

We also had to train ourselves to control our facial expressions. When we were called for questioning, the interrogators would turn their back to the light while we had to sit facing the light so that they could watch our facial expressions. This made it necessary to control it so that neither our thoughts nor our feelings could be betrayed by the alternating expressions in our eyes.

We were in the habit of never asking each other questions which did not concern us. When I was in charge of the technical phase of our work, I knew, of course, the comrades who were engaged in propaganda and agitation, but I did not know their assistants, that is to say, the people who attended the meetings of their circles. They might give me instructions to have the literature brought to such and such an address for the workers. But I had no idea which circle it was or who was at the head of it, nor did I ask about it.

The observance of all the rules of conspiratorial work and the ability to exercise self-control frequently saved one from failure and arrests. Leaning on the shoulders of people such as Elena Stasova, Lenin and Lenin's *Iskra* were able to proceed successfully with the preparations for the summoning of the Second Congress of the R.S.D.R.P.

The Congress met clandestinely in the summer of 1903, starting its sessions in Brussels and continuing in London. It discussed and adopted the party program drafted by Lenin and Plekhanov at the bidding of the editorial board of *Iskra.* The program avowed the proletarian nature of the party, its role as the vanguard of the workers' movement, and advocated the idea of the hegemony of the working class in the Russian revolution.

In the struggle against those who, failing to appreciate fully the organizational principle, sought to transform the party from one of social revolution to one of phrase-mongering and shop talk, an independent political trend emerged at the Second Congress and with it an independent party, the party of the Bolsheviks. This is the name given to the supporters of Lenin, who received a majority in the voting for a Central Committee. His adversaries, who received a minority vote, were henceforth referred to as the Mensheviks.

The founding of a revolutionary party of the working class was the greatest landmark in the history of Russia. The party not only rallied the proletariat, which had emerged as a serious political force at the close of the nineteenth century, but it also furnished the proletariat with a single, centralized, fighting organization that solved theoretical, practical, tactical and organizational problems.

The adoption by the Second Congress of the R.S.D.R.P. of

a revolutionary Marxist program was of great importance. It formulated both the immediate tasks of the proletariat in the bourgeois democratic revolution—the task of overthrowing tsarism and establishing a democratic republic (the minimum program); and its ultimate goal, a victory for the socialist revolution to establish the dictatorship of the proletariat and put an end forever to the exploitation of man by man (maximum program). "Several years before the revolution," Lenin wrote at a later time, "the Social Democrats came out with a most consistent and uncompromising program, whose correctness was borne out by the class struggle and by the action of the masses during the 1905 Revolution."

The Dress Rehearsal. The fire of the revolution was fanned into a bright conflagration from the spark of revolutionary consciousness dropped by the socialists on the rich soil of the Russian workers' movement. The twentieth century ushered in a new and higher form of class struggle. The proletariat of the empire turned from economic strikes to political strikes and demonstrations. On May 1, 1900, a mass political demonstration took place in Kharkov. Ten thousand workers issued a demand for an eight-hour workday and political freedoms. In 1901, on May 1, strikes spread through St. Petersburg, Moscow, Tiflis, Ekaterinoslav and other large industrial centers. On May 7, 1901, a strike was called at the Obukhov military works in St. Petersburg in protest to the dismissal of a group of workers in retaliation for their participation in the May 1 demonstration. All of the 5,000 workers in the plant demanded the reinstatement of their comrades and the dismissal of the most hated foremen.

"The next demand you people will perhaps make is to fire the ministers?" the assistant plant director queried in a mocking tone.

"Not only the ministers but the tsar himself!" the men of the Obukhov works replied.

The strikers met the police, the gendarmes and two companies of soldiers with a hail of stones. The battle of the unarmed workers against the regular troops of the tsar lasted for more than three hours.

In the summer of 1903 the individual strikes at different enterprises in the south of Russia developed into a general strike.

The Russo-Japanese War, which began in January 1904, further deepened the crisis throughout the country. The general strike of the workers of Baku, which broke out in December, bore witness to the serious resurgence of the revolutionary movement in the outlying national districts of the Russian empire. The workers of nearly all the larger cities and industrial centers of the country went out on strike as a show of solidarity with the proletarians of Baku. "We, the workers of St. Petersburg, salute you cordially in your glorious struggle," the workers of the capital wrote. "In your new action we see the beginning of the revolutionary movement of the broad masses which will once and for all sweep away the autocracy that is hateful to us."

All signs pointed to the approach of the revolution in Russia, Maxim Gorky wrote as follows in "Song of the Stormy Petrel":

"A storm! Soon the Storm will come crashing with thunder!"

And the storm did crash.

In the early days of January 1905, in a protest against the dismissal of a number of workers by the administration, 13,000 proletarians of the Putilov works called a strike. They received the support of all the large plants in the capital. By January 8 the strike had spread throughout St. Petersburg. It turned into a general strike and blazed up into a class struggle of unbelievable proportions.

To crush it, the ruling circles again had recourse to their favorite device, armed suppression and provocation. The priest Gapon, one of the organizers of the Russian Association of Workers of Plants and Factories, which had been founded at the initiative of S. V. Zubatov, chief of the secret police, came forward with the proposal of staging a peaceful procession to the Winter Palace (the tsar's residence in St. Petersburg). He proposed that a petition be submitted to Nicholas II. The petition read:

We, wretched and abused slaves crushed by the burden of despotism and arbitrary power . . . We who have come here, thousands of us, are deprived of all human rights, as are the rest of the Russian people . . .

Your Majesty! Deny not the help that the Russian people ask of You! Bring down the wall which stands between You and Your people! Deign and condescend so that our pleas may be heeded, and you will bring happiness to Russia; if you will not we are prepared to die right here. We have only two ways open to us: freedom and happiness or the grave.

The second path was being readied for them. The map of the city had been marked with the places where the soldiers and the Cossacks were to be brought into action, and where the demonstration was to be stopped at any price. But the faith in the tsar, in his "mercy," was still alive among the masses:

". . . Deny not the help which the Russian people ask of You!"

The Bolsheviks were opposed to the petition. "Freedom cannot be purchased," one of the leaflets of the St. Petersburg Committee warned, "at so paltry a price as one petition. . . . Freedom is paid for with blood, freedom is won with arms in hand, in fierce battles. No supplications are to be addressed to the tsar, and not even demands. One must not humble oneself before our accursed enemy, but topple him from the throne and drive him out together with his autocratic clique—this is the only way in which freedom can be won."

It was impossible to halt the procession and the Bolsheviks stood by the people. On their motion, political demands were included in the petition, among other things, the calling of a Constituent Assembly, transfer of the land to the peasants, freedom of speech, press and assembly, and an eight-hour day.

However, this did not alter the obsequious tone of the petition. On January 9, the peaceful demonstration was met by the bullets and bayonets of the soldiers, by the sabres and the knout of the Cossacks.

They sank down, women, old men and children, in a gory harvest of death, as they were stabbed with bayonets and riddled with bullets at point-blank range.

". . . We are being scoffed at; they do not regard us as humans, they treat us like slaves who must bear their bitter fate and remain mute . . ."

More than a thousand killed, some five thousand wounded; that was the price they paid for trying to feel human. The ninth of January remained in the memory of the people as Bloody Sunday, and in the history of Russia it became known under that name. What the bullets riddled on that day was faith in the tsar. The First Russian Revolution started on that day.

The Bolsheviks called the people to battle, to vengeance.

"Citizens! Yesterday you witnessed the bestiality of the autocratic government," they wrote on the day following the bloody reckoning with the demonstrators. "You saw the blood which bespattered the streets. Who was it that summoned the army and its weapons, who aimed the bullets at the hearts of the workers? It was the tsar, the grand dukes, the ministers, the generals and the riff-raff of the court. They are the killers! Death to the killers!!!"

The proletariat replied to the tsar's repressions with political strikes. In St. Petersburg the armed clashes between the workers and the troops were still continuing when the Moscow proletariat called a general strike. On January 13, 1905, the workers of Riga called a strike and staged a political demonstration. On January 14 a general strike broke out in Warsaw, and on January 18 a general strike was called in Tiflis, ushering in a series of political strikes in the towns of Transcaucasia. During the period from January to March of 1905 alone, 810,000 industrial workers went out on strike, twice as many as during the entire preceding decade. "Dormant Russia," wrote Lenin, "was transformed into a Russia of a revolutionary proletariat and a revolutionary people."

The May 1 celebrations turned into an imposing demonstration of proletarian solidarity among the various nationalities of the empire. The total number of workers participating in the strikes on that day amounted to 220,000.

The greatest of all the May actions was that of the textile workers of Ivanovo-Voznesensk. Their strike lasted from May 12 to the end of July. A total of seventy-two days of uninterrupted strike action, the degree of organization which prevailed among the workers of Ivanovo-Voznesensk, and their solidarity, served as a great school for the political education of the masses. The Bolsheviks were in the leadership of the strike. The masses held in admiration Fyodor Afanasev, a worker Bolshevik, and Mikhail Frunze, who subsequently became a prominent figure in the Communist Party and the Red Army.

For the purpose of directing the strike and carrying on negotiations with the employers, the workers of Ivanovo-Voznesensk created a Soviet of Representatives. This was the first Soviet of Workers Deputies, and in it Lenin detected the emergence of a new form of power created by the masses themselves.

The Ivanovo-Voznesensk Soviet acted as a full-fledged organ of power. It created a militia and detachments of armed workers to maintain public order and repulse the police and the troops. It established control over the printing shops, while also ensuring freedom of speech and assembly, conducting negotiations with the government and organizing a strikers' fund. The strike was terminated only at the instructions of the Soviet. It demonstrated the advanced political maturity of the workers.

The flame of revolution blazed with an ever higher intensity. Strikes and demonstrations, which were occasionally fought on the barricades, rolled across Lodz in May, spreading to Warsaw, Odessa, Rostov, Novorossiisk and other cities. In the summer of 1905 there was a total of 895 peasant actions. Particularly stubborn and well organized were the battles waged by the peasants in Georgia, in the Ukraine and in the Volga Area.

The military, which was the last bastion of tsarism, also began to waver. In the summer of 1905 the great battleship *Potyomkin* aligned itself with the revolutionary people for the first time. For more than a week it navigated the Black Sea under a red flag, and in the words of Lenin it was "the unconquered territory of the revolution." Short of water supply, coal and provisions, it was forced to steam to Rumania and surrender to the Rumanian government. The *Potyomkin* incident served as a spur to a whole series of mutinies in the army and the navy.

The country saw the spread of a general strike. In September the Moscow printers went out on strike, followed by the bakers, trolley car workers and the workers of other branches. Tsarism again attempted punitive measures. In response, the metal workers joined the struggle. The events occurring in Moscow evoked sympathetic reactions in many cities throughout the country.

The Bolsheviks worked to impart an organized and purposeful character to the struggle being waged. On October 7 the railroad workers of many railway lines were already out on strike. The strike enveloped the entire Moscow network of railroads (with the exception of the Nikolayev line linking Moscow with St. Petersburg, which was guarded by troops). Commencing on October 11, on the decision of the Moscow Conference of the Bolsheviks, the strike became general throughout the city. Moscow was supported by St. Petersburg and within a matter of days the strike blanketed the country. A total of 519,000 plant and factory workers, 700,000 railroad workers, and in sum total no less than two million people participated in the All-Russian October political strike of 1905.

In his attempt to bedevil the revolutionary movement,

Nicholas II published a manifesto on October 17, "granting most graciously" freedom of speech, assembly and trade unions, personal immunity and an elective legislative body or State Duma. The liberals received the tsar's manifesto with jubilation. They regarded the revolution as ended and its goals achieved. Parties were founded, clearly reflecting in their very names their political platforms.

The Union of October 17 (Octobrists) joined together the large industrialists, the merchants and those landowners who had shifted to capitalist methods. It was headed by a well-known industrialist and Moscow landlord A. I. Guchkov and a major landlord, V. M. Rodzyanko. The manifesto of October 17 was entirely in keeping with their interests. The Octobrists had no wish to go beyond this.

The Constitutional Democrats' Party (Cadets) was the leading party of the liberal-monarchist bourgeoisie. It included the representatives of the financial and industrial circles, some of the landowners and the intelligentsia. Prominent among the leaders of the Cadets were P. N. Milyukov, S. A. Muromtsev, V. A. Maklakov, A. I. Shingarev, P. B. Struve and F. I. Rodichev. They did not go beyond a demand for a constitutional monarchy.

The "freedom" proffered by the tsar proved to be a barefaced fraud. Immediately after the "Monarch's graciousness" followed merciless repression, a slaughter of the vanguard of the workers, students and prominent Bolsheviks (one of those killed during this time in Moscow was N. E. Bauman, and in Ivanovo-Voznesensk it was F. A. Afanasev), pogroms against the Jews swept the country and demonstrators were shot down. Within less than a month after the manifesto was promulgated nearly four thousand people were killed and more than ten thousand wounded and mutilated. It was no wonder that the song then going the rounds was:

The tsar was seized with fear and made a proclamation:
Give freedom to the dead and jail the living nation.

The Manifesto of October 17, 1905, did not halt the spread of the revolutionary movement. The revolution continued growing at an increasing rate while the events multiplied daily. The October events and especially the All-Russian political strike gave impetus to the peasant movement. It blanketed half the Russian districts. Out of a total of 3,328 peasant actions in 1905, half occurred in the autumn. A total of two thousand country estates were destroyed during that year, which is to say every fifteenth estate.

The revolutionary movement was embracing ever greater numbers of soldiers and sailors. An uprising of the Kronstadt sailors flared towards the end of October. The uprising was crushed and the mutineers faced a death sentence. The proletariat of St. Petersburg rose up in their defense and prevented the implementation of the death sentence that had been handed down by the tsar's court against the insurgent sailors and soldiers. Within a few days an uprising of sailors took place in Vladivostok, and in November in Sevastopol, one of the largest military ports on the Black Sea. The uprising of the sailors of the naval division took place aboard the cruiser *Ochakov* and on the battleship *Panteleimon* (the former *Potyomkin*) as well as on a number of minesweepers, supported by the workers of the Admiralty and by the soldiers of the Forty-ninth Brest Infantry Regiment.

The ferment in the Black Sea Fleet did not subside following the disturbances on the battleship *Potyomkin,* and it grew particularly intense in the autumn. Gatherings and meetings took place. One of the meetings of the sailors and workers was fired on by the police. This was the drop that filled the cup of patience to overflowing, and a mutiny broke out. It was headed by the Soviet of Sailors', Soldiers' and Workers' Deputies, while the military leader of the mutiny was Lieutenant P. P. Schmidt. He dispatched the following telegram to the tsar: "The glorious Black Sea Fleet, sacredly guarding its loyalty to the people, demands of you . . . the immediate convening of a Constituent Assembly and that you cease obeisance to your ministers." Schmidt hoisted the red flag on the cruiser *Ocha-kov* and proclaimed himself commander of the fleet. This not-withstanding, the insurrection was of a defensive nature and lacked a clear-cut plan. It was not supported by the other ves-sels or by any of the military units. The insurgents let time slip by and the government was able to rally its forces in order to force their submission. The vessels that took part in the upris-ing came under artillery fire. Lieutenant Schmidt and the leaders of the Soviet Bolsheviks were executed under court sentence.

However, the situation in the country was such that an armed uprising became the only possible course of action. The Bolshevik Party prepared the masses for this decisive struggle with the autocracy. On November 8 Lenin arrived from abroad. On the very same day he paid a visit to graves of the victims of "Bloody Sunday" at the Preobrazhensky Cemetery in the capital, in tribute to those who lost their lives during the January days of 1905.

Lenin's interest centered unflaggingly on the Soviets, as he considered them to be the organs of the uprising and of revo-lutionary power. While preparing the masses for the struggle, Lenin time and again stressed the absolute need for a broad cooperation between the workers through their Soviets and the non-proletarian masses, with a view to isolating the liber-als. The tactic of a left bloc was emerging during those days.

On December 5, 1905, expressing the will of the workers, the citywide Moscow Conference of the Bolsheviks adopted a decision to call a general strike and to launch an armed strug-gle. On December 7, a general political strike began in re-sponse to the call issued by the Moscow Soviet. On December 10 the strike turned into an armed uprising. In the streets of Presnya, Zamoskvorechye, the Rogozhsko-Simonovsky Dis-trict and in the district of the Kazan Railroad desperate bat-tles were waged over a period of nine days. The insurgents had no experience at all in armed combat, and they suffered from a shortage of arms. Nor did they have competent leadership, as the workers of the Moscow committee of the Bolsheviks were arrested at the very outset of the uprising. The St. Petersburg Soviet headed by the Mensheviks failed to come to the support of the Muscovites. The government moved reinforcements by way of the Nikolayevsk Railroad from St. Petersburg to Moscow for the support of the Moscow garrison, which was isolated from the insurrectionists. Towards the middle of December the tsarist government had in Moscow eleven infantry and five cavalry regiments as well as five artillery batteries against two thousand armed and four thousand unarmed combatants. A joint appeal of the leaders of the R.S.D.R.P., Bolsheviks and Mensheviks, on December 13, calling for the support of the Moscow uprising, failed to bring the intended results. All of this determined the outcome.

On December 17 the counterrevolution launched its attack and the insurrection was savagely crushed. The center of the uprising, Presnya, flowed with blood. The Moscow Committee of the Party and the Moscow Soviet adopted a decision to end the armed uprising on December 19 in order to preserve the revolutionary forces and prepare for further struggles.

". . . We have started and we are ending," wrote the staff of the detachments of armed workers in its appeal. "Blood, violence and death will dog our steps, but it doesn't matter. The future belongs to the working class. Generation after generation will learn a lesson of endurance from Presnya throughout the world."

Following the events in Moscow in December 1905 and January 1906, insurrections flared up in Nizhny Novgorod, Rostov-on-the-Don, Novorossiisk, Donbass, Ekaterinoslav, Perm, Ufa, Krasnoyarsk and Chita. Large-scale armed actions took place in Transcaucasia, Poland, the Baltic area and Finland. However, all of these separate insurrections were savagely suppressed by the tsarist government.

The December armed uprising was the climax of the 1905 revolution. The difference in their attitudes towards it put an even greater distance between the two wings of the Social

Democratic Party. The Mensheviks condemned the heroic struggle of the Russian proletariat who took the path of armed uprising. "There was no need for taking up arms," declared Plekhanov. On the other hand, the Bolsheviks maintained that it was necessary to take up arms more resolutely. They explained to the masses that the victory of the revolution could be won only in armed conflict. Holding that the December uprising was of great significance, Lenin wrote that the people "had gone through its baptism of fire. It had become steeled in the insurrection and brought forth numerous fighters who triumphed in 1917 . . ."

After the defeat of the December armed uprising, there followed a period of gradual decline in the revolution. It retreated fighting. The strike movement still continued vigorously, and the level of peasant agitation remained high. (In 1906 there was a total of 2,600 peasant actions.) In Sveaborg, in Kronstadt and in a number of garrisons of the Turkestan area there were insurrections of the soldiers. All of them suffered crushing defeats.

The speeches of the peasant deputies in the First and Second State Dumas, demanding land and freedom for the people, made it clear to the tsar that even though it was shorn of any real power, being dependent on the government and tributary to it, the Duma could serve as a platform for the exposure of tsarism and the survivals of serfdom. Seeing that the revolution was on the decline, Nicholas II dispersed the Second Duma on June 3, 1907. All the members of the Social Democratic faction of the Duma were arrested. The tsar's Manifesto of October 17, 1905, and other laws promulgated during the course of the revolution were rudely violated. All impartial observers described these events as the Third of June Coup. It signified the victory of autocracy and the end of the last stage of the first Russian Revolution. There ensued a prolonged period of reaction which was not followed by a new wave of the revolutionary movement before 1910.

Notwithstanding its defeat, the struggle of the Russian proletariat in the years of 1905 to 1907 remained one of the most remarkable pages in the history of the liberation movement. The revolution was unable to gain a victory but the working class proved itself potentially capable of victory.

The first popular revolution of the twentieth century was of great significance. It was in the nature of a dress rehearsal without which the revolution of 1917, either in its bourgeois-democratic phase in February or its proletarian phase in October, would not have been possible. It was a prologue to the coming revolutionary explosions both in Europe and Asia.

The Gathering Revolutionary Crisis and the First World War. The beginning of the First World War cut short the new upsurge of the revolutionary movement that had occurred following the Lena carnage, which took place in 1912. The patriotic demonstrations, the philanthropic collections of contributions at soirées, balls, and concerts, and the speeches delivered by Menshevik leaders, particularly those of George Plekhanov, advancing such slogans as "Defense of the Motherland," caused the first flush of chauvinistic intoxication to engulf quite a considerable section of the workers, and especially the peasantry.

At the time the war was declared, hundreds of Bolshevik party workers were in prison or in exile, and a great many of them had emigrated. The scale of the repression undertaken against the Bolsheviks can be gauged from an inquiry made of the delegates to the Sixth Party Congress, which convened in Petrograd after the overthrow of tsarism in August 1917. E. Drabkina, who was in charge of distributing the questionnaires to the delegates at the Congress, recalls the following:

"One hundred and seventy-one delegates filled out the questionnaires. They had spent in the revolutionary movement a collective total of 1,721 years. They had undergone 549 arrests, or an average of three each. They spent in jail, in exile and at hard labor a total of about 500 years."

The destruction of the Bolshevik party organizations in a number of large cities, including the capital, could not but have an effect on party relations and working conditions which had already become unwieldy as a result of the war. Nevertheless, the only party in Russia that openly and straightforwardly raised its voice in protest against the war and declared a revolutionary struggle against it was the party of the Bolsheviks under the leadership of Lenin.

The Bolshevik deputies of the Fourth State Duma, A. E. Badayev, M. K. Muranov, G. I. Petrovsky, F. N. Samoilov and N. P. Shagov, came forward with a statement of the Social Democratic faction roundly condemning the war, naming as its perpetrators the rulers of the belligerent countries. When the adoption of the war budget came under discussion, they not only refused to vote for it but they walked out of the session in protest. This action resounded throughout the entire world. Subsequently, the Bolshevik deputies of the Duma were placed under arrest, condemned and sentenced by the tsarist court to be exiled to Siberia for life.

Lenin was again abroad when the war broke out. In the autumn of 1907 the first volume of his *Works, In Twelve Years*, was published in St. Petersburg. It included the principal articles printed during the period of 1895 to 1905. The volume was confiscated by the police and it brought Lenin face to face with the prospect of being placed on trial. In hiding from the police, Lenin walked across the Gulf of Finland on the perilous ice in December 1907, and eventually reached Stockholm. A second and prolonged emigration now began for him. He lived for a while in Geneva and in Paris, then in London, Berlin and Rome, and went to Capri to see Gorky. In 1912, to be nearer to Russia, where once again an upsurge of the revolutionary movement was being felt, Lenin reached Cracow where he took up residence, spending the summers in Poronino. He was living there at the outbreak of the First World War.

Austrian gendarmes arrested Lenin. However, with the aid of some friends he managed to obtain a release some two weeks later. Within a matter of days he delivered a speech before the Bolsheviks in Bern (Switzerland) on the position of the Party towards the imperialist war. The theses of the revised speech were subsequently published as a party document in the form of a manifesto of the Central Committee of the R.S.D.R.P. entitled *The War and Russian Social Democracy.*

The manifesto stressed that the purpose of the war was to seize territories and to subjugate other nations, while disuniting and stultifying the workers' movement, and exterminating its vanguard. The manifesto considered the task of the Social Democrats to be to struggle against the chauvinism of their country, and find the best possible way out of the war, by bringing about the defeat of the government and turning the imperialist war into a civil war.

Lenin's slogan of bringing about the defeat of the country's own government in the imperialist war received a hostile reception from the social chauvinists. They sought to brand it as treachery to the national interests of the country. Lenin replied in a remarkable article entitled "The National Pride of the Great Russians." In it he made the point that the war was being waged in the interest of a group that was disgracing the national dignity of the Great Russians. One could defend the native land under such circumstances only by fighting with every means at one's command against the Romanov clique and against the ruling circles, who were the deadliest enemies of the native land.

These were the only tactics suited to the occasion. They were in keeping with the aggressive, predatory aims of all belligerent countries, with the exception of Belgium and Serbia.

The Left-Social Democrats throughout the world came out against the war. Karl Liebknecht, Rosa Luxemburg and Clara Zetkin in Germany, Dimitry Blagoyev and Vasil Kolarov in Bulgaria, D. Maklin in England, and Fritz Platten in Switzerland all raised their voices in opposition to the war and against the treachery of the rightist leaders of Social Democracy who voted in favor of war loans and supported their governments.

The longer the war lasted the stronger and more widespread

became the general discontent with and bitterness against the ruling classes. The situation was taking a revolutionary turn. The organizing and directing force in the process was the Party of the Bolsheviks. Outlawed by the tsarist government as the only party which openly opposed the war, it continued to fulfill its revolutionary obligation with an unbending will. Despite the terror, the growth of the Party was not diminished. New party members were added to replace those who had been arrested because of their struggle against tsarism. More than two thousand regular dues-paying members belonged to the Party in Leningrad in the year 1916.

The strike movement intensified, beginning in the spring of 1915. The struggle flared up with particular force in Moscow and Petrograd. The autocracy dealt with the workers in a most savage manner. The police fired on demonstrations in Kostroma and Ivanovo-Voznesensk. The workers of Petrograd* responded to this crime by calling a political protest strike. A total of more than half a million workers took part in the strike movement of 1915. It took on an even wider sweep in 1916, involving more than one million people. Many of the strikes were of a political nature and were conducted under the slogans "Down with the war!" and "Down with the autocracy!"

The village poor joined the movement of the city. In 1916 it was reported from the Yadrinsky District of the Kazan province to the center that:

"There is every reason to fear that the peasant movement will assume the proportions it reached in 1905–1906."

About three hundred peasant actions against the kulaks, the landowners and the government's agrarian policy took place during the war years.

The new year of 1917, which was ushered in to the accompaniment of the thunder of cannon seemed to carry a forebod-

---

* At the beginning of the war, to fan the mood of chauvinism, the government changed the name of St. Petersburg to Petrograd.

ing that it would be a year of changes. This feeling became more and more widespread. The poet Vladimir Mayakovsky wrote about the "revolutionary crown of thorns." Another poet of those days, and one of no lesser fame, Velemir Khlebnikov, citing a long array of historical dates that at first sight appeared to be incomprehensible, pointed to the conclusion that the fall of the monarchy was inescapable. Even as rightist a paper as *Novye dni* wrote in its issue of January 3:

"Never before have the circumstances of life been such as to make one feel at so close a range that something higher was so near. . . . And anyone feeling this something higher becomes filled with concern, with a sense of sacred disquiet, and gazes questioningly forward into the distant future, sensing the alarm and singularity of each living day. . . ."

Everything combined to inspire uneasiness, from the assassination of Grigory Rasputin, to the "ministerial cabal," to the alarming news from the front.

During that period there was a renewed contact between the ruling circles of Russia and the Central Powers. (The reference here is primarily to the well-known meetings between Rizov, the Bulgarian Ambassador to Berlin, and the Russian representatives in Switzerland and Norway, Neklyudov and Gulkevich.) The talks that were underway with the Bulgarians, who did not conceal the fact that they were acting with the knowledge and blessing of Germany, were continued in neutral Switzerland. The tsarist government evidenced an interest in the advances made by the opponent. The autocracy proceeded on the premise that it must free its hands on the outside to be able to deal more effectively with the domestic enemy (the ever-mounting wave of the revolutionary movement), which was more dangerous than the enemy without.

Information to the effect that a shift was imminent in the foreign policy of the government led to the hatching of a "palace coup" by the bourgeois landowning opposition. In this they were aided by the Allied Powers, fearful lest Russia withdraw from the war. The conspirators planned to overthrow

Nicholas, send the tsar's wife to some monastery, crown the under-age Alexius as emperor, and appoint the Grand Duke Mikhail Alexandrovich, the tsar's brother, to the Regency, as he was famed for his pro-British sentiments. They hoped to wean the masses away from the revolutionary movement by the activities of the Duma. The bourgeois leadership concentrated all of their fire on the Minister of the Interior, Protopopov, and took the allies under their wing, protecting them against the attacks of the Germanophile party.

In the Duma rumors began to circulate to the effect that there had been an incident between the Chairman of the State Duma, Rodzyanko, and Protopopov on the occasion of the exchange of New Year's wishes. The latter walked up to Rodzyanko and addressed to him some words of salutation. Rodzyanko avoided a handshake and turned away from Protopopov abruptly. The Minister felt offended and there was talk of an impending duel. However, no duel took place. The revolution headed it off completely. It swept away both the conspiracy of the autocratic government and the planned palace coup.

The severe winter of 1917 imposed new privations and a general price boost on the workers and toilers of the country. Commencing January 1 even trolley fares were increased by five kopecks. The economy of backward Russia patently failed to withstand the wartime strain. Economic disorders began to reach the point of complete dislocation both in industry and transportation. The mobilization had torn out of the village millions of the most highly skilled workers. According to the 1917 census, up to 50 per cent of the workers had been removed from the villages. Those who went into the army were replaced by women, children and old men. Some 600,000 prisoners of war and 250,000 refugees were drafted for work in the villages but their labor proved inefficient and low in productivity. The planted area shrank and crop capacity dropped while cattle breeding also suffered a decline. While in the prewar period more than 79.4 million tons of grain were harvested annually, the harvest in 1917 amounted to no more than 52.1 million tons. In December 1916 the government adopted a decision to introduce compulsory requisitioning of grain and cattle.

The economic dependence of the tsarist clique on the Allies continued to grow, and in fact, as far as the latter were concerned, aid to the partner became a purely commercial undertaking. Thus Great Britain confirmed its readiness to supply Russia with 3.72 million tons of freight "related to defense requirements," but in recompense for it demanded, in addition to 529,500 tons of wheat that had been preempted earlier, 100,000 tons of flax, 250,000 to 300,000 hectolitres of alcohol, a large quantity of timber and a considerable number of other products, such as manganese, asbestos, potash, eggs, lentils, and beans. Hungry Russia, freezing on account of a shortage of fuel, was exporting everything, even what she herself needed desperately, under conditions of the most serious food crisis. Long queues of people waiting for an opportunity to get some bread trailed along the streets of all the cities. All the newspapers carried an item concerning the wife of a merchant who had shot herself in Odessa at the end of January. In the note which she left she stated that the endless standing in queues had made life intolerable for her. However, such things were not a frequent occurrence. More often the people in the queue charged forward and looted the bakeries.

In their January reports the secret police stated as follows:

"Mothers of families, in a state of complete exhaustion from standing in queues and waiting at stores, worn out with suffering at the sight of their half-starved and sick children, were to be sure now closer to revolution than Messrs. Milyukov, Rodichev and Co., and also a good deal more dangerous, since they represented an accumulation of fuels which one spark was sufficient to inflame."

Seeking to prevent the conflagration, and employing the usual device, they endeavored to shift the "primordial force" into the channels of anti-semitism. In the early days of January, as the newspaper *Rech* reported, an order was promulgated according to which all persons of the Jewish faith employed in the Union of Cities and in the Union of the Zemstvos, excepting doctors and their assistants (it seems they were needed!) were to be immediately replaced by persons "of other faiths." And what brazen hypocrisy was evinced in an accompanying announcement of the Ministry of the Interior which recommended to the provincial and regional chiefs that they not put any obstacles in the way of Jewish disabled veterans staying in localities outside of the Jewish pale "for the purpose of securing artificial limbs, that is to say prosthetic appliances." According to these instructions they were also permitted to settle "in Siberian health resorts." However, there were no "health resorts" in Russia either for Jews or for other nationalities of the "one and indivisible" empire, which was a prison of nations, where Poles and Armenians, the Kirghiz people and Kalmyks, the Finns and the Ukrainians were equally victimized.

The flame of insurrection among the peoples of Central Asia blazed up for some months in 1916. A new tide of the revolutionary movement could not be stemmed by any means whatsoever, although the chief of the Petrograd Secret Police Department, Globachev, in his report to his superiors concerning the clandestine revolutionary mood then prevailing, stated that "the proletariat is now less affected by propaganda" and declared that "a number of liquidations in recent days have considerably weakened the forces of the underground."

Enormous strikes broke out throughout the country on the anniversary of the shooting down of the members of the workers' demonstration in 1905. On the eve of the strike, the Petrograd Bolshevik Committee called on the workers to stage anti-war demonstrations. The Russian Bureau of the Central Committee of the Bolsheviks addressed an identical directive to Moscow, and meetings were organized in many plants and factories on January 9. Workers surged into the streets holding aloft red banners. In the Vyborg, Moscow and Narvsky Districts of the capital, nearly all of the enterprises stopped work. Workers' demonstrations also took place in Baku, Nizhny Novgorod, Voronezh and other cities.

The Moscow Committee of the Bolsheviks organized a demonstration of two thousand on Tverskoy Boulevard, but the mounted police dispersed the rally. Towards three o'clock in the afternoon a group of workers and students appeared on Teatralny Square carrying red banners displaying the slogans "Down with the war!" "Long live the Russian Social Democratic Labor Party!" The demonstration soon swelled in number to one thousand and set out toward Okhotny Ryad, covered half the distance between Neglinnaya and Okhotny Ryad and turned back. The trolley cars stopped running. The crowds of watchers continued to grow. Many of them joined the demonstrators in singing: "We shall renounce the old world." Near the Metropol Hotel, police officers blocked the demonstrators, while two ensigns rushed at them with bared sabers. The policemen also drew their sabers out of their scabbards and began laying about them with the flats of the blades. Mounted police detachments appeared on the scene, rushing at the demonstrators from the rear and sides. A few people were arrested.

Violence against the strikers was raging in every city. However, new strikes broke out within a few days. Through the month of January more than 200,000 workers struck throughout the country, not counting those in Petrograd. No such strikes had ever occurred before during the war. An extremely tense situation developed in the capital.

Overthrow of the Autocracy. When in the last third of February Nicholas II made a trip to military headquarters to see the Chief of Staff of the Supreme Command, General Alekseyev, he had no idea what events were maturing in the country.

On February 10 at Tsarskoye Selo he found himself listening to the sad words of the Chairman of the State Duma, Rodzyanko, who had come there to render his report. In it he contended that Russia was on the eve of great events the outcome of which could not be anticipated. So far as Rodzyanko was concerned, one could brush him off with cavalier treatment and the job of warding off his prognostications had to be entrusted to the loyal minions of the autocracy.

However, the first symptoms showing that Rodzyanko was nevertheless right were not long in coming. On February 14, 1917, sixty enterprises went on strike, involving some tens of thousands of workers. They followed the lead of the Bolsheviks, organizing a demonstration under the slogans "Down with the autocracy! Down with the war!" Police who sought to disperse the demonstration encountered resistance.

On the same day meetings were held in a number of institutions of higher learning in the capital. The revolutionary parts of the student bodies at the university, the polytechnic, the forestry school, the psychoneurological institute and other institutions of higher learning declared themselves ready to support the proletariat in its struggle against tsarism.

On the thirteenth and fourteenth of February the representatives of the Russian Bureau of the Central Committee of the Bolshevik Party delivered speeches in the shops of the Izhorsky plant at Kolpino. Hundreds of the plant's workers responded to their appeals. The chief of the secret police department, when reporting to the Petrograd gendarmerie department concerning the meetings and strikes at the Izhorsky plant, called attention to the helpless state of the administration. The Cossacks and soldiers who were sent to "establish order" almost completely avoided any recourse to violent measures against the workers. The gendarme reported as follows:

"It should be noted that the Cossacks showed an amicable disposition towards the workers and they obviously considered the demands of the workers to be justified and that no steps should be taken by the government against the movement; on the whole, the impression was produced that the Cossacks were on the side of the workers."

Further events showed that the "impression" was well-

The last Russian Emperor, Nicholas II (1868–1918), and
Empress Alexandra wearing Russian national costumes.

Young Fyodor Chalyapin at a soirée in St. Petersburg.
The composer I. Cui (in a general's uniform) stands at the piano, and
in the corner are N. Rimsky-Korsakov and A. Glazunov.

The Alexander III Bridge.

Rasputin.

BOTTOM:

"Thou art plentiful, and thou art impoverished," the poet Nekrasov wrote about the Russian land. There were a great many villages like this one.

INSET:

A stove in a peasant's hut.

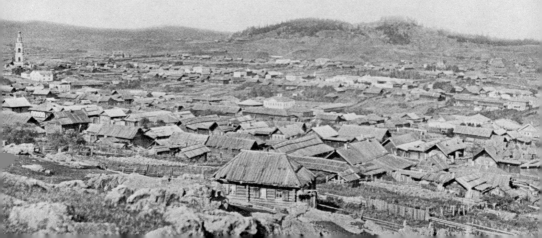

UPPER LEFT:
Peasant women reaping rye.

UPPER RIGHT:
Workers crushing stones for
paving the parade grounds,
Mounted Guards' billets, St. Petersburg.

January 9, 1905.

The Russian section of the Paris Exposition, 1900.

The pavilion of the wine and vodka monopoly was the largest among the Russian pavilions at the Exposition.

The people's way of life as depicted at the Exposition.

After a battle, World War I, 1915.

Barricades in Lityeini Prospekt
in St. Petersburg during the
February Revolution of 1917.

The May Day demonstration in St. Petersburg, 1917.

Pravda—Issue No. 1,
March 5 (18), 1917.

grounded. The atmosphere became more heated day by day. On February 18 one of the shops of the Putilov Works went out on strike. In reply to the demands of the workers, the administration closed down the works on February 22 and the Putilov workers moved out into the streets.

On February 23 (March 8 according to the new calendar) * on the occasion of Women's International Day, new ranks of men and women workers joined the demonstration started the day before at the closure of the Putilov Works. In response to the appeal issued by the Bolsheviks fifty-nine enterprises struck, involving a total of some 83,000 people.

Tsar Nicholas II dispatched a telegram on that day to the Commander of the Petrograd Military Area, General Khabalov, reading as follows: "I command you to stop all disorders in the capital no later than tomorrow, such disorders being inadmissible during the difficult days of the war with Germany."

The tsar had not yet grasped the full extent, the force and the full meaning of the events that were taking place. Having dispatched the telegram to Khabalov, he sat down to address a letter to the empress:

"My dear beloved sunshine!" he wrote. ". . . I miss very much the half hour of solitaire every evening. As soon as time permits I will again get down to playing dominoes."

By February 24 the number of strikers had reached 200,000. On the twenty-fifth, the Petrograd strike turned into a general political strike. On that day the Bolsheviks issued an appeal that formulated the political objectives of the movement and called on the workers and soldiers to turn the strike action into a decisive battle with tsarism.

"The time has come for open warfare!" the Bolsheviks proclaimed. ". . . Better die a glorious death for the workers' cause," they wrote, "than pay with your head for the profits of

---

* All the dates in the text concerning the revolution are given according to the old, Julian calendar, which differs from the European calendar by thirteen days.

capital at the front or perish from hunger or back-breaking toil.
. . . Struggle lies ahead. Sure victory awaits us! Everyone
rally to the red banners of the revolution!"

On February 26 the political strike and demonstrations in
Petrograd developed into an armed uprising.

"Your Majesty," Rodzyanko wired that day to the tsar, "the
situation is grave. Anarchy rules the city. The government is
paralyzed. Transportation, food supply and fuel deliveries are
in complete disorder. General discontent is growing. Confused
shooting is heard in the streets. Army detachments are firing
at each other. Absolutely essential to entrust a person enjoying
the confidence of the country with the task of forming a new
government. Not a minute to be lost. All delay spells death. I
pray to God that in this hour the responsibility may not come
to rest on the monarch."

But it was too late in fact. Nearly all of the military units
proved "unreliable." On February 26, the Fourth Company of
the Reserve Battalion of the Pavlosk Regiment, outraged by
the participation of the training command of its regiment in
the shooting down of the workers, poured out into the streets
seeking to turn back the men of their regiment to their barracks, and along the way they fired on the mounted detachments of police.

This action of the soldiers, which was still an isolated occurrence on February 26, did not as yet signify the complete shift
of the garrison to the forces of the revolution.

On February 27 the soldiers of the Volyn Regiment allied
themselves with the insurgents. By evening more than 66,000
soldiers of the Petrograd garrison were aligned with the
revolution.

"Please report to His Majesty," wired General Khabalov to
M. V. Alekseyev, "that I was unable to fulfill the command to
restore order in the capital. Most of the units, one after the
other, turned traitor and refused to give battle to the mutineers. Other units fraternized with the mutineers and turned
their guns against the troops loyal to His Majesty. Those who

remained loyal to their oath fought against the mutineers all day and sustained heavy losses. Towards evening the mutineers held most of the capital. Only small units of the different regiments have remained faithful to their oath, and these units are concentrated about the Winter Palace under the command of Major-General Zankevich, and I will continue fighting with their aid."

The Petrograd insurrection was victorious. It received the support of revolutionary forces throughout the country.

Everywhere the workers and peasants in soldiers' uniforms were setting up their revolutionary organizations—the Soviets of Workers' and Soldiers Deputies, which emerged as the organs of the insurrection. Leaning on the armed workers and peasants, the Soviets proceeded immediately to perform the functions of organs of state power, invalidating and declaring null and void certain orders and instructions issued by municipal authorities and those of high-ranking military chiefs; conducting searches and arrests among the police and gendarmerie, and resolving all sorts of economic problems.

On the evening of February 17 there appeared in the Tauride Palace the first deputies elected to the Petrograd Soviet from plants, factories and units of the army. The unconditional support given to the Soviet by the Petrograd garrison conferred on it all the attributes of power, something that even Rodzyanko wrote about with bitterness. However the Bolsheviks were not in control of the Soviet. There were many reasons for this, among them the fact that the leaders of the Bolshevik Party, pursued by the tsarist government, were at the time either abroad or in exile or prison. The Bolsheviks were the first to be drafted into the army and sent to the front lines under the hail of enemy fire. While all the available Bolsheviks were at the time occupied with directing strikes, meetings and mass demonstrations, the Mensheviks and Socialist Revolutionaries were launching into a spate of varied organizational combinations. Moreover, those class-conscious proletarians who had been sent to the front were being replaced by people who were poorly oriented as to the nature and purposes of the political struggle. This is the reason why the leadership of the Soviets fell into the hands of the Mensheviks and Socialist Revolutionaries, who regarded them as provisional organizations needed only until such time as a Constituent Assembly were called into session.

The ruling circles were also endeavoring to organize. On February 27 a group of deputies of the Duma organized a Provisional Committee of the State Duma with Rodzyanko at the head. At first this committee had no intention of taking power into its own hands. V. Shulgin, who was at the time a self-confessed monarchist, recalls in his book *Dni (Days)*:

> . . . Rodzyanko long remained irresolute. He kept on querying, "What is this leading to, and will it or will it not be a mutiny?
>
> ". . . I have no desire to mutiny. I am not a mutineer, I have not made any revolutions nor do I wish to make any. The only reason why it came about is that they would not listen to us . . . But I am not a revolutionary. I will not nor do I want to go against the supreme power. But then again, the fact is that there is no government. They are calling on me from all sides . . . They are tearing down my telephone. They want to know just what they are to do. How is one to act? Step aside? Wash one's hands of it? Leave Russia without a government? After all this is Russia! . . . We have an obligation to our native land, don't we? . . . How is one to act?"
>
> I answered him, unexpectedly even to myself, in a very categorical manner:
>
> "Take it, Mikhail Vladimirovich. There is nothing mutinous about it. Take it as a loyal subject."

And to be sure, the Provisional Committee did act in the spirit of "loyalty." Trying to save the monarchy, it first of all dispatched a delegation to Nicholas II asking that he abdicate in favor of his son. On February 28 the tsar still failed to appreciate how far things had gone. "Considerable armed forces have been sent from the front. My warmest regards," he wired to his wife. On March 2 the demand was reiterated by the commanders of all fronts, who declared that they could not vouch for the army. The tsar's diary described this as follows:

2 March. Thursday. In the morning Ruzsky* arrived and read to me the entire long conversation he had with Rodzyanko over the telephone. According to him the situation in Petrograd is such that the Ministry will now be helpless to do anything without the Duma since the Soc.[ial] Dem.[ocratic] Party in the guise of a Workers' Committee is at loggerheads with it. My abdication is necessary. Ruzsky conveyed this conversation to Headquarters and Alekseyev conveyed it to all commanders-in-chief. By 2:30 replies had been received from all. The fact is that in order to save Russia and to keep the army at the front undisturbed, this action must be taken. I agreed. They sent me a draft manifesto from Headquarters. In the evening Guchkov and Shulgin arrived from Petrograd, whereupon I discussed with them and handed them the signed and revised manifesto. One o'clock in the morning I left Pskov, my heart heavy with what transpired.

Anywhere you turn you find treason, cowardice and deception!

Nicholas II signed the manifesto abdicating his sovereignty, both on his own behalf and on behalf of his son, in favor of his brother Mikhail.

However, there was no way of saving the monarchy. The indignation of the masses also forced Mikhail to abdicate. Anxious not to permit the revolution to spread farther, and acting in concert with the leaders of the Executive Committee of the Petrograd Soviet, the Provisional Committee of the State Duma established a provisional government on March 2, 1917.

It was made up as follows: Chairman of the Council of Ministers and Minister of Home Affairs, Prince Georgy Lvov, landowner and one of the leaders of the All-Russian Union of the Zemstvos; Ministers: Foreign Affairs, Pavel Milyukov, publicist and historian, founder and chairman of the Constitutional Democrats' Party, confirmed upholder of the monarchy; Minister of the Army and Navy, Alexander Guchkov, State Councillor, scion of a rich merchant family, head of a large trading firm in Moscow and member of the management and board of directors of many joint-stock companies; Minister of Communications, Nikolai Nekrasov, member of the bar,

---

* N. V. Ruzsky was the General and Commander-in-Chief of the armies of the northwestern and northern fronts.

professor and landlord in Tomsk, and one-time mayor of the city; Minister of Trade and Industry, Alexander Konovalov, secretary of the bar, a large manufacturer and landlord, assistant to the chairman of the Moscow Merchants' Exchange; Minister of Finance, Mikhail Tereshchenko, one of the largest sugar refinery operators; Minister of Education, Alexander Manuilov, professor of political economy, representative of the Constitutional Democrats' Party; Minister of Agriculture, Andrei Shingarev, one of the leaders of the Duma faction of that party; Minister of Justice, Alexander Kerensky, attorney, landlord, nobleman; Attorney General of the Synod, Vladimir Lvov, Councillor of State, landowner; State Controller, Ivan Godnev, reader at the University of Kazan.

As can be seen, the provisional government was composed of monarchists, large landowners, manufacturers and landlords representing certain specific interests. Although the overthrow of the autocracy was a great achievement for the revolutionary movement in Russia, it was still far from attaining the age-long dream of the people: Complete freedom with the earth a place of bountiful nurture to man. The policy of the new government, which safeguarded the interests of the same social strata as were the concern of tsarism, differed but little from that of the previous government.

The following joke was published in a satirical periodical *Bich*:

"Say, what is the strange piece that the orchestra is playing so poorly?"
"Don't you recognize the Marseillaise?"
"What are you saying? It is not at all like it!"
"That's because the musicians are playing it from the score for 'God Save the Tsar.' "

The Bolsheviks explained to the workers the true meaning of the events, stressing the fact that the victory of the February Revolution was but the first step towards the victory of the socialist revolution. *Pravda*, the central organ of the party, publication of which was renewed on March 5, and the Bolshevik newspapers which began appearing anew in Moscow, Kiev, Kharkov, Baku, Tiflis and other towns and cities, called on the workers not to surrender their weapons, the Bolsheviks basing their appeal on the fact that they would be needed to continue the struggle.

The fact that the revolution had not yet been consummated was also realized in the circles close to the government. General A. Lukomsky, at the time Quartermaster General of the Supreme Commander, wrote subsequently as follows:

. . . A sense of depression hovered over the Stavka. There was no confidence abroad that the new Provisional Government which was being set up in Petrograd, headed by Prince Lvov, would prove equal to the occasion.

A feeling prevailed that only the first stage of the revolution had been passed; that the State Duma, which had to some extent guided the course of events until the Tsar's abdication and on whose initiative the Provisional Government had been formed, was beginning to let events take their course and to go into an eclipse before the new organ that was moving into the forefront, the Council of Workers' and Soldiers' Deputies.

Dual power came to prevail in the country. Along with it, the provisional government, lacking the effective power that would enable it to repress the masses, continued clinging to power thanks only to the agreement it had entered into with the Soviets. The prospect of a victory of the proletarian revolution by peaceful means at the time stemmed from the fact that the government would have been powerless to stand up against the Soviets in the event that the latter should proclaim Soviet Power. The slogan "All Power to the Soviets!" advanced by Lenin on his return to Russia in April came as a rallying call to move ahead to a new stage of the revolution, setting a course towards peaceful victory for the socialist revolution.

PART II

THE BIRTH OF A NEW WORLD:

OCTOBER 1917

4 ALL POWER TO THE SOVIETS!

No sooner had the news of the February Revolution reached Switzerland than Vladimir Ilyich Lenin became obsessed with the single thought of how to return to Russia. Obviously, neither England nor France would tolerate the idea of the Bolsheviks being allowed passage to Russia, and Lenin had to find other ways.

"Some of the most impossible plans were being laid night after night," states N. K. Krupskaya in her reminiscences of those days. "Such plans could have been entertained only in the semi-delirious atmosphere of those nights. You only had to utter them aloud and it at once became obvious how impractical and absurd such notions were in actual fact.

". . . One will have to obtain the passport of some foreign national of a neutral country, preferably a Swede if the likelihood of arousing suspicion is to be reduced to a minimum. . . . Ignorance of the language poses a problem, to be sure. Perhaps not so serious after all? . . . But no, one might give himself away."

In the midst of this mental torture, having concluded that "all further delays must be avoided at all costs," Lenin dispatched a letter to Yakov Ganetsky, an activist who had joined the social democratic movement in 1896 and was now a member of the Foreign Bureau of the Bolshevik Central Committee:

"Waiting at this point is out of the question; all hope of an official sanction for a passage is futile. No matter what, it is necessary to set out for Russia at once and the only workable plan is for you to find a Swede bearing likeness to me. However, I do not know Swedish, and so he would have to be a deaf-mute. To cover all eventualities I am sending you a picture of myself."

"Having read the note," Yakov Ganetsky writes in his memoirs, "I sensed at once the agony of Vladimir Ilyich's suspense, but I must say in all candor that this extravagant plan moved me to a fit of laughter."

But Lenin had to act, to depart immediately, and it was hard for him to bear the thought of losing as much as a single day in waiting. Again he wrote, but this time to Vyacheslav Karpinsky in Geneva, a Bolshevik who had become a member of the Party as far back as 1898:

Dear Vyach. Al.,

I am considering every possible way of travelling. [Of returning to Russia.] The following is an absolute secret. Please reply to me immediately and, perhaps, best by express (I think we won't ruin the Party by a dozen extra express letters), so that I can be sure no one has read the letter.

Make out papers in your own name for travelling to France and England, and I will use them to travel through England (and Holland) to Russia.

I can put on a wig.

A photograph will be taken of me with the wig on, and I shall go to the Consulate in Bern with your papers and wearing the wig.

You must then disappear from Geneva for a minimum of a few weeks (until my telegram arrives from Scandinavia): for this period you must hide yourself well away in the mountains, where, we shall, of course, pay for your board and lodging.

If you agree, begin preparations immediately in the most energetic (and most secret) fashion, and drop me a line at once in any case.

Yours, Lenin

Think over all the practical steps involved and write to me in detail. I am writing to you because I am convinced that between us everything will remain absolutely secret.

This plan also proved impractical because the risk of discovery was too great.

Early in March, Lenin addressed his first letter to *Pravda* dealing with the revolution. This was the first of a series of letters in which he gave an appraisal of the nature, the course and the motivating forces of the February Revolution. "Letters from Afar" was the title he gave to these articles.

In "Letters from Afar" he formulated the problem of a transition to a socialist revolution, the establishment of a proletarian state, a prototype of which was the Paris Commune. He emphasized that even after the overthrow of tsarism, the peace program proposed by the Bolsheviks would remain in force. This included immediate publication and abrogation of the tsarist treaties; an immediate armistice; peace predicated on freedom for the colonies, for the subject and oppressed nations, and for those deprived of their civil rights. The Bolshevik program was an appeal to the workers of all countries to take power into their own hands and repudiate the repayment of loans contracted by their governments for the waging of a predatory war. Lenin's peace program shed light in many directions upon practical operations. It answered the question of what must be done to cast off the yoke of the war, and by what means a just and democratic peace could be achieved.

Lenin's letters of those days breathed a feeling of elation because of the events that had taken place. They set forth the prospects lying ahead—searching, ever searching and untiringly searching for paths that would lead him back to his homeland. These letters were full of eagerness and optimism.

"Congratulations on the Russian revolution," he writes to Mikhail Tskhakaya, a figure in the Russian revolutionary movement since 1880. ". . . I am preparing for the journey, and packing my baggage. What are you doing?"

Tskhakaya was doing the very same thing as all the other Russian exiles, that is, endeavoring by every means to arrange a homeward journey with all possible speed. Feverish discussions continued day and night. Finally, on March 6 (19 according to the new calendar) in Bern, at a private conference of the Russian party centers, one of the Social Democratic (Menshevik) leaders, Yuly Martov, proposed a plan through which the exiles could make the journey across Germany in exchange for the Germans who had been interned in Russia. This plan was met with a guarded response, and only Lenin seized on it.

"Martov's plan is good," he wrote to Karpinsky, "it should be furthered."

". . . Besides Martov," he continued, "it is necessary that other non-party and patriotically-minded Russians approach Swiss ministers, influential people, lawyers, and whomever (which can likewise be done in Geneva), with a request to discuss the matter with the ambassador of the German government in Bern. We cannot take part in this either directly or indirectly; our participation would spoil everything. However, the idea in itself is very good and very well suited."

Robert Grimm, one of the leaders of the Social Democratic Party of Switzerland and member of the Swiss parliament, was delegated to conduct the negotiations with the Swiss government. However, nothing came of this.

It was then that Lenin insisted that negotiations be initiated with Germany, by-passing the Swiss government, through the intermediary of Fritz Platten, a Swiss socialist-internationalist. Platten concluded a detailed written arrangement with the German ambassador in Switzerland. The salient terms of the agreement were as follows: 1) All of the exiles, regardless of their position concerning the war, were to be included in the party slated for departure. 2) Nobody would be admitted into the railroad car accommodating the exiles without Platten's permission. All formalities and passports, as well as baggage, would be ruled out. 3) The exiles granted permission to make the journey undertook to agitate, upon their return to Russia, for the exchange of a corresponding number of Austro-German internees.

"When a letter was received from Bern with the news that Platten's negotiations were successful, that it remained only to sign a protocol and forthwith start on the journey to Russia," Nadezhda Krupskaya relates, "Ilyich immediately exclaimed: 'We will take the first train.' We had to leave in two hours, and in two hours it was necessary to dismember our entire 'household,' settle accounts with the landlady, return the books to the library and pack. 'Go alone and I will follow tomorrow.' But Ilyich insisted: 'No, we will go together.' We took the earliest train to Bern."

From Bern thirty Russian Social Democrats started on the journey across Germany in a special railroad car. On March 18 (31) they were already in Stockholm.

On April 3 (16) Petrograd turned out to greet Lenin at the Finland Station. Addressing himself to the people in his first speech, on the square opposite the terminal, Lenin called on them to take up the struggle for a socialist revolution. "All Power to the Soviets!" he proclaimed, and the revolutionary proletariat and revolutionary soldiers supported him.

Towards a Socialist Revolution. On the morning of April 4, brushing aside the effects of a long night during which he had delivered frequent speeches, and after a tumultuous meeting prompted by his arrival, Lenin began his first day's work in Russia.

He took up residence in a quiet apartment, No. 24, at 49–9 Shirokaya Street on the Petrograd Side, where his sister Anna Ulyanova-Elizarova was then living. Lenin arrived there near nightfall, but left almost immediately for the Tauride Palace, accompanied by friends who had dropped in on him. A meeting of the Bolsheviks, members of the All-Russian Conference of Soviets of Workers' and Soldiers' Deputies, was already in progress at the palace. It was there that the first clear-cut words of Lenin's theses, to become known in history as the April Theses, rang out. They contained Lenin's analysis of the situation, outlined the goals to be striven for, and established the avenues for their achievement.

Everyone was eager to hear Lenin. A messenger arrived from the Mensheviks, who were holding a meeting on the floor below, asking that Lenin address them. But the Bolsheviks adopted a decision to the effect that Lenin was to deliver the identical report at a joint meeting of the Menshevik and Bolshevik delegates.

They convened in the large hall of the Tauride Palace. And here Lenin again branded the war as predatory; again he called for withholding all support from the Provisional Government and returned to the slogan "All Power to the Soviets!" He spoke for about two hours.

The events of the days that followed demonstrated to what degree Lenin was correct in his assessment of the policy of the Provisional Government and of the nature of the continuing war.

On April 18 (May 1) when the people for the first time openly celebrated the day of international proletarian solidarity, the Provisional Government came out with explanatory statements about its foreign policy.

As large crowds of demonstrators appeared, carrying streamers and banners that proclaimed such slogans as: "Hail the Brotherhood of Nations!", "Peace Without Annexations or Indemnities!", "Proletarians of the World Unite!", the Provisional Government's foreign minister, Milyukov, issued a note assuring the Allied Powers of the "entire nation's aspiration to conduct the war to a decisive victory." At the same time the official press unleashed a vast campaign of vilification of the Bolsheviks. Lenin characterized this as a counterrevolutionary eruption aimed at provoking a spontaneous revolutionary response among the people, which would then be used as a pretext for disbanding the Soviet and the use of reprisals.

On April 20, the day on which the text of Milyukov's note was made public, the heads of the army met in Petrograd at the home of War Minister Guchkov. They included the new commander-in-chief, General Alekseyev, the commander of the Petrograd military district, General Kornilov, and the commander of the Black Sea fleet, Admiral Kolchak. They deliberated on what steps could be taken at the right moment to restore "order." After the meeting Alekseyev went to the General Headquarters, intent upon organizing a demonstration of the army in support of the government, if need be.

Immediately after the publication of the note in the press, protest meetings began in the factories and barracks of Petrograd. As early as April 20 a spontaneous demonstration of soldiers and workers demanded "Down with Milyukov!" Throughout the night and day of April 21 large demonstrations and meetings continued without let up in Petrograd. The protest movement spread in the army and to the provinces. But at the same time, the supporters of the Provisional Government sought to organize their own demonstrations. According to the newspaper *Novaya Zhizn,* the British Ambassador, George Buchanan, then launched his appeal to a crowd assembled before the British embassy, calling for the support of the Provisional Government as "the true defender of the nation's interests."

Meanwhile the Provisional Government attempted to disperse the "mob," as it referred to those whom it demagogically claimed to defend. Kornilov ordered the artillery to scatter the demonstrators with a barrage of fire. However, the soldiers refused to obey and declared that the command lacked authority without the sanction of the Soviet of Deputies.

The Petrograd Soviet was then in a position to take the reins of power by peaceful means. The Mensheviks and the Social Revolutionaries found it ever more difficult to speak out in opposition to Lenin's clear-cut and lucid position. Nevertheless the Menshevik-Social Revolutionary majority of the

Petrograd Soviet was content with the absolutely noncommittal "Explanation" of the Provisional Government and made every effort to smother the protest movement in the capital and throughout the country.

With this in mind, the Provisional Government began a new test of strength. On April 21 the judicial arm of the government was ordered to initiate an investigation of an alleged firing by Lenin's supporters on demonstrators. On April 22 Kornilov, using the pretext of a German threat to Petrograd, issued an order that the reserve units of the district be reorganized, to be "prepared for the defense of civil rights, and in the event of the enemy's assault on Petrograd, to meet and rout the enemy on the approaches to the capital."

But Kornilov's attempt to stage a *putsch* foundered. On the same day, a meeting of the representatives of the capital's garrison adopted a decision to accept the authority of nothing less than the Petrograd Soviet, and the Soviet of Viborg District called on the Executive Committee to investigate the matter of Kornilov's order to fire on the demonstrators in the Palace Square. The leaders of the Petrograd Soviet were forced to raise the question of establishing control by their representatives over Kornilov's orders.

The Provisional Government's attempt to appeal to the army also failed. General Alekseyev was not only unable to find reliable units for an assault on Petrograd, but his efforts to produce a show of moral support for the government by issuing a special appeal of the generals, also miscarried. It was then that Guchkov seized on his last resort, namely a demonstrative resignation, declaring that he did so in protest against the impossibility of restoring discipline in the army. He planned in this manner to precipitate a governmental crisis which he could, in concert with the allies and the generals, exploit as a means of bolstering the power of the Provisional Government.

Milyukov hastened to Headquarters hoping to prevail upon Alekseyev to reconsider his decision to delay the offensive that was to be mounted on the German front. An immediate revival of military operations, so it appeared to him, would have regained the favors of the Allies and afford the best chance "of normalizing the situation in the country, and particularly in the capital." However, the army was in no position to launch an offensive.

The secret negotiations with Germany initiated by Milyukov in Stockholm during March and April 1917 came to nothing, as related in the memoirs of Reichstag deputy M. Erzberger, the German representative and leader of the Catholic Center. Within three days after Guchkov's resignation, Milyukov, seeing the fruitlessness of all his efforts, also tendered his resignation.

"The causes of the crisis have not been removed," wrote Lenin on the subject, "and the recurrence of such crises is unavoidable."

In the resolution of the Central Committee of the R.S.D.R.P. (B)*, adopted on the morning of April 22 (May 5), 1917, Lenin pointed out that "the organization of our Party, and the consolidation of the proletarian forces clearly proved inadequate at the time of crisis." He considered the key tasks of the moment to be: 1) Explanation of the course of the proletariat and its plan to end the war; 2) Criticism of the policy of confidence and collaboration with the government; 3) Propaganda work in every regiment and in every factory, particularly among the most backward masses, household servants, unskilled workers, etc., since during the crisis the reactionaries sought to gain support among them; 4) Organization of the proletariat, on which Lenin laid particular emphasis.

These and other questions claimed the attention of the Seventh All-Russian Conference of the R.S.D.R.P. (B). It opened on April 24. Lenin was elected to chair the Conference. He spoke before it concerning the current situation, the

---

* (B) stands for "Bolsheviks."

review of the party program and the agrarian question. In these addresses Lenin brought to light the fundamental question of the party's strategy and tactics during a period that he characterized as the period of transition from a bourgeois-democratic revolution, which overthrew the monarchy, to the stage of a socialist revolution that would deliver power into the hands of the proletariat. The Conference adopted Lenin's guidelines as the party's platform.

"We have little time and a lot of work," declared Lenin in his concluding remarks to the Conference. ". . . The proletariat will find in our resolutions material to guide it in its movement towards the second stage of our revolution."

The question of power for the first time came into the open at the First All-Russian Congress of the Soviets. At its opening session on June 4, the Menshevik leader Tsereteli declared:

"At the present moment there is no political party in Russia to come forward and say: Deliver power into our hands, depart and we will take your place . . ."

Lenin, remaining in his seat, cried out:

"There is such a party!"

The sponsors of the Congress greeted Lenin's statement with laughter and disparaging comments.

"You may laugh as much as you please," was Lenin's answer, "but as the Minister confronts us with this question side by side with the party of the Right, he will receive a suitable reply. . . . Give us your confidence and we shall give you our program.

"This program was presented at our Conference on April 29. Unfortunately, it is being ignored and not taken as a guide."

Discontent with the policy of the coalition government gained daily in the country, and a protest move was gathering momentum in Petrograd. The Central Committee of the Bolshevik Party adopted a decision "to direct the movement into the channel of an organized and peaceful demonstration against the counterrevolution."

The demonstration was called for June 10. The leaders of the Mensheviks and Social Revolutionaries, aware that they were losing influence over the masses and that the prestige of the Bolsheviks was growing, made every possible move to have it canceled. They did succeed in having the demonstration banned by the Congress of the Soviets. A similar decision was adopted by the Provisional Government. The Bolsheviks complied and announced that the demonstration was called off. But this did not stop one faction from vilifying the Bolsheviks by circulating a canard about a "Bolshevik military conspiracy" which imperiled the "achievements of the revolution."

Of course, it did not escape even the Socialist Revolutionary and Menshevik organizers in the Congress that, as a matter of fact, the demonstration could not be called off. Resorting to sideline maneuvers, they rescheduled it for June 18, thinking that they would organize a new demonstration under the slogan of "confidence to the government."

Wishing to lessen the growing popular influence of the Bolsheviks by all possible means, the Provisional Government began rapidly preparing for an offensive at the front. They hoped that the first rumors of a successful advance by the Russian army would dissolve the masses' opposition to such an offensive. According to their strategy, the demonstration that was being prepared would serve to show popular and unchallenged backing of the government's policy and the parties of conciliation.

This offensive, which had been anticipated so eagerly, did not bring any glory to its organizers. It began June 18 and at the outset did well. Then, under the retaliatory blow of the German armies, which had received reinforcements from the western front, the Russian armies began reeling back swiftly, almost without any show of resistance. From June 18 through July 6, when the breakthrough occurred at the Russian front, the Russian army lost in excess of fifty-eight thousand men; seven thousand of them were killed and more than thirty-six thousand wounded. By the middle of July the enemy had hurled back the Russian armies far behind the initial position and captured all of Galicia and Dobruja.

As a consequence of this adventure into which the Provisional Government had plunged, the Russian army soon forfeited what fruits of victory it had purchased during the three years of war at the price of enormous sacrifices. The Provisional Government itself described its venture as a catastrophe which cost the country "heavy losses in men and territory."

On June 18 a mighty demonstration took place in Petrograd in which half a million people participated. Not a single regiment, not a single factory carried slogans calling for confidence in the Provisional Government. Thousands of banners and streamers displayed the Bolshevik slogan: "All Power to the Soviets!"

The Petrograd demonstration reverberated powerfully throughout the country. On that day in Moscow, Kiev, Riga, Ivanovo-Voznesensk and in other cities, the workers and soldiers poured out into the streets. These demonstrations showed the extent to which the influence of the Bolshevik Party had grown among the masses, and served as a kind of survey of its combat strength. Lenin wrote: "The demonstration in a few hours scattered to the winds, like a handful of dust, the empty talk about Bolshevik conspirators and showed with the utmost clarity that the vanguard of the working people of Russia, the industrial proletariat of the capital, and the overwhelming majority of the troops support slogans that our Party has always advocated."

The collapse of the June offensive launched by Kerensky, and the enormous sacrifices made for the sake of obliging the Allies, served to heighten the revolutionary mood of the masses. The prestige of the Provisional Government, and of the parties which backed it, declined catastrophically. The situation grew more acute early in July.

Taking advantage of the defeat at the front, the reactionary wing of the Provisional Government decided to put an end to dual power. The Cadet Ministers—Manuilov, Shakhovsky and Shingarev—resigned with the aim of precipitating a government crisis. They calculated that the parties of conciliation would shrink before the prospect of remaining alone in the government face to face with the revolutionary masses and would make concessions to the bourgeoisie. This in fact happened. An attempt was made to persuade the Cadets to remain in the government.

The revolutionary masses viewed the situation differently. At midday on July 4 a demonstration started in Petrograd, involving nearly half a million workers and soldiers. The Peter and Paul fortress sided with the demonstrators. Sailors arrived from Kronstadt. That day Lenin spoke before them. He called on everyone to manifest self-restraint, staunchness and vigilance.

Exemplary order prevailed in the city. The demonstrators committed no violence nor did they try to capture any of the institutions. Their demand that the Central Executive Committee of the Soviets take power into its own hands met with refusal from the Committee's Menshevik and Socialist Revolutionary leaders. The Provisional Government, with the consent of the Central Executive Committee, hurled detachments of military cadets and Cossacks against the peaceful demonstrators and fired on them at the corner of Nevsky Prospect and Sadovaya Street. Counterrevolutionary military units had been commandeered from the front for the purpose.

At the conference of the Central and the Petrograd Party Committees, which took place under the guidance of Lenin during the night of July 4 to 5, a decision was adopted concerning an organized halt to the workers' and soldiers' demonstrations. Thanks to this well-timed maneuver the Party was able to save the main forces of the revolution from a rout. The firing on the demonstration of July 4, in which units of the army had been employed, signaled the end of the peaceful stage of the revolution. The Soviets no longer exercised power. They surrendered it. Dual power had come to an end. The counterrevolution went over to the assault.

Reprisals were aimed first and foremost against the Bolsheviks. The newspapers *Pravda*, *Soldatskaya Pravda* and others were shut down. The *Trud* printing plant, purchased with the contributions of workers, was destroyed. Those units of the army which, to use the language of the government, "were infected with the bacillus of Bolshevism" were dispatched to the front. Detachments of workers were disarmed. Searches and arrests commenced.

All newspapers started a savage, defamatory campaign against the Bolsheviks. Paying no heed to the protest lodged by the Chairman of the Central Executive Committee of the Soviets, Chkheidze, the newspapers published a forged document over the signature of Aleksinsky, a former Social Democrat and deputy of the Second State Duma who disgraced himself with the purveying of slander and unprincipled conduct. The document alleged that Lenin maintained contact with the German General Staff. The purpose of this forgery was not only to discredit the leader of the Bolsheviks, but also to cast a shadow on the Party as a whole, to make it responsible for all the victims and the fiasco of the ill-prepared and senseless July offensive, and to unleash a new tide of "ultrapatriotism" which the deplorable situation at the front rendered extremely urgent.

"The counterrevolutionary bourgeoisie flavor their political baiting of the Bolsheviks, the party of the international revolutionary proletariat, with the foulest slander and campaigning in the press that is quite like the campaign of the French clerical and monarchist papers in the Dreyfus case," wrote Lenin on the subject.

In recalling the efforts expended by the reactionary-monarchist circles of the French military in the nineties of the nineteenth century, who brought an indictment against an officer of the French General Staff, the Jew Dreyfus, charging him with high treason, Lenin underscored the fact that the same attempt was now being made to bring the same accusation against someone among the Bolsheviks. He declared bitterly:

"It is a veritable Dreyfusiad, a campaign of lies and slander stemming from fierce political hatred. . . ."

After the publication of the defamatory charge against Lenin in *Zhivoye Slovo*, a newspaper which reflected the policies of the Black Hundreds, the Central Executive Committee (CEC) of the Soviet of Workers' and Soldiers' Deputies, upon the insistence of the Bolshevik faction, established a commission to conduct an inquest into the false accusations directed at Lenin and other Bolsheviks. However, the commission of the CEC tendered its resignation when the following day, July 7, the Provisional Government issued an order for Lenin's arrest as well as that of other prominent leaders of the Party, charging them with "the organization of an armed uprising in Petrograd on July 3 to 5, 1917, against the government." On July 13, at the joint session of the CEC of the Soviet of Workers' and Soldiers' Deputies and the Executive Committee of the All-Russian Soviet of Peasants' Deputies, the Mensheviks and the Socialist Revolutionaries managed to force through a resolution stating that it was absolutely inadmissible for Lenin to avoid standing trial.

Profoundly resentful of the calumny, Lenin was at first inclined to appear before the court of the Provisional Government. But as events began to unfold, it became obvious that the question would never come to trial. His guards had been given orders to kill Lenin on the way to court on the pretext that he had attempted to flee.

"The authorities need not a trial but a persecution campaign against the internationalists," Lenin wrote.

The Party saw to it that its leader went underground. On July 9 he traveled under cover of secrecy to Razliv, a suburb of Petrograd, where he was received in the home of a worker, N. A. Emelyanov. There he lived for a time in a barn loft and shortly moved to a hut beyond the nearby lake, disguised as a field worker. At Razliv Lenin wrote eleven articles, as well as letters and notes. He worked there on his book *The State and Revolution*, developing a theory of the socialist state, the establishment of which was the task of the coming proletarian revolution, and in whose victory he had an unshaken faith.

While underground, Lenin maintained steady contact with the Party. On the instructions of the Central Committee, Shotman called on him almost daily and reported on the activity of the Party and all its decisions. G. K. Ordzhonikidze also came to see him on two occasions. The hut occupied by Lenin became the headquarters for the preparation of the Sixth Congress of the R.S.D.R.P. (B), which would have before it the task of deliberating on issues relating to the further development of the revolution, including the issue of new tactics required to meet the changed situation.

The Congress, which represented the largest political party in the country, was forced to convene in an atmosphere of semi-legality. A notice appeared in the press only to the effect that a Congress was to convene but no mention was given of the place where the sessions were to be held. It opened July 26. Of the delegates, 157 were qualified to cast deciding votes while 110 participants could cast deliberative votes. Representatives of the most important regions of Russia took part in the Congress.

One of the very first questions to come up for deliberation was that of Lenin's appearance before the court. Following a discussion that involved all those present, a decision was adopted by unanimous vote resolutely opposing Lenin's appearance before the court.

All decisions of the Congress, which closed on August 3, were subordinated to the principal aim, that of preparing the masses for an armed insurrection.

The counterrevolution was not slumbering either. An unofficial meeting of the State Duma, a session of the members of all four Dumas, a conference of the commissars of the provinces, a conference of tradesmen and industrialists, a joint conference of public figures with the Union of the Cossack armies, the Officers' Union and the Union of the Bearers of the Georgievsky Cross—all of these formed the social milieu for a coalition between the government, the Mensheviks and the Socialist Revolutionaries. The counterrevolution wove a golden halo about the name of General Kornilov, presenting him as the "future savior" and transforming him into a rallying point for all counterrevolutionary forces.

It had been planned that the coup would be carried out early in August, while the Council of State, composed of representatives of all the propertied strata of the population, was convening in Moscow. The confidence of the counterrevolutionaries in the idea of agitating Moscow to work against revolutionary Petrograd stemmed from their impression that the July events in the capital had failed to awaken any significant response in Moscow. However, reality disappointed such hopes. Because of the enormous organizational efforts that the Bolsheviks expended among the masses and because the revolutionary mood in the country grew swiftly in the wake of the July events, Moscow soon caught up with Petrograd, as did other industrial centers, and forged ahead to become one of the prime movers in the revolutionary thrust.

A one-day strike of 400,000 Moscow workers shattered the plans of the reactionary bourgeoisie. It manifested the unity and the spirit of organization that prevailed among the working class, and displayed the actual influence wielded by the Bolsheviks.

Shortly after the conference and the fiasco of the coup in Moscow on August 27, the commander-in-chief of the Russian army, would-be dictator General Kornilov, moved against the capital with the Third Mounted Corps, aiming to take possession of Petrograd and foist a military dictatorship on the country. Kerensky, who at the outset supported Kornilov, now broke with him fearing that, with the onset of the revolt, he would be swept away with the rest.

The Bolsheviks played a great part in the struggle against the Kornilov revolt. The Party's appeal to the workers and soldiers, calling on them to take into their own hands the cause of defending the revolution, found a warm echo among the masses. The Bolsheviks were successful not only in gaining a nationwide response to the struggle against Kornilov, but also in completely unmasking Kerensky, who by other means was seeking to smother the revolution.

Within a few days an odd state of affairs emerged in the country. Lenin described it as "a drastic and unique turn of the Russian revolution." Once again the extremely rare and promising prospect of a peaceful development of the revolution had opened up.

For the sake of this peaceful onward movement, as Lenin said, the Bolsheviks were prepared to enter into a compromise with the parties constituting a majority in the Soviets and to propose to them the formation of a government made up of Socialist Revolutionaries and Mensheviks, responsible to the Soviets. Power was to be transferred at once to the Soviets.

"The compromise would amount to the following:" wrote Lenin, "the Bolsheviks, without making any claim to participate in the government (which is impossible for the internationalists unless a dictatorship of the proletariat and the poor peasants has been realized), would refrain from demanding the immediate transfer of power to the proletariat and the poor peasants and from employing revolutionary methods of fighting for this demand. A condition that is self-evident and not new to the S.R.s and Mensheviks would be complete freedom of propaganda and the convocation of the Constituent Assembly without further delays or even at an earlier date."

The freedom of propaganda and the immediate establishment of a new democracy, both in the composition of the Soviets and in their functioning, would of itself ensure the peaceful advancement of the revolution, and the peaceful overcoming of party strife within the Soviets.

Lenin drafted all of this on Friday, September 1. The heading of the article was "On Compromises." It was intended for publication in the newspaper *Rabochy Put* (one of the names under which *Pravda* appeared following the July events). However, it failed to reach the desk of the editor of the paper that day. In the postscript to the article of September 3, Lenin explained wryly just how this came about.

After reading Saturday's and today's (Sunday's) papers, I say to myself: perhaps it is already too late to offer a compromise. . . . Yes, to
all appearances, the days when by chance the path of peaceful development became possible have already passed.

All that remains is to send these notes to the editor with the request
to have them entitled: "Belated Thoughts." Perhaps even belated
thoughts are sometimes not without interest.

What did in fact happen during those two days? On September 2, at a joint plenary meeting of the Central Executive
Committee of the Soviets of Workers and Soldiers' Deputies,
the Mensheviks and the Socialist Revolutionaries passed a
resolution supporting the composition of the new government. Thus, once more, by making a verbal display of
their break with the Cadets, the Mensheviks and the S.R.s
aided the ruling groups in the retention of power. Having been
granted authority to form a government to his own liking,
Kerensky further pursued his course of smothering the revolutionary movement.

The formation of a new government and the renewed capit-
ulation of the Menshevik and Socialist Revolutionary leaders
before the representatives of big capital, who had been granted
the principal posts, failed to deliver the country from a crisis
that was deepening by the hour.

"The crisis has matured," Lenin wrote on September 29.
He detected symptoms of this crisis in the peasant movement, which had brimmed over by then into an outright insurrection against the Kerensky government. He furthermore saw
symptoms of it in the more vigorous upsurge of national
movements (in Central Asia, in Finland and in the Ukraine);
in the army's break with the government; in the fact that the
people, having lost faith in the policy pursued by the Mensheviks and the S.R.s, gave a majority in the Soviets to the Bolsheviks and the Left-Socialist Revolutionaries who opposed a coalition with the government. Among the symptoms that had
not only a diagnostic but also a most concrete significance,
Lenin also included the nationwide strike of the railroad
workers and employees, which commenced during the night

of September 23 to 24 and embraced the entire network of railroad lines, as well as the strike of the postal workers.

"The crisis has matured," Lenin repeated persistently.

"The whole future of the Russian Revolution is at stake. . . . The Bolsheviks must take power. . . . To wait is to doom the revolution to failure."

The Salvo from the Aurora.   The fateful days of preparing the uprising had arrived. Lenin returned to Petrograd illegally. "Delay is fatal," he wrote to the Bolsheviks participating in the Congress of the Soviets of the Northern Region.

On October 10 he took part in the session of the Central Committee (CC) that adopted the resolution calling for an armed insurrection. Ten members of the CC, headed by Lenin, voted in favor of armed insurrection, while Zinoviev and Kamenev opposed it. At this particular session the Politbureau, under the leadership of Lenin, was created to head the insurrection.

Numerous conferences and meetings passed resolutions calling for the transfer of all power to the Soviets. But throughout the country, nearly everywhere, the Soviets were in fact already taking power into their own hands.

On October 11 a meeting of the Putilov workers unanimously adopted a resolution demanding the transfer of all power to the Soviets and the arming of the workers.

On October 11 to October 13 a Congress of the Soviets of Workers' and Soldiers' Deputies of the Northern Region was held in Petrograd under the guidance of the Bolsheviks. On October 15, in the city of Minsk, only Bolsheviks were elected to the Presidium of the Executive Committee of the Soviet of Workers' and Soldiers' Deputies. On October 16 the Regional Congress of the Soviets of the Volga Area in Saratov adopted a resolution transferring power to the Soviets. On the same day, the Congress of the Soviets of the Vladimir province elected a Bolshevik Executive Committee. Thus, power had been transferred into the hands of the Soviets.

From October 16 to 24 the first All-Siberian Congress of

Soviets took place in Irkutsk. A resolution was adopted transferring power to the Soviets. This Congress elected the first Central Executive Committee of the Soviets of Siberia (Centrosibir).

On October 17 the regional session of the Soviets of Workers' and Soldiers' Deputies of the Southwestern Territory in Kiev adopted a resolution transferring power to the Soviets.

The Provisional Government tried to use force against the Soviets. On October 19, it attempted to disband the Kaluga Soviet. The Kaluga garrison, which favored the Bolsheviks, put up armed resistance.

Intensified preparations for the insurrection were proceeding throughout the country. The question had now moved into the realm of concrete decisions. Carrying out Lenin's instructions concerning a legal staff to head the insurrection, the Executive Committee of the Petrograd Soviet established a Revolutionary-Military Committee (RMC) by its decision of October 12. The RMC was composed of representatives from the Soviet; the Centrobalt and the Finnish Regional Committees; the factory committees; the trade unions, including the members of the CC of the R.S.D.R.P. (B): A. S. Bubnov, F. E. Dzerzhinsky and M. S. Uritsky; the members of the Military Organization of the CC of the R.S.D.R.P. (B): V. A. Antonov-Ovseyenko, N. V. Krylenko, K. A. Mekhonoshin, V. I. Nevsky, N. I. Podvoisky and other Bolsheviks.

At a closed session of the Petrograd Committee on October 15, Central Committee member A. S. Bubnov delivered a report dealing with the practical questions concerning preparations for an armed insurrection. He gave special attention to organizing liaison between the center and the regions, and to the combat readiness of the Red Guard detachments.

Preparations for the insurrection entered the decisive stage. An enlarged session of the Central Committee met on October 16, which was attended also by representatives of the party and trade-union organizations. Lenin announced the resolution of October 10 and proceeded to substantiate the directives, which it embodied, with profound logic. An analysis of the political state of affairs in Russia and in Europe, he stressed, showed the unavoidable necessity for a decisive preparation of the insurrection.

Here again Zinoviev and Kamenev came out in opposition to the course which Lenin advocated for the Central Committee. They reiterated their arguments, claiming that the Bolsheviks lacked sufficient strength to ensure a victorious uprising. The call for an uprising, Zinoviev declared, was sheer adventurism. This precipitated a heated debate which lasted all night. Sverdlov, Rakhya, Krylenko, Dzerzhinsky, Kalinin and others supported Lenin. With nineteen votes against two, and four abstentions, the Central Committee carried the resolution that it had made on October 10. Party organizations of workers and soldiers were now called on to intensify preparations for an insurrection. At this session the Revolutionary Military Center (A. S. Bubnov, F. E. Dzerzhinsky, Y. M. Sverdlov, J. V. Stalin and M. S. Uritsky) was established.

During the night of October 17 to 18, at the home of the worker D. A. Pavlov, Lenin met the leaders of the Military Organization of the Central Committee, N. I. Podvoisky, V. A. Antonov-Ovseyenko and V. I. Nevsky, listened to their reports on the progress of preparations for the armed insurrection in Petrograd, and gave them instructions and advice.

He frequently met with the representatives of the Moscow Bolshevik Party organization to elicit from them information concerning the preparations underway in Moscow. The Moscow District Bureau of the Central Committee of the R.S.D.R.P. (B), had as far back as October 14 adopted without debate the directive on the armed insurrection, and proposed to the local organizations "to have the start of their action coincide with the action at the center."

It was precisely then, during the days that were heavy with great responsibilities and fateful decisions, when the October Revolution was facing the question of "to be or not to be," that two members of the Central Committee, Kamenev and

Zinoviev, dealt the Party a treacherous blow. On October 18 Lenin learned of a notice captioned "Y. Kamenev on the Insurrection," which had been placed in the semi-Menshevik newspaper *Novaya Zhizn*. In his own name and in that of Zinoviev, Kamenev made public the decision of the Central Committee on an immediate insurrection. Lenin indignantly denounced these strike-breakers of the revolution and demanded Kamenev's and Zinoviev's expulsion from the Party. The Central Committee adopted a resolution accepting Kamenev's resignation from the Central Committee and ordered both Kamenev and Zinoviev to abstain from any pronouncements on behalf of the Party. The opponents of an armed uprising now found themselves isolated.

The Party continued vigorous preparations for the insurrection. On the night of October 21, the Revolutionary-Military Committee appointed commissars to all units of the Petrograd garrison.

On the same day, at a session of the regimental committees of the Petrograd garrison, a resolution was adopted to extend full support to the Revolutionary-Military Committee for the immediate summoning of a Second Congress of the Soviets. The session proposed that a review of the forces of the Petrograd soldiers and workers should take place on "Petrograd Soviet Day" (scheduled to be celebrated on October 22).

On Petrograd Soviet Day, huge meetings in army units, plants and factories revealed the actual strength of the Bolsheviks, who were ready to go into action. The government even lacked authority to command the cruiser *Aurora* to leave its dock. Instead, the ship remained in the city in response to the instructions issued by the Petrograd Soviet.

On October 23, the Revolutionary-Military Committee appointed commissars to take up their posts not only with the military units, but also at the most vital points of the capital and its surroundings. By order of the RMC all military units were placed on combat readiness.

The Provisional Government made rapid preparations to

head off the uprising. On October 24, patrols of military cadets occupied the key points of the city. The newspapers *Rabochy Put* and *Soldat* were closed. An order was issued for the immediate arrest of the Bolsheviks and the participants in the July demonstrations. The military district staff issued orders for the removal and prosecution of the commissars of the Revolutionary-Military Committee assigned to military units. The commander-in-chief of the Petrograd Military Area issued orders that the telephone lines of the Petrograd Soviet be immediately cut off, and the bridges raised to isolate the proletarian districts from the center.

In "A Letter to the Central Committee Members," Lenin wrote: "To delay action is fatal." He proposed the immediate arrest of the Provisional Government and the seizure of power. Late in the evening of October 24 he reached the Smolny Institute secretly and personally took charge of the armed uprising.

At 1:25 A.M. on the night of October 25 the Central Post Office was occupied by a combat unit of seamen, Red Guards and soldiers. At 2:00 A.M., armed units of the Revolutionary-Military Committee occupied the Nikolayevsky and Baltic railway stations. At 3:30 A.M. the cruiser *Aurora* dropped anchor at the Nikolayevsky Bridge and armored cars were stationed outside the Winter Palace. On the orders of the Petrograd Revolutionary-Military Committee, preparations were made for a crossing by the eight-thousand-strong force of armed sailors from Helsingfors, Kronstadt and Revel. The State Bank and the offices of the principal newspapers were occupied towards six o'clock in the morning on orders of the Revolutionary-Military Committee. Towards seven o'clock in the morning, the military cadets protecting the Palace Bridge were dislodged, and the torpedo boats from Helsingfors sailed into the Neva and took up battle stations in front of the Winter Palace.

At ten in the morning on October 25 (November 7), not waiting for the fall of the Winter Palace where the Provisional

Government, now completely shorn of power, was under blockade, Lenin addressed an appeal on behalf of the Revolutionary-Military Committee:

To the Citizens of Russia:
The Provisional Government has been deposed. State power has passed into the hands of the organ of the Petrograd Soviet of Workers' and Soldiers' Deputies—the Revolutionary-Military Committee, which heads the Petrograd proletariat and its garrison.
The cause for which the people have fought, namely, the immediate offer of a democratic peace, the abolition of landlord ownership, workers' control over production, and the establishment of Soviet power— this cause has been secured.
Long live the revolution of workers, soldiers and peasants!
—The Revolutionary-Military Committee of the Petrograd Soviet of Workers' and Soldiers' Deputies.

At 2:35 P.M. on October 25 an emergency session of the Petrograd Soviet convened. It heard a report by the Revolutionary-Military Committee on the overthrow of the Provisional Government and the victory of the revolution. Delivering a report on the tasks of Soviet power, Lenin stated:

"We have now learned to make a concerted effort. The Revolution that has just been accomplished is evidence of this. We possess the strength of mass organization, which will overcome everything and lead the proletariat to the world revolution."

At 10:40 in the evening the Second All-Russian Congress of Soviets of Workers' and Soldiers' Deputies opened in the Smolny Institute. A total of 670 delegates took part in the Congress, 390 of them Bolsheviks, 179 Left-Socialist Revolutionaries,* thirty-five Social Democratic Internationalists,†

---

* "Left-Socialist Revolutionaries" refers to the left wing of the Socialist Revolutionary Party, which broke away, forming an independent party, following the October Revolution.
† "Social Democratic Internationalists" (Menshevik-Internationalists) represents a movement among the Mensheviks which participated during the First World War in the Zimmerwald and Kienthal anti-war conferences. After the February Revolution they supported the Bolsheviks on many issues relating to domestic and foreign policy.

etc. The presidium consisted of Bolsheviks and Left-Socialist Revolutionaries. The Menshevik and Right-S.R. factions resolved to bolt the Congress but many of their delegates refused to abide by the decision and remained. The estimates of the number of delegates that actually bolted the Congress vary from twenty-five to fifty-one, according to different accounts.

When the Congress was already in session, the Revolutionary-Military Committee dispatched an ultimatum to the Winter Palace, where the Provisional Government had taken refuge, calling on it to order the units defending the Winter Palace to surrender their arms to avoid bloodshed. The time limit elapsed but no reply was forthcoming. It was then that under the orders of the RMC the cruiser *Aurora* fired a blank round to signal the storming of the Winter Palace.

At 3:10 in the morning of October 26 the Winter Palace was captured. The Provisional Government was placed under arrest. The Chairman of the Council of Ministers, A. F. Kerensky, had fled the city as early as the morning of October 25, on the pretext of a mission to rally forces against the Bolsheviks. He had departed in a car flying the American flag, as this was the only ruse that could give him a sense of security.

At five o'clock in the morning on October 26, the Second Congress of the Soviets adopted an address written by Lenin to the "Workers, Soldiers and Peasants!" announcing that all power throughout the country had passed into the hands of the Soviets, that the revolution had won a final and irrevocable victory without bloodshed. "All of us who had taken part in the armed uprising in Petrograd," wrote Sofia Shchulga, who had been a member of the Party since 1916, "well remember the elation we experienced on account of this bloodless victory of the uprising, and how proudly resounded at the time these words bearing witness to an authentic triumph of our Party, and to the masterful leadership it gave to the uprising."

The second session of the Congress opened in the evening.

Lenin addressed it on the two fundamental questions of peace and land. By eleven o'clock that evening the Decree on Peace was adopted by a unanimous vote. "The Workers' and Peasants' Government," it read, "created by the revolution of October 24–25, basing itself on the Soviets of Workers', Soldiers' and Peasants' Deputies, calls upon all the belligerent peoples and their governments to start immediate negotiations for a just, democratic peace.

"By a just or democratic peace, for which the overwhelming majority of the working class and other working people of all the belligerent countries, exhausted, tormented and racked by the war are craving—a peace that has been most definitely and insistently demanded by the Russian workers and peasants ever since the overthrow of the tsarist monarch—by such a peace the government means an immediate peace without annexations (that is, without the seizure of foreign lands, without the forcible incorporation of foreign nations) and without reparations."

At two o'clock in the morning a second historical Decree was adopted—the Decree on Land, which proclaimed immediate abolition, without compensation, of the private ownership of land by the landlords. All land was declared to be the property of the people.

The Congress furthermore established a government of workers and peasants known as the Council of People's Commissars. Those Left-Socialist Revolutionaries who threw their support in the Congress to the Bolsheviks rejected participation in the Soviet government, and the first government was made up exclusively of Bolsheviks.

The Second All-Russian Congress of the Soviets adjourned at about six o'clock in the morning on October 27. The will of the revolutionary people prevailed, and the first government of workers and peasants anywhere in the world became a reality. Its powers had received a firm sanction. The first legislative acts it promulgated were the Decree on Peace and the Decree on Land—and both of them were adopted. October started its triumphant march through the land, implanting throughout its length and breadth the power of the Soviets.

The dismemberment of the old and the mounting of a new state apparatus was a complex undertaking. In the course of the severe political struggle the principal guidelines emerged that were to define the functions and interrelationships of the higher administrative bodies—those between the Congress of the Soviets and the All-Russian Central Executive Committee (VTsIK) elected by it and the Council of People's Commissars (SNK). The All-Russian Congress of the Soviets became the supreme governing body. During the periods between Congresses the functions of the supreme governing body were performed by the VTsIK. The Council of People's Commissars was responsible to the All-Russian Congress of the Soviets and the VTsIK, which were endowed with the power to control and remove the government.

The most characteristic and distinctive feature of the new state power, which distinguished it to good advantage from all forms of parliamentarianism known at the time, was that it combined the legislative and executive powers. Through the departmental structure which it created, VTsIK administered the corresponding branches of the governmental structure and guided the political life of the country. The Council of People's Commissars, which had been invested with the right to take all measures directly, without any prior deliberation by VTsIK (while being responsible to the latter) in waging the struggle against the counterrevolution, was also given the privilege of initiating legislation. This did not at all signify that any of the supreme Soviet governing bodies, either VTsIK or SNK, endeavored to legislate and act independently of the others. Quite to the contrary, the merging of the legislative and executive powers presupposed unity in the performance of these functions by the supreme Soviet organs.

At its sessions, the Council of People's Commissars deliberated on the most important questions that came within the competence of the different departments of the VTsIK.

Hence, at the session of October 30, the Council of People's Commissars examined the activities of the Cossack Department of the VTsIK and approved the proposal of that Department to formulate draft laws aimed at safeguarding the interests of the toiling masses of the Cossacks. When the question of sending abroad a delegation of Soviet representatives came before the session of the Council of People's Commissars, the latter referred the matter to the VTsIK. The Chairman of the VTsIK, Yakov Sverdlov,* attended the sessions of the Council of People's Commissars and took a most active part in the work it performed. The Chairman of the Council of People's Commissars, Lenin, spoke at the sessions of the VTsIK on the most vital issues of state. The members of the SNK, the People's Commissars, were, as a rule, members of the VTsIK, and they submitted for deliberation both to the SNK and to the sessions of the VTsIK major problems concerning the activities of the People's Commissariates.

The victory of the Soviet wing at the Second Congress of Peasants' Deputies called for November 10 consolidated the achievements of the proletarian revolution. The Congress expressed absolute confidence in the power of the Soviets and approved their decrees.

The Left-Socialist Revolutionaries, who headed the Congress of the peasantry, and who had earlier refused to enter into the government without the other "socialist parties," new preempted the posts of the SNK and so A. L. Kolegayev became People's Commissar for Agriculture, P. P. Proshyan, People's Commissar for Post and Telegraph, and I. Z. Steinberg, People's Commissar for Justice. At the Third Congress of the Soviets of Workers', Soldiers' and Peasants' Deputies, M. A. Spiridonova was elected to the chairmanship of the Peasant Section of the VTsIK.

On November 21, the Bolshevik faction introduced a draft

---

* Y. M. Sverdlov was elected to the Presidency of the Soviet Government on November 8, 1917, on the recommendation of Lenin.

decree concerning the right to recall any deputy failing to vindicate the trust which the people had placed in him. In the discussion on the draft, those who principally came out in support of the right to recall constituted a majority of the members of the VTsIK, with two votes against and one abstention. The draft was then handed over for some finishing touches to the Coordinating Commission, with the participation of the Left-S.R.'s. The draft decree submitted to the Coordinating Committee was unanimously adopted by the VTsIK and published on November 23. Following the lead of this decree, a number of peasants' and army congresses adopted decisions providing for the recall from the Constituent Assembly of the deputies of the Right-S.R.'s and the Mensheviks, among them Aksentiev, Gots, Milyukov and others.

"Everything had to be taken by storm," G. I. Petrovsky commented sometime later in his remarks about that period. It was difficult to manage the work of the former ministries with the officials on strike. Food rationing also presented a difficult problem.

The food situation was serious in the capital. On October 27 Petrograd had its disposal barely 1,080,000 pounds of grain, not enough to satisfy the needs of the population even at the rate of half a pound per person according to the prevailing norm. A careful search was launched for all possible food reserves that might be in the hands of private organizations, on the exchanges, in warehouses and on railroad sidings. A total of some eleven million pounds of grain was requisitioned, and a supply made available for a period of ten days. Special detachments to carry out requisitions of grain among the landowners and propaganda among the peasants were dispatched to the grain-producing districts. Nevertheless, early in November no more than some fifteen cars of grain daily reached the capital. The bread ration was reduced to one-eighth of a pound daily. A relentless war was declared against speculators and everything found in hiding was confiscated. It was the middle of November before the ration was again increased to half a pound per day, and it was raised to three-fourths of a pound commencing on November 30. Food supplies began arriving with a greater frequency. A total of some thirty-three million pounds of grain was supplied to Petrograd from November 1 to November 30. Starting in the middle of November a supplementary food ration was issued to younger children.

On November 14 the VTsIK ratified the decree that came to be known as the "Regulations on Workers' Control," the draft of which had been prepared by Lenin. Henceforth workers were to assume control over the production and distribution of the industrial output. This represented an important step towards the nationalization of industry.

On December 5, 1917, a decree was published establishing a Supreme Council of National Economy, a body which was invested with the management of the industry of the young republic.

On December 14, countering the sabotage carried on by bank operators, detachments of workers and Red Guards, acting under orders of the Soviet government, occupied all banks and credit institutions in Petrograd. On the same day, at a session of the VTsIK, decrees were adopted concerning the "nationalization of the banks" and the "inspection of safe-deposit boxes in banks."

In complete accord with the nationalities policy proclaimed by Lenin on December 18, 1918, the SNK, responding to the wishes of the Finnish Seim, adopted a resolution extending independent statehood to Finland. At the session of the Council of People's Commissars, Lenin personally handed over the text of the decree to the Prime Minister of Finland, P. E. Svinhufvud, who then headed the Finnish state delegation. On December 22 the decree granting independence to Finland was ratified by the VTsIK.

The Soviet government was successful in saving the highest achievements of Russian culture in the past, its material treasures and monuments, along with the enduring works in the spheres of science, literature and art. It also attracted the main body of the progressive democratic intelligentsia by affording it a proper atmosphere where its creative work could thrive and prosper. Aligned with the people from the very first days of the revolution were A. Blok, V. Mayakovsky, V. Bryusov, V. Meyerkhold, A. Sumbatov-Yuzhin, S. Chekhonin, N. Andreyev, K. Timiryazev, N. Zhukovsky, A. Ioffe, S. Chaplygin, N. Marr and others.

Questions relating to the cultural legacy of the past and the nature and limits within which it might be utilized, as well as those dealing with the enlistment of the old intelligentsia for active work, confronted the Soviets from the very beginning.

During the days of the armed insurrection the Petrograd Revolutionary-Military Committee assigned commissars (G. S. Yatmanov and B. D. Mandelbaum) to the protection of museums, palaces and art collections. Reliable protective guards were posted at the Hermitage, the Winter Palace and the Anichkov Palace, and at the Public Library, with the aid of military units of the garrison and detachments of the Red Guard. The commissars took effective steps towards the removal of valuable manuscripts of the Public Library from Petrograd to Moscow and organized a fire-fighting brigade in the library building. The People's Commissar of Education, A. V. Lunacharsky, announced on October 30, 1917, that the Winter Palace had been turned into a state museum, along with the Hermitage. He recommended to the Commission on Art, under the chairmanship of V. A. Vereshchagin, that a descriptive catalogue of the property of the former palace curatorship be compiled.

Petrograd's Red Guards exhibited a unique vigilance and a spirit of self-sacrifice in the defense of what have come to be regarded as the material and spiritual treasures of the nation. After receiving a report to that effect, A. V. Lunacharsky wrote:

"As the People's Commissar of Education, I am deeply concerned about the intact survival of the people's treasure. I cannot but voice with rapturous joy my profoundest thanks to the newborn and magnificent offspring of the Petrograd proletariat, the Red Guards, for having set examples worthy of admiration in their defense of the people's treasures."

The supervision of the buildings and possessions of the palaces at Tsarskoye Selo, Peterhoff, and Gatchina was placed in the hands of the local Soviets, which set up a protective watch over architectural monuments and the priceless objects of culture that they housed.

The Soviets displayed true solicitude towards everything that embodied the pride of the people in its culture. The Tula Soviet of Workers', Soldiers' and Peasants' Deputies took charge of safeguarding the home of L. N. Tolstoy in Yasnaya Polyana. The Soviet of Klin saved the house of P. I. Tchaikovsky from being requisitioned. When the matter of evicting N. I. Goncharova from her estate in Lopasnya came up for consideration, the following resolution was adopted: ". . . to allow an exception in the case of the landed gentry living in the said museum, by virtue of their being the grandchildren of A. S. Pushkin."

The triumph of the October Revolution inaugurated a series of events that is recognized as a "cultural revolution." It signified a qualitative turn in the spiritual life of society and in the consciousness of man. The events embraced in their unfolding such achievements as the end of illiteracy among the adult population and the development of scholastic education oriented so that it would accommodate all of the upcoming generation. The events led to the reform of the higher educational system, and the utilization of the full spectrum of knowledge that mankind had accumulated through time. Of course, this could not be achieved all at once.

By foiling the sabotage practiced by the officials and the reactionary members of the teaching profession, overcoming the enmity of a segment of the intelligentsia, introducing control over industry and the distribution of its output, and planning and directing the economic life of the country under a centralized system, the young government was making giant strides with ever-growing confidence in the structuring of a new social order. The accomplishment of these changes demanded a solution of the peace question before anything else.

In view of the patent reluctance of the Entente to enter into negotiations aiming towards peace with Germany, the Soviet government was compelled to conclude an unavoidable though burdensome peace at Brest-Litovsk. It afforded the country a much-needed breathing spell, which unfortunately was only short-lived.

The Struggles of the Revolution. As early as the beginning of March 1918 alien soldiers invaded Soviet soil. The Entente initiated open intervention, bringing aid and comfort to the counterrevolution inside Russia. The British cruiser *Glory*, the American ship *Olympia*, the French *Amiral Aube* and other vessels of various navies disembarked interventionist units in Murmansk and Archangel.

In April 1918, the Japanese landed in Vladivostok. They were eventually joined by detachments of the armed forces of the United States, Great Britain, France and Italy.

At the same time, the Germans, in disregard of the Treaty of Brest-Litovsk, occupied the Crimea, invaded Finland and put Hetman Skoropadsky into power in the Ukraine. On May 8 German units occupied Rostov-on-the-Don, aiding the creation of the anti-Bolshevik "Almighty Army of the Don," headed by Ataman P. Krasnov. In the middle of May the Germans landed on the Taman Peninsula. On May 25, summoned by the Georgian Mensheviks, the German army appeared in Georgia.

In Transcaucasia, Turkey unleashed a widespread intervention.

In May of the same year the revolt of the Czechoslovak corps began, engineered and provoked by the Entente. This corps had been formed sometime earlier by the Provisional Government, and incorporated Czech and Slovak prisoners of war. With the consent of the Soviet government, this corps was making its way to Vladivostok for repatriation. The mutiny of the Czechoslovak legionnaires, which served as a signal to the domestic counterrevolution, sought to unite the different anti-Soviet mutinies into a single arm. Moreover, the capture of a number of sections of the Samara-Far East railroad line and the establishment of control over vast industrial and productive regions of the country was undertaken to solve the problem of supplying this single stream of a country-wide counterrevolution directed by the Entente. The mutiny of the Czechoslovak corps thus played a singular part in the scheme of the interventionists.

In May–June the Czechoslovak legionnaires and the White Guard detachments that emerged under their cover seized Syzran and Samara on the Volga, Zlatoust and Chelyabinsk in the Urals, Omsk and Novonikolayevsk in Siberia, and other cities, as well as industrial and railroad centers along the entire stretch from Penza to Vladivostok. They helped to consolidate the anti-Soviet governments in the Volga Area, such as the Socialist Revolutionary and Menshevik Committee of the Constituent Assembly with its center in Samara, and the Provisional Siberian Government in Omsk.

The very fate of the Republic of the Soviets, as Lenin declared, was now being decided on this most important and most dangerous front, which came to be known as the Eastern front. The situation assumed greater gravity as a result of the simultaneous outbreak of a revolt by Left-Socialist Revolutionaries against the Soviet government. As far back as June 24, 1918, the Central Committee of the party of the Left-Socialist Revolutionaries had adopted a treacherous resolution which read in part: "It is essential to put the speediest possible end to the so-called breathing spell. With this in view, the Central Committee of the party regards it as both feasible and expedient to organize a series of acts of terrorism against the more prominent representatives of German imperialism." The launching of the resolution by the Left-Socialist Revolutionaries was scheduled to coincide with the Fifth All-Russian Congress of the Soviets, which had convened in Moscow early in June. Under the camouflage of pseudo-revolutionary phrases, they appealed for war against Germany. Realizing that they would not be able to count on a majority of the Congress to support their plans, they proceeded to carry out the intent of the resolution by acts of terrorism against the representatives of Germany in Russia. On July 6 the German Ambassador, Count Mirbach, was assassinated. Along with this the Left-S.R.'s launched an open assault against the Soviet power.

In Moscow the revolt was quelled swiftly. A prominent role in these events was played by Latvian infantry units under the command of I. I. Vatsetis, a colonel of the former tsarist army who from the beginning of the October Revolution took an active part in the civil war, heading armies, commanding at the front, and at one time even leading all of the Red Army.

The treacherous attempt on July 11 by the then commander of the Eastern front, Left-S.R. Colonel M. A. Muravyov, to open a front to the Czechoslovak legionnaires, and to move with them against Moscow was thwarted with equal swiftness. When Muravyov showed up in Simbirsk at a meeting of the Provincial Executive Committee, with the aim of dictating his conditions to them, the local Communists were prepared. Muravyov was surrounded, isolated from his followers and shot for treason to his country.

Simultaneously with the organization of this mutiny, the Socialist Revolutionaries launched their program of terrorism. On August 30 the director of the Provincial Extraordinary Commission for Struggle Against the Counterrevolution (Gubcheka), M. S. Uritsky, was killed in Petrograd, and on the same evening Lenin was gravely wounded at the Mikhelson factory.

However, the Soviet government and the people everywhere replied with red terror to the terror that was hurled against them. "Red terror was nothing else but the expression of the inflexible will of the poorest peasantry and the proletariat to crush all attempts at uprisings against us," wrote F. E.

Dzerzhinsky, head of the All-Russian Extraordinary Commission for Struggle Against Counterrevolution (VChKa).

In the summer of 1918, the Soviet government was able to score decisive gains in the organization of the poor peasants in the central regions of the country. ". . . The working and exploited country people . . . are rising up everywhere and coming out in alliance with the urban proletariat . . ." wrote Lenin, "and we have now taken the first and the most momentous step of the socialist revolution in the countryside." At this point he summed up his thoughts with the statement that it was ". . . only in the summer and autumn of 1918 that the urban October Revolution became a real rural October Revolution." This made it possible for the Soviet power to crush in July the counterrevolutionary mutinies in the central districts of the country. At the same time the Eastern front was consolidated and strengthened.

I. I. Vatsetis was appointed as the new commander of the front. The Party sent the best of her sons to the Eastern front. The orders issued by Mikhail Tukhachevsky before his departure stated that he was commanded "to carry out assignments of exceptional importance," adding that "he should be entrusted with the most responsible and exacting tasks, since according to the testimonial of the VTsIK he is one of the best military specialists of the Communist Party." The twenty-five-year-old ensign became the organizer and commander-in-chief of the First Revolutionary Army. One just as young was in command of the Volga flotilla. He was the "Red Admiral" Fyodor Raskolnikov.

On September 10, 1918, the Red Army launched an offensive on the Eastern front and liberated Kazan, then on September 12, Simbirsk, and on October 7, Samara. The Soviet armies continued their advance to the Urals. The authority of the "Constituent" leaders was undermined once and for all. On November 18, in the city of Omsk, the Minister of War of the Siberian government, an ally of the Entente, Admiral A. V. Kolchak, staged a *coup d'état*. He was proclaimed the

Commander-in-Chief and "Supreme Ruler" of Russia, and acknowledged as such by all of the leaders of the Russian counterrevolution.

The successes scored by the Red Army on the different fronts, the termination of World War I, which ended in the defeat of the Austro-German bloc, the revolution in Germany and the downfall of the kaiser's rule, made it possible for the Soviet government to nullify the piratical treaty of Brest-Litovsk. There now began mass expulsions of the German invaders from the regions that they had occupied. In December 1918 the VTsIK promulgated a decree granting independence to the Latvian, Lithuanian and Estonian Republics. On January 1, 1919, the founding of the Soviet Republic of Byelorussia was proclaimed. "We are scoring gigantic victories," wrote Lenin, summing up the results of the first year of struggle against the interventionists and White Guards.

However, as early as March 1919 a new peril loomed up in the east: the forward surge of the White Guard army of Kolchak, 300,000 strong and bolstered by the interventionists. On March 4 the Kolchak troops launched an offensive. Debilitated and exhausted by the battles they waged in the autumn and winter of 1918–1919, deprived of the most essential forces and supplies, which were being routed at the time to the Southern front where the White Guard units were in action under the command of General A. Denikin, the Red Army of the eastern front began a retreat. The enemy occupied a number of the largest industrial centers (Ufa, Sarapul, Bugulma) and moved towards the Volga. On April 11, the White Cossack Orenburg Army of Ataman Dutov captured Aktyubinsk, and cut the communications between the central part of the Republic and Turkestan. Capturing vast stores of bread that had been stocked in Siberia and the Volga Area, Kolchak's hordes further aggravated the country's food situation, which was grave enough already.

It was then that the appeal of the Party, "Everything for the struggle against Kolchak," resounded throughout the country.

On April 11, 1919, the Organizational Bureau of the Central Committee of the Bolshevik Party endorsed the "Theses of the Central Committee of the Russian Communist Party (Bolsheviks) in Connection with the Situation on the Eastern Front," written by Lenin.

"All our energies must be exerted to the extreme," it was stated in the "Theses," "to smash Kolchak."

The Party, the Komsomols,* the trade unions and the peasantry proceeded to mobilize. The republic marshaled all the forces at its command. Reinforcements one hundred thousand strong were rushed to the Eastern front in a short time. Fifteen thousand Communists and a few thousand Komsomol members formed its backbone.

The Communists and the Komsomol members labored unremittingly in the rear. Lenin described as "A great beginning" the people's drive for a boost in the productivity of labor, the like of which had never been seen in terms of scope and enthusiasm.

"The starving workers," wrote Lenin, "surrounded by the malicious counterrevolutionary agitation of the bourgeoisie, the Mensheviks and the Socialist Revolutionaries, are organizing 'Communist Subbotniks,' working overtime without any pay, and achieving an enormous increase in the productivity of labor in spite of the fact that they are weary, tormented and exhausted by malnutrition. Is this not supreme heroism?"

As early as the end of 1918, the Workers' and Peasants' Defense Council (subsequently renamed the Council of Labor and Defense) was set up under the leadership of Lenin. The Council was charged with the task of mobilizing all the industrial and other national resources to help the front and heading all military operations. In his capacity as leader of the su-

---

* Komsomols: Members of the Young Communist League which was founded in the summer of 1917 and officially established at its First Congress in October 1918. In 1924, after the death of Lenin, the Sixth Congress of this youth organization adopted a decision to add the name of Lenin to the Komsomol.

preme defense organization Lenin personally steered and guided all war operations.

"Lenin's conduct of the Civil War . . . constitutes an accomplished course initiating the entire country into the science of war," recalled S. S. Kamenev, who was at the time in command of the Eastern front, and subsequently (beginning June 1919, and to the end of Civil War) Commander-in-Chief of all of the Armed Forces of the Republic. "Day in and day out he commanded the Red Army in person. Lenin's command did not express itself only in the fact that the communiques and frequently also written reports of the RVSR were submitted to him daily.* He organized the struggle of the country as a whole, the struggle in which the operations of the Red Army were but a part of the other means of struggle."

The steps taken soon had their effect on the situation at the Eastern front. On April 28 the armies of the southern sector of the front went over to the offensive, and commanding them was one of the earliest members of the Bolshevik Party, the revolutionary fighter and outstanding proletarian leader Mikhail Vasilyevich Frunze.

Despite the fact that the enemy had an appreciable superiority of forces, it now suffered one defeat after another. This was because the armies of Kolchak and the interventionists had no support among the people. Comparing the contending forces, the Minister of War of the Kolchak "government," Baron Budberg, observed: "If you tally our assets and liabilities, the conclusions would be most dismal. . . . We have on our side the officers, but this is not all . . . we have on our side the affluent bourgeoisie, the speculators, the merchants, for the reason that we are defending their material goods. . . . Everything else is against us, partly in terms of active par-

---

* RVSR (Revolutionary Military Council of the Republic): A supreme military operative body, established by resolution of VTsIK on September 2, 1918. L. D. Trotsky was appointed Chairman of the Revolutionary-Military Council. It was entrusted with the guidance of all organs of the Red Army.

ticipation. . . . Nothing can be accomplished without solid reliance on the sympathy of the entire population."

In the struggle for the Urals, the units of the Red Army exhibited an exceptional endurance and heroism.

Here is an incident that occurred during the crossing of the Belaya River: The regiment, which was made up of the workers of Ivanovo-Voznesensk, crossed over to the side occupied by the enemy, descended on the White Guards and in the action used up all its shells, so that it was forced to dig in and wait for reinforcements. The enemy took advantage of this. "And so," related Dmitry Furmanov, Commissar of the regiment of Ivanovo-Voznesensk, who later became a well-known Soviet writer, "when instead of feints the enemy unleashed a real attack along a wide front, the fighting men gave way and fell back. The commander and commissar rushed to the flanks calling to the retreating men to halt, explaining to them fast and furiously that come what might, there was no place to run to; behind them was the river with no way of crossing it; that nothing else remained but to be resolute, dig in and go over to the attack. Men who had faltered for a moment stopped in their retreat. At that moment some horsemen leaped from their mounts, which they had galloped into front units of the line. There among them was Frunze, and with him the chief of the political section of the army, Gronin, and a few men closely associated with them. . . . He rushed ahead, rifle in hand: 'Hurrah! Hurrah! Forward, Comrades!' Everyone nearby recognized him. With the speed of lightning the news flashed through the lines. The fighting men were fired with a new spirit, and they rushed forward in a frenzy. This was a decisive moment. But firing became sporadic—there was a shortage of cartridges—and they hurled themselves with bayonets levelled at the advancing enemy. So massive was the surge of the heroic onrush that the enemy lines wavered, broke and went into retreat. . . . The breakthrough was accomplished, and the situation retrieved."

The Twenty-fifth Division battled with utter self-renunciation under the command of Vasily Chapayev. The third son of a poor Russian peasant, Vasily worked as a carpenter up to World War I. In that war he was decorated four times with the Cross of St. George and received a medal for bravery and valor.

Non-commissioned Officer Chapayev, a member of the Bolshevik Party since September 1917, commanded first a regiment, then a brigade and then a division in the Red Army. His very name struck terror into the heart of the enemy. His military talent was acknowledged by everyone, both friend and enemy. He was no more than thirty-two years old when an enemy bullet ended his life. He died on September 5, 1919, in the battle on the outskirts of the Cossack village of Lbishchenskaya.

The regular units of the Red Army received great assistance from the underground and the partisans behind the lines of the Kolchak army. The Siberian Bureau of the Central Committee of the Party was established for the purpose of directing all of the party work in Siberia. More than 100,000 partisans, joined together into a partisan army, waged a heroic struggle against the White Guards and interventionists. Heading the movement were S. Lazo, P. Postyshev, F. Mukhin, I. Gromov, E. Mamontov, A. Kravchenko, Y. Yakovenko, P. Shchetinkin and others.

In July the Red Army liberated Ekaterinburg, Chelyabinsk and many other cities. "The Urals are in our hands. We are now moving on to Siberia!" the Red Army men of the Eastern front cabled to Lenin. The demoralized army of Kolchak was on the retreat. Forging ahead, fighting over a distance of thousands of kilometers, the Red Army utterly routed the enemy in a last huge battle against Kolchak's men between Tobol and Irtysh. In January 1920, Kolchak and the members of his "government" were arrested and sentenced to be shot.

In May 1919, after a breakthrough on the front between the Narva River and Lake Chudskoye, the Northwestern Corps of Volunteers of the White Guard moved against Petrograd, under the command of General A. P. Rodzyanko. The entire White Guard corps was under the command of General Yudenich. This put Petrograd into a grave predicament. All Communists and Komsomol members had gone off to the front. On June 10, 1919, the Central Committee of the Bolshevik Party, responding to Lenin's recommendation, shifted its prime efforts to the Petrograd front. Units of the Eastern front and the reserve forces of the General Headquarters were dispatched to that city. The situation began to take a turn for the better as they were approaching and in July Yudenich's army was hurled back to Yamburg and Gdov.

Following the catastrophic fiascoes in the east and in the northwest in the summer of 1919, the White Guards shifted the mainstay of their operations, staking everything on their southern armies. Crack units of officers were concentrated there. The Entente furnished them all kinds of supplies, from uniforms to cartridges. The United States maintained a special mission at the General Staff headquarters of the Commander-in-Chief, A. I. Denikin. On July 3 Denikin issued orders for an offensive against Moscow.

In August the troops of Denikin drove back units of the Red Army, occupying the entire right bank of the Ukraine, occupying Odessa on August 23, and entering Kiev on August 31. Units of the Forty-fifth, Fifty-eighth and Forty-seventh Divisions were cut off from the main forces of the Red Army and found themselves far behind the enemy's rear positions. They formed the Southern Group of the army and were placed under the command of Ion Yakir. He had just turned twenty-three that year. The son of a Jewish pharmacist, Yakir aspired to become a chemist, but the revolution turned him into a soldier. His outstanding military talents, a formidable will, energy and the diversified attainments which he acquired subsequently, placed him in the category of prominent Soviet military leaders. Following Vasily Blucher, the first man to be awarded the highest military distinction of the Republic, the Order of the Red Banner, Yakir was the second to receive this award. Appointed as commander of the Southern Army Group, Yakir was determined to break through to the north and join the main forces of the Red Army. Under the most difficult conditions, the fighting men of the Southern Group staged a four-hundred-kilometer raid through the rear lines of the enemy, finally joining units of the 12th Army.

On October 1, 1919, Lenin signed the decision of the Defense Council to award the Forty-fifth and Fifty-eighth Infantry Divisions the Distinguished Banner of the Revolution in recognition of their heroic advance, and to bestow a cash award on the entire roster of men in the Group. On October 30, 1919, Yakir was for a second time decorated with the Order of the Red Banner, a distinction which he earned because of this operation.

The counterattack mounted by the Red Army on the Southern front in the summer of 1919 was unsuccessful. In the autumn, Denikin's White Guard armies occupied Kursk, Voronezh and Orel and approached Tula. Moscow was in grave peril; at the same time, Yudenich's army again reached the Pulkovsky Heights on the outskirts of Petrograd. Intending to turn the Ukraine into an underling government, the chief of the Polish extremists, Marshal Jozef Pilsudsky, also joined the fray. His armies occupied Minsk. The press the world over predicted the impending and inevitable doom of "Bolshevism." However, these and all later prophecies proved futile.

Reinforcements were repeatedly added to the ranks of the Red Army. The Party continued to grow during those days with uncommon speed. In the Central provinces alone, 200,-000 men came to join it. Thousands of workers and peasants joined the partisans. A Home Defense Bureau of the Central Committee was set up, headed by Stanislav Kosior, a worker of Polish descent, and a Party member since 1907, whose function was to direct the operations of the partisans in the Ukraine, in which more than fifty thousand were taking part. Stanislav Kosior directed all of the underground operations behind Denikin's lines. Komsomols courageously fought in the underground side by side with the Communists in the Ukraine, Don and North Caucasus. In Odessa, the Komsomol underground numbered in excess of three hundred men, and in Riga some two hundred. Underground groups were formed in Ekaterinodar, Semfiropol, Nikolayev, Valmier, Tiflis and other cities.

The underground endured many sacrifices. The slightest carelessness brought on the risk of failure and ruin. In Kharkov, the White Guards were able, with the aid of provocateurs, to annihilate three staffs of the Underground Provincial Committee of the Party. Among the many who met their deaths was the remarkable underground personality, Mikhail Cherny. Also a victim was the secretary of the Ekaterinoslav Provincial Party Committee, Maks. In Lugansk among those who died before a firing squad was a young Communist woman, Dusya Zeldovich, whose devotion to the revolution knew no bounds. The loss of the leader of military operations of the Provincial Committee, Aleksandr Khvorostin, was a serious blow to the Odessa underground. Denikin's hangmen subjected him to tortures, attempting to learn from him the names of the other members of the underground, but they failed to extract from him even a single name. In the city of Nikolayev, sixty-one people were executed before the firing squad on the night of November 20. Among them were the leader of the Komsomol organization of the town, Grisha Khazanov, and the Komsomol girl, Tamara Malt. Tamara was suspended by her hair, while Grisha's heels were roasted on a fire and a red-hot needle was driven into the soles of his feet. But the hangmen failed to elicit from him the name of a single underground member. In his last agony he exclaimed: "Long live the power of the Soviets!"

In October 1919, the Central Committee of the Bolshevik Party approved a strategic plan devised to rout Denikin's army. The main blow was to be dealt the enemy through the regions of the Donets coal basin (Donbass), in which the working population predominated, and whose support played a prominent part in the successful execution of the plan. In the second half of October, the armies of the Southern front inflicted a serious defeat on the armies of General Denikin under Oryol, Kromy and Voronezh. On the Southeastern front, the Ninth Army, reinforced with the merged Mounted Corps of B. M. Dumenko and the Cavalry Group of M. F. Blinov, filled the breach between the Southern and the Southeastern fronts on November 12.

Boris Dumenko was known as the Commander of the Red Cavalry. Many famed cavalrymen entered their service in the Red Army under his command, among them Marshal S. M. Budyonny, Marshal S. K. Timoshenko, General of the Army A. V. Khrulev, Lieutenant-General O. I. Gorodovikov and many others.

Commissar P. S. Dyachenko, of the Cavalry Brigade of the Thirty-second Infantry Division (Tenth Army), gives the following account concerning his first meeting with Dumenko:

In the autumn of 1919 our division, then taking part in the general offensive of the army, approached the Don River through the Arched station and dug in on the sandhills of the left bank of the Don. Our cavalry brigade, in which I then filled the post of commissar, was occupying a farmstead on the right flank of the division. All at once our reconnaissance reported that a mounted group had been observed on our side of the river, some eight to ten kilometers away. We reported a concentration of the enemy to the field headquarters of the army. They informed us in turn that Dumenko had been instructed to dispatch one cavalry brigade and to destroy the cavalry division under Glubintsev which had crossed over to our side of the river during the night. . . . Some time later I saw through the field glasses that a black cavalry column was sweeping across the hill—that was Dumenko coming to our aid. Then a few minutes later a horseman came racing towards us across the knoll on a magnificent tall dark bay horse. The rider was broad shouldered, about thirty years of age, with a broad, handsome, though slightly pale face and a keen, grave expression.

. . . The enemy did not observe the approach of the brigade from the Dumenko corps, and therefore boldly advanced to the onslaught on our numerically small brigade. The Whites advanced as far as the farmstead, and it was only then that they became aware of the presence of another cavalry column. Our two brigades rushed in to meet them, and a savage encounter of sabers ensued. The enemy was unable to withstand it and turned tail, but it was too late.

When I had hewed down to the ground two Cossacks and the heat of the first skirmish had subsided, I should rather say in the midst of this raging sea, I saw Dumenko on his spirited horse sailing into the multitude and laying about him with the blade of his sword right and left and mowing down Cossack heads as he did so. It was a frightful carnage. After all, more than three thousand horsemen had converged from both sides in the cavalry onslaught. The following day they counted more than four hundred bodies among the Whites. Many White Cossacks and saddled horses were taken prisoner. . . .

This battle proved to me that Dumenko had honestly earned the spurs of a legendary chief of the Red Cavalry. . . . Both on account of his conduct with us, and in battle, Dumenko found favor with me. I admired him for his heroism, for his mighty willpower, and for his calm sobriety of judgment. I became his staunch admirer for all time.

The endeavor of the White Guards to take up a defensive stance proved of no avail. In December 1919 they were driven out of Kharkov and Kiev. At the same time the army of Yudenich was shattered beyond redemption on the outskirts of Petrograd. Early in January 1920 the Red Army entered Rostov-on-the-Don, and in March Novorossiisk. The White Guard army of Denikin and its accomplices suffered a complete collapse. Remnants of that army fled abroad and some of them went into hiding in the Crimea. Early in 1920, when the Red Army liberated Archangel and Murmansk, it swept the Soviet north clean of the interventionists. The blockade was broken and a peaceful breathing spell won.

However, the calm was short-lived. A new offensive was launched from the west. Playing on the national feeling of the Poles, who had been cruelly trampled underfoot by tsarism, the followers of Jozef Pilsudsky deceived the Polish people, declaring to them that the interests of "independence and territorial integrity" of Poland dictated the undertaking of a war against Soviet Russia. They were spreading mendacious rumors to the effect that the people of Russia were preparing to seize Poland and to impose Communism on the people of Poland by force of arms, and that the Polish Communists were seeking to hasten this seizure, etc.

In its efforts to repudiate this lie, the VTsIK promulgated

an appeal to the people of Poland as early as February 1920. The appeal said in part: "The Russian workers and peasants were the first to adopt a resolution granting independence to the Polish people, recognizing it unconditionally and for all time." Even before independence was restored to the Polish state, the Soviet government promulgated a decree on August 29, 1918, abrogating all treaties and instruments imposing the partition of Poland concluded between tsarist Russia, Prussia and Austria-Hungary. Refuting false rumors, the appeal published by VTsIK stated categorically: ". . . All that the Communists of Russia are now seeking to accomplish is to defend their own soil, their peaceful, constructive tasks, and they do not nor could they seek to impose communism on foreign countries by force. The transformation of Poland in accord with the interests of the toiling masses of Poland must be left to the decision of these toiling masses." The supreme organ of the Soviet Republic appealed to the Polish government to establish peaceful relations between the two governments. On April 25 Pilsudsky's armies launched an offensive. The following day they occupied Korosten and Zhitomir, on April 27 Kazatin and on May 6 they entered Kiev. The White army of General P. N. Wrangel moved out of the Crimea to aid them.

And once again all life in the young republic, which had begun to settle down to peaceful pursuits during the few months of breathing spell, had to give way to the exigencies of war. Lenin wrote that the old rule to which the Russians had adhered during all the previous wars must be restored at this moment. The rule presupposed that during the war everything should be subject to the interests of war, the entire internal life of the country should be subordinated to war and not the slightest vacillation in this connection was permissible.

Large numbers of reinforcements were on the way to the Polish front as soon as various units of the Red Army could be supplied with uniforms, equipment and food. Thousands of agitators explained to the Red Army men the special nature of the Polish-Soviet war, its aims and tasks. "The rout of the Polish White Guards that attacked us does not by a single jot make any change in our attitude towards the independence of Poland," was the categorical assertion in the theses of the Central Committee of the Russian Communist Party (R.C.P.) (B) entitled "The Polish Front and our Tasks."

In May, units of the Red Army of the Western front under the command of Mikhail Tukhachevsky launched an offensive. In so doing they relieved the situation on the Southwestern front, where the army then began inflicting blows on the enemy, soon driving them in the direction of Lvov. Fighting on that front were Grigory Kotovsky, the hero of the Civil War, Aleksandr Parkhomenko, and Semyon Budyonny's Red Cavalry. The armies of the Western front liberated Minsk, the capital of Byelorussia, on July 11, 1920, and the enemy began beating a swift retreat towards Warsaw. The units of the Red Army pursuing them pushed forward over a distance of seven hundred kilometers in one continuous advance. "Only those who measured the stretch from the Berezina to the Vistula by their strides," wrote Vitovit Putna, commander of the Twenty-seventh Omsk Infantry Division, "know how difficult it is to become a hero. It is even more difficult to win a victory." By the admission of Pilsudsky himself, this headlong advance of the Red Army created panic in the government of Poland.

However, the success of this brilliant breakthrough was not consolidated. The armies of the Western front broke away from their bases in the rear and suffered heavy losses. The Central Committee of the Bolshevik Party adopted a special resolution concerning aid to this front at the expense of the Southwestern front. However, the shift of the Budyonny Cavalry from the approaches to Lvov in the direction of Warsaw was delayed. Pilsudsky's armies struck at the exposed flank of the Western front, forcing the Red Army to retreat hastily.

This failure on the outskirts of Warsaw did not mean that the Soviet Republic was no longer capable of waging war;

however, true to its peace-loving policy, the Soviet country did not wish to prolong it, and on October 12, 1920, the preliminary peace terms were signed in Riga.

The cessation of military operations on the Western front enabled the Soviet High Command to bring down the might of the Red Army on Wrangel's White Guard armies. Mikhail Frunze was appointed to the command of the Southern front. The membership of the Revolutionary War Council included one of the oldest activists of the Communist Party, Sergey Gusev, and a prominent figure of the international movement of the working class, the Hungarian Communist Bela Kun. Many figures well-known in the Party, in the government and in the conduct of the war were dispatched into the zone of military operations. Among them were Mikhail Kelinin, who in March 1919 on the death of Yakov Sverdlov succeeded him in the Presidency, Anatoly Lunacharsky, Dmitry Kursky and others.

The armies on the Southern front were faced with the task of routing the White Guard armies in Northern Tavria, and liberating the Crimea before the onset of winter.

At the end of October they launched an offensive, setting out from Kakhovka. Within a matter of a few days Wrangel's army in Northern Tavria suffered a complete rout. Its remnants retreated into the Crimea and took shelter behind fortifications which they erected on the isthmuses of Perekop and Chongar. These fortifications were defended by lines of trenches and barbed-wire barriers, ditches, ramparts, reinforced concrete, machine guns and artillery. They were thought to be impregnable.

There were three possible routes open to the Red Army for a breakthrough to the Crimea, namely the Perekop Isthmus (eight kilometers at its widest point), the Chongar Isthmus and the Arabat Crescent, which skirted the western part of the Sea of Azov. The Perekop Isthmus afforded the best prospects for maneuvering and it was here that the main blow of the Southern front was aimed.

The advance preparations for the decisive struggles for the Crimea were conducted under the most difficult circumstances. Freezing temperatures, which suddenly descended to fourteen degrees Fahrenheit, found the men of the fighting forces in their threadbare summer uniforms. Most of the units were camped in the open fields, lashed by a sharp, icy wind. There was a shortage of drinking water. (All the reservoirs of the Sivash region contained salt water.) "Only the uncommonly cheerful mood of the entire body of the army," wrote Frunze, who personally visited all of the units in the days of the assault, "enabled the accomplishment not only of the impossible but also brought it about that one could not hear anywhere any grumbling about the outrageous conditions under which combat operations had to be waged. Every Red Army man, commander and political worker was preoccupied solely with the one aspiration which had taken root in the consciousness of all, down to the last man: To surge into the Crimea at all costs because it meant an end to all privations."

During the night of November 7 to 8, which was the third anniversary of the October Revolution, the assault began on Perekop. The attack against the forts of Perekop and Chongar took place in an area which was entirely exposed and which was under artillery and machine-gun fire. The crossing was made on the bed of the Gulf of Sivash during the few brief minutes of low tide, while the onrush of water tailed the fighting men and threatened to engulf everything and everybody, or at least cut them off from the rear and their reserves. It was an unforgettable page of heroism in the history of the Red Army.

The Isthmus of Perekop was seized and Wrangel's armies tried to reach the sea. But on November 16, 1920, Frunze sent a telegram to Lenin: "Today our cavalry occupied Kerch. The Southern front is no more." Even before Wrangel's armies were defeated, the armies of the Turkestan front routed the interventionists and the nationalist counterrevolution in Central Asia and in Kazakhstan. Soviet power was established throughout the area. Joining ranks with the Turkestan Autonomous Soviet Socialist Republic, which was proclaimed on April 30, 1918, the Soviet People's Republic of Khorezm was constituted in April 1920, and the Soviet People's Republic of Bukhara in October. The Red Army also came to the aid of the people of Transcaucasia. Here again the forces of the domestic and foreign intervention were crushed. Subsequently, the People's Soviet Republics of Azerbaidzhan, Armenia and Georgia came into being.

Towards the end of 1920 the main forces of the interventionists and the White Guards were crushed. By the autumn of 1922 the last nucleus of civil war, in the Far East, was destroyed. In the battles on the outskirts of Volochayevka and Spassk, the Red Army shattered the White Guard army beyond redemption. Vladivostok was liberated from the interventionists.

Summarizing the victories of the Soviet people and its Red Army, Lenin observed: "Soviet power accomplished what could well be termed a miracle because in its struggle against international capital it was able to win an unprecedented and improbable victory, the likes of which the world had never before witnessed."

5 DICTATORSHIP AND DEMOCRACY

M an is intolerant of brute force. It is repugnant to him in any form. The word "dictator" is uttered with hostility, anger and pain by everyone alike. Dictatorships have worked much evil in the world. But what means other than force would one employ in the struggle for its defeat? And, in fact, is it possible at all to struggle against it without force?

The surgeon in his efforts to arrive at a diagnosis not infrequently causes acute pain when probing for the causes of an illness. This is force. However, it is unavoidable if one is to be effective in combating a disease.

Society isolates criminals of every kind—thieves, murderers, rapists, etc. This is force. It is unavoidable, not only as a means of self-defense, but also as a means of outright attack in behalf of man at his best, in behalf of his right to realize his best and in behalf of his right to feel at his best.

The dictatorship of the proletariat is the political power of the working class won by virtue of the victory of the socialist revolution. Here again is force. However, as force in the hands of the toiling majority exercised over the exploiting minority it has as its aim the dismantling of the old, seemingly immutable relations between people; the final abolition of the exploitation of man by man; the breaking of the will of those who have turned the labor of man into an object of unremitting speculation.

The dictatorship of the proletariat is the struggle against a society which has become enfeebled with chronic diseases; it is furthermore the isolation of those who would inhibit this struggle. Being the most democratic of all regimes so far as the majority of workers is concerned, it proceeds differently in posing the question of the relationship between dictatorship, equality and democracy.

With the setting up of its dictatorship, the proletariat takes a step, a most resolute step (in terms of magnitude, scope and speed) in the direction of true freedom, true equality and democracy.

People have not in the past, nor do they now accept the notion of "equality" between the exploiter and the exploited, between the well-fed and the hungry. They do not grant the "freedom" of the former to plunder the latter. Genuine equality calls for the abolition of exploitation, and the abolition of classes. True freedom means freedom from class oppression. True democracy is democracy predicated on the struggle for the liquidation of private property, since the latter is the seedbed both of violence and exploitation.

The broadening of democracy to the level of universal socialist democracy is feasible only on the basis of the dictatorship of the proletariat which continues to pursue the class struggle to the point where all classes are abolished. From the earliest days of its existence, the dictatorship of the proletariat carried within it the features of universal socialist democracy, and the potential for its transformation into a state of the entire people. This potential was realized in the Soviet country where, as stated in the program adopted by the Twenty-second

Lenin in hiding at the station of Razliv (near Petrograd), carrying a passport in the name of Ivanov, a worker.

The shooting of the July demonstration marked the end of the peaceful development of the Revolution.

Smolny, the headquarters
of the Revolution.

Cadets guard the Winter Palace, the
last bulwark of the Provisional Government.

The revolutionary cruiser *Aurora*.

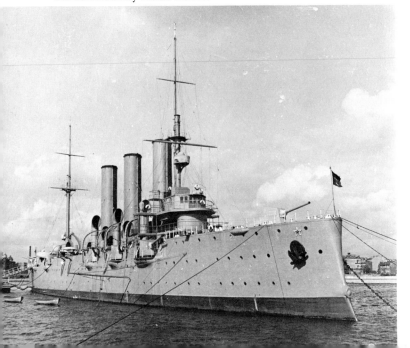

Lenin at the unveiling of the memorial plaque
in honor of the fallen in
the October days, 1917. Moscow.

The Kschesinskaya Palace in Petrograd,
where the Central and Petrograd Committees
of the Bolsheviks were located.

Meyerhold, Shostakovich, Mayakovsky and artist Alexander Rodchenko at a rehearsal of Mayakovsky's play *The Bedbug*.

Free meals for children at
the Petrograd commune.

INSET:
Everybody studied—
the victory against illiteracy.

The Magnitogorsk Iron and Steel Mill.

The Dnieper Hydroelectric Power Plant.

A station of the Moscow Metro.

Kerch, 1942. Searching for relatives among victims of the Nazis.

Military equipment left behind by the retreating enemy near Voronezh, 1942.

Soldiers reading an announcement of the
Soviet Information Bureau, First Baltic Front, 1944.

INSET:
Major General Baklanov,
whom the United States Government
awarded the Distinguished Service Cross for
his part in the Battle of Stalingrad.

Stalingrad, 1943.

The Victory Banner over the Reichstag, Berlin, May 1945.

The Grave of the Unknown Soldier—"Your name is unknown, your deed is immortal."

Congress of the Communist Party of the Soviet Union, "Having brought about the complete and final victory of socialism —the first phase of communism—and the transition of society to the full-scale construction of communism, the dictatorship of the proletariat has fulfilled its historic mission and has ceased to be indispensable in the U.S.S.R. The state, which arose as a state of the dictatorship of the proletariat, has, in the new, contemporary stage, become a state of the entire people, an organ expressing the interests and will of the people as a whole."

Distorting the essence of the dictatorship of the proletariat, the opponents of Marxism, the anti-communists, following the precedent of dogmatists and revisionists of every stripe, more often than not reduced it to sheer force. Lenin time and again pointed out that the essence of the proletarian dictatorship does not lie in force alone, and not so much in the use of force. What lies at the core of the dictatorship of the working class, its constructive tasks and functions, is the fact that the proletariat embodies and achieves a higher stage in the social organization of labor as compared with any preceding stage. This is the root and core of it.

Lenin emphasized that in order to achieve victory, the proletariat must fulfill a double task: First of all, it must enlist all of the laboring and exploited masses to overthrow the ruling class and crush all resistance that might come from that quarter; secondly, it must stimulate the workers to follow along the road of new economic construction, the creation of a new socialist economy and new social relations. "This is the second task," Lenin observed, "more difficult than the former, since it cannot under any circumstances be resolved by heroism at one single sweep, but calls for the most sustained, the most stubborn, the most exacting heroism of collective and routine labor. Moreover, this task is also more essential than the former since in the last analysis only a new and higher method of social production can serve as the deepest wellsprings of stability and inalienability of these victories."

Force or Organization?   If one analyzes carefully everything the Soviet people have accomplished from the very first days of the October Revolution, it will become apparent to what extent the second task took precedence over the former and how every step of the new government was subordinated to its achievement.

The bitterness of the class struggle in Russia was determined not by the striving of the working class to use force, but by the desperate resistance of the overthrown classes, whose strength was enhanced tenfold by enormous assistance given them from the outside precisely because they had been overthrown. Adversaries of the new republic unleashed a savage campaign of defamation in the entire press, organizing acts of sabotage, mutinies, and treacherous assassinations at a time when the Soviet government had not shut down a single hostile newspaper, had released Kerensky's ministers, and even General Krasnov, who had waged war against Soviet Russia (merely on his word of honor as an officer, which he broke almost instantly). "It was only after the enemies of the Soviet state had begun developing their resistance," wrote Lenin, "that we began to crush that resistance systematically, applying even terror." However, the fundamental goal of the dictatorship of the proletariat has always been the transformation of the country's hybrid economy into a socialist economy, the emancipation of man and the opening up of unlimited prospects for the development of the people's capabilities and talents.

This was very clearly underscored in the four variants of the political report presented by the Central Committee of the Bolsheviks to the Eleventh Congress of the Party, framed by Lenin:

"Item: The gulf between the world-historical magnitude of the goals, both advocated and embarked on, *and* the material as well as *cultural* poverty."

In the second variant:

"What is 'the link in the chain'? . . ."

"1922: The *gulf* between the immensity of the tasks and the material poverty and cultural poverty."

"The abyss to be filled."

In a matter of some twenty years this historical abyss was filled. Tens of millions of the Soviet people gave living reality to these jottings of Lenin concerning the creation of a huge machinery industry, the electrification of the country, the collectivization of agriculture and the development of science and culture. Lenin declared: One must "become civilized in good time," before the next military clash with imperialism. The land of the Soviets reached this goal in good time by maintaining the organizational aspect as the focal point of all efforts.

It was generally acknowledged that tsarist Russia was some fifty to one hundred years behind the developed capitalist countries in the volume of its industrial production and in terms of the level of its technical development. In 1918, the country's per capita industrial production was 21 times below that of the United States, 13 times behind Germany, 14 times behind Great Britain and 7.7 times below that of France. Russia imported from abroad about 20 per cent of its coal consumption, 80 per cent of its lead, 30 per cent of its copper, 80 per cent of its mineral fertilizer and 85 per cent of its metal-cutting lathes. Even plows, scythes and other agricultural tools were imported.

The situation was further aggravated by the fact that the civil war had left a legacy of chaos in industry and in transportation, shortages in raw materials and fuel, mass unemployment, a critical shortage in food supplies, particularly in urban communities and at the front. In 1920 industrial output in the Soviet country amounted to no more than one-seventh of its output in 1913, and an even lower fraction of the output of metal—that is, only 5 per cent of the 1913 level. Some five to seven years were required to restore the country's economy to its 1913 level, while many more were necessary to go on and attain rates of production in industry and socialist agriculture of which one could not even begin to dream at the beginning of the twenties.

H. G. Wells, the well-known British writer of science fiction, referred to Lenin as "the dreamer in the Kremlin," regarding Lenin's plans for the development of the land of the Soviets as Utopian.

"I cannot see anything of the sort happening in this dark crystal of Russia," he wrote in his book *Russia in the Shadows*, "but this little man at the Kremlin can; he sees the decaying railways replaced by a new electric transport, sees new roadways spreading throughout the land, sees a new and happier Communist industrialism arising again."

However, Lenin spoke more concretely and with greater precision concerning his plans. In February 1920 he granted an interview to Lincoln Eyre, a correspondent of the American newspaper *The World*. "In the past," Lenin stated, "we made every possible sacrifice to defeat our armed enemies, and from now on we will commit every sinew to our endeavor to rebuild our economy. It will be a matter of years but ultimately we will win. . . . We mean to electrify our entire industrial system through power stations in the Urals and elsewhere. Our engineers tell us it will take ten years. When the electrification is accomplished it will be the first important stage on the road to Communistic administration of public economic life. All our industries will receive their motive power from a common source, capable of supplying them all adequately. This will eliminate wasteful competition in the quest of fuel and place manufacturing enterprise on a sound economic footing—without which we cannot hope to attain the level in the exchange of goods of prime necessity that would be consistent with the principles of communism."

Lenin's chat with Eyre lasted an hour. It was conducted in English, first in Lenin's study, and later at his apartment in the Kremlin. At the end of the talk Lenin said, smiling: "Incidentally in three years we expect to have 50,000,000 incandescent lamps burning in Russia. There are 70,000,000 in the United

States, I believe, but in a land where electricity is in its infancy, more than two-thirds of that number is a very high figure to achieve. Electrification is to my mind, the most momentous of the great tasks that confront us."

It was no wonder, therefore, that the earliest plan advanced for the restoration and development of the people's economy of the Soviet Republic was the plan of the State Commission for the Electrification of Russia (GOELRO Plan), the targets of which were set by Lenin. In that plan, which was to cover a period of ten to fifteen years, the goal was the construction of twenty thermo-electric power stations (Kizelovskaya, Kashirskaya, Shterovskaya, and others) and ten hydroelectric stations (Dnieper, Svirsk, Volkhov, and others) with an over-all power output of 1.5 million kilowatt-hours. The over-all annual electrical power output projected was calculated at 8.8 billion kilowatt-hours, as against 1.9 billion kilowatt-hours produced in Russia in the year 1913.

The GOELRO Plan traced out the principal channels of socialist industrialization, including rational distribution of industry, industrial development of the Eastern regions, maximum utilization of natural resources, and the industrialization of the Urals and Siberia. It also proposed a series of more concrete goals, particularly the combining of the ores of the Urals and the coal of Kuznetsk, and the building of metallurgical complexes out of the enterprises of Kuznetsk and Magnitogorsk, the development of new channels of communication, development of the northern sea route, and construction of the Turkestan-Siberian railroad. The plan provided for an increase in industrial production of 80 to 100 per cent as compared with the 1913 level, and by a large multiple as compared with the production level of 1920.

The years of the first Soviet five-year plans (1928–1941) surpassed some of the most daring dreams. Even during the years preceding the Second World War, industry in the U.S.S.R. ranked first in the world in its rate of growth and occupied one of the ranking places in volume of output.

During the period from 1945 to 1965, industry in the U.S.S.R. made another stride forward. During the years of the Soviet state's existence, the total volume of industrial output of the U.S.S.R. increased more than sixty-three-fold, and the production of the means of production rose more than one hundred-fold. In the year that saw the end of the Second World War, the United States of America produced 75 million tons of steel, while the Soviet Union's output was only 12 million tons. In 1965 the U.S.A. produced 125 million tons of steel, an increase of 67 per cent as compared with 1945, while the Soviet Union produced 96.9 million tons in 1966, which is to say that it had boosted its steel production eight times. Lenin's behest regarding electrification of the country was fulfilled. In 1940, the U.S.S.R. produced 48.3 billion kilowatt-hours of electrical power, and in 1966 it reached 545 billion kilowatt-hours—or something in excess of eleven times greater. The output of petroleum and gas expanded to enormous proportions, and along with it the production of cement. All of these constitute the very foundations of present-day construction.

In 1913, tsarist Russia ranked fifth in the world in its volume of industrial output, and fourth in Europe. About 4 per cent of the world's industrial output came from Russia in 1913, but machine building in the country was poorly developed and it was dependent on the importation of machinery and equipment. Today, in 1967, the U.S.S.R. ranks second in the world in volume of industrial output, while holding first place in Europe, and it produces about 20 per cent of the world's industrial output. Moreover, it relies only on its own potential for the production of all essential machinery and equipment.

In 1913, at one of the sessions of the Fourth State Duma, the Chairman of the Council of Ministers of tsarist Russia, Kokovtsev, declared: "To suggest that over a period of some twenty years we could catch up with nations with a century-old culture, gentlemen, is making demands which one should not venture to advance." What was an inconceivable demand in prerevolutionary Russia became a reality in Soviet Russia within a short period of time—ten to thirteen years.

In his broad plan of socialist transformation Lenin devoted considerable attention over and above the problem of industrialization to the problem of transition from small individual peasant holdings to the socialist form of organization. This was a complex problem rooted first and foremost in the impediments created by peasant leanings towards private ownership of land, which stemmed from an age-long hunger for land. Now, at long last, the peasant found himself in possession of his own little patch of soil. The task of the proletariat, Lenin pointed out, was one of guidance and of bringing its influence to bear on the peasantry to serve as a bellwether to the vacillating and those lacking in firmness of purpose. Lenin stressed the fact that it involved a struggle, one of a different kind, the overcoming of the known—a quite different type of resistance and a quite different sort of overcoming.

In a speech delivered at the Eighth Congress of the Party in March 1919, Lenin declared: ". . . . Coercion on this point would ruin the whole cause. What is required here is prolonged educational work. We have to give the peasant . . . concrete examples to prove that the 'commune' is the best possible thing. . . . The aim here is not to expropriate the middle peasant but to bear in mind the specific conditions in which the peasant lives, to learn from the peasant acceptable methods of transition to a better system, and not to dare to give orders!" The decisions of the Eighth Congress reaffirmed the principle of the voluntary nature of collectivization: "Associations are only worthwhile when they have been set up by the peasants themselves, on their own initiative, and their benefits verified in practice. Undue haste in this matter is harmful, for it can only strengthen prejudices against innovations among the middle peasants.

"Representatives of Soviet power who permit themselves to employ not only direct but even indirect compulsion to bring peasants into communes must be brought strictly to account and removed from work in the countryside."

In 1927 there were more than 27 million individual peasant holdings in the country. No more than 15.2 per cent of them had horse-drawn agricultural machinery available; 28.3 per cent of the farms had no beasts of burden whatsoever, and 31.6 per cent lacked all tilling implements.

The poor peasants were unable to obtain a living from their own farms. They were forced to lease out their land, to hire themselves out, or to rent beasts of burden and implements from prosperous peasants, who owned one-third of all agricultural machinery.

The prosperous peasants (known as kulaks) represented 4 to 5 per cent of the whole peasantry, but owned a large proportion of the means of agricultural production—15 to 20 per cent. They waged a fierce propaganda campaign against the collective farms (*kolkhozy*) and state farms (*sovkhozy*).

The kolkhoz is a collective enterprise founded on the voluntary association of the toiling peasants for the purpose of conducting large-scale agricultural production. Collectivized in the kolkhoz are the beasts of burden and the productive cattle, the agricultural implements, the seed, fodder and the farm buildings. The land, which is the property of the entire people, is allotted to kolkhoz members for free and perpetual use. The kolkhoz retains ownership of the output of the collective farm, namely seed, meat, butter, vegetables and fruit, cotton, flax, beets, as well as ownership of the buildings. The income of the collective farm is distributed among its members according to the work they have invested in it. Each collective farm household retains personal ownership of the subsidiary holdings on a personal plot, namely a dwelling house, dairy-producing cattle, fowl, farm buildings essential for the housing of the cattle, and a stock of small agricultural implements. Life has completely proved the correctness of the cooperative plan formulated by Lenin and conceived to accomplish the socialist transformation of the rural economy "by the simplest, easiest means accessible to the peasant."

The state farms (sovkhozy) represent large-scale state socialist enterprises. All the means of production of the state farm and all the production coming out of it are the property of the state.

The attacks that the kulaks launched against the collective and state farms and their dissemination of all sorts of rumors for the purposes of provocation, including the most patent absurdities, were intended to check the shift of the peasants to the path of collective farming.

A worker on the state farm "Gigant" wrote to his brother from the town of Salsk in August 1929:

How are you, dear brother Shura! They say that the kulaks are spreading all kinds of rumors about the sovkhoz, such as that the grain did not come up in "Gigant," that a good deal of the grain rots on account of the combine, that the combine spills a large quantity of grain. . . .

As you well know, I have been working in the sovkhoz for quite some time, and I can therefore tell you this: All the things that the kulaks are saying about the sovkhoz are sheer lies. The grain came up fine in the sovkhoz, in some cases as much as 3,600 pounds of it from a single hectare. There is no better machine than a combine. It is something to see how neatly she mows and threshes. We will harvest all of the grain on time.

Those of us who work in the sovkhozes try to harvest the grain on time and conscientiously because we are aware of one thing: this is ours, our very own farm.

The kulaks are spreading lies about the sovkhoz, realizing as they do that Soviet farming spells their extinction.

The kulaks can see how the poor and the middle peasants, as they look at the sovkhoz, become convinced that it pays better to work as a collective, on a large scale. . . .

The sovkhoz spells extinction to the kulak, and so he vents his malice. . . .

Shura, you must tell everyone about the sovkhoz, so that they may join it more confidently and strike back strongly at the kulaks.

Respectfully,
Your brother F. K. Novobrantsev

Extending his felicitations to the workers of the "Gigant" sovkhoz on the occasion of the first anniversary of their enterprise, the famous Soviet writer Maxim Gorky, wrote: "It seems to me that this is striking proof of the fact that the working class is truly a giant who has come to the forefront for the purpose of accomplishing unprecedented tasks. Having asserted their dominion over factories, they demonstrated in a single year that they are also able to govern the land. Undertakings such as yours are not isolated instances. The dictatorship of the working class is growing with an incredible swiftness, spurring on increasingly the creative energies of the masses."

Today there are 36,280 kolkhozes and 11,681 sovkhozes in the U.S.S.R. In 1965, the area sown in the kolkhozes and the sovkhozes, including all agricultural crops, was 209.1 million hectares, as compared with 118.2 million hectares for all types of farms in tsarist Russia in 1913. Soviet industry has made powerful machines available to the rural economy. Thus, for example, in 1965, 1,613,000 tractors and 520,000 combines were operating in the country's fields.

But the most essential component of Lenin's plan for building socialism was the carrying out of the cultural revolution. Not only the face of the earth had to be transformed in the intervening years, but people also had to be transformed. The country had to absorb knowledge. It was concerned above everything else with wiping out illiteracy. The primer came into everyone's hands, and age made no difference. To many the primer became the stepping stone to the world and education.

Wiping out illiteracy among the adult population aided in the rapid solution of one of the root problems of socialist rehabilitation of the people's economy, namely that of training cadres on a mass scale.

A name widely famed in the Soviet Union is that of Alexei Stakhanov, a coal cutter of the mine known as Tsentralnaya Irmino. On August 31, 1935, having decided to celebrate International Youth Day by establishing an all-Soviet record of productivity, he achieved a dazzling quota, namely 102 tons of coal within a period of six hours. A mass movement striving for increased labor productivity assumed his name, becoming known as the Stakhanovite movement. Likbez* has earned

---

* *Likbez:* the name of the Movement for the Liquidation of Illiteracy in its abbreviated form.

the merit of turning an illiterate laborer into a hero of socialist construction. Stakhanov came to the mine as an illiterate and decided to gain an education only under the prodding of his comrades.

P. I. Kalinkina, who started as a semi-literate cook, graduated from an adult education school and rose to the position of Minister of the Food Industry of the Chuvash Autonomous Soviet Socialist Republic. Neither M. Ryskulov, a People's Artist of the U.S.S.R. and formerly a poor Kirghiz peasant, and Gafur Gulyam, the People's Poet of Uzbekistan, knew how to read or write. M. G. Egorov encountered the revolution as an illiterate Yakut, but today he is a scholar who has been awarded a State Prize. In Central Asia, among the people who triumphed over illiteracy was a young Tadzhik girl, Khamra Tairova. Back in the thirties she earned her degree in construction engineering and became the first woman engineer in the Tadzhik Republic. Some years later Tairova was elected Deputy of the Supreme Soviet, and became Minister of Urban and Rural Construction of the Tadzhik Soviet Socialist Republic.

Within a period of twenty years (from 1920 to 1940) some sixty million people learned to read and write, bringing efforts to overcome the problem of mass illiteracy to a successful conclusion.

There is a rise of culture in town and country. To cite an example let us take Stalingrad (now Volgograd), famed for its heroic exploits in the Second World War. We shall cite but a few figures which brilliantly illustrate the changes that have occurred in the cultural physiognomy of the city:

1917	1967
Population: 135,000.	*Population:* Close to 800,000.
Industry: Primarily small woodworking ventures.	*Industry:* Some 165,000 people working in 196 large and middle-sized enterprises. Output exported to 44 countries.

1917

Electricity: None. At night 745 kerosene lanterns illuminated the streets.

Education: Two secondary schools and no institutes.

Health: 30 medical workers, of whom 17 were physicians.

Arts: One library with a meager stock of books, and one theater.

Other: Some 30 shops, eating-houses, pubs.

1967

Electricity: Largest power center in the Volga Area. The hydroelectric station alone has produced from the day of its inauguration in excess of 70 billion kilowatt-hours of electricity.

Education: 800 schools, 6 universities, 224,000 pupils, some 28,000 students.

Health: 4,079 physicians and 8,700 nurses.

Arts: 260 libraries, 5 professional theaters, dozens of cinemas.

Other: More than 850 shops, 840 cafés, restaurants and snack bars.

What changes have taken place in the villages of the Volgograd region? During the last seven-year plan more than seven hundred thousand square meters of floor space were constructed. Houses with central heating, sewage disposal and running water systems are being built in ever greater numbers, and many villages have their own gas supply. The kolkhozes have built two hundred clubs and palaces of culture, more than one hundred day nurseries and kindergartens, and schools accommodating some fifteen thousand pupils. In the last two years alone, 350 new shops and dining halls were opened; 250 of these were built with the resources of the kolkhozes and the sovkhozes. Trading centers have been constructed in many villages.

Take as an example the district town of Dubovka. Only recently its shops and dining halls were housed in dilapidated quarters. Today, modern foodstores and shops retailing manufactured goods have sprung up on the main street. There is also a bookshop and a cafe. And, generally speaking, in the Volgograd Region as many as 80 per cent of the villages are well built, with all amenities. The villages have a total of 130,000 radio loudspeaker stations, more than 80,000 receiver sets and some 25,000 television sets.

The conditions of work in the village have likewise changed radically. In field work, all essential tasks have been mechanized. In the sovkhozes and kolkhozes of the Volgograd Region one finds today upward of twenty-three thousand tractors, eleven thousand combines and eleven thousand automobiles.

The tractor operators, combine operators, trained cattle-breeders in the ranks of the workers, agronomists, livestock experts, engineers, doctors, teachers—these are the people who make up the professional segment of the population in the villages. More than nine thousand teachers and some three thousand medical workers are doing their work in the country-side.

Concern and apprehension for the cultural legacy of the past have prompted a rapid growth, unprecedented prior to the revolution, and flourishing of science, literature and art.

The entire world is well acquainted with the names of the outstanding scientists in whose behalf the Soviet government has done everything possible, from the earliest days of the revolution, to ensure suitable conditions of work. Among them are I. Pavlov, physiologist, awarded the Nobel Prize; K. Tsiolkovsky, whose work has hastened the day of cosmic flights; A. Ioffe, an outstanding Soviet physicist; N. Vavilov, greatest among geneticists, and many others. Prominent among their pupils and successors are academicians P. Kapitsa, S. Korolyov, I. Kurchatov, S. Sobolev, M. Keldysh, A. Kolmogorov, L. Landau, the brothers Alikhanov, P. Cherenkov, N. Semyonov, I. Tamm, I. Frank and others.

At the beginning of the thirties the words of Maxim Gorky, the great Russian writer, resounded throughout the world. The verse of Vladimir Mayakovsky, which had in it the ring of a tocsin, and the poetry of Anna Akhmatova and Boris Pasternak were known to all. Mikhail Sholokhov, Alexander Fadeyev, Nikolay Ostrovsky, Mikhail Svetlov, Iosif Utkin, Yuri Olesha, Yuri Tynyanov—what a diversity of names, what a profusion of talents blossomed out during the prewar years. Sergei Eisenstein, a celebrated figure in worldwide cinematography, was the creator and innovator of forms of expression of the young art form and one of its earliest and most profound theoreticians. His film *The Battleship Potyomkin* is still projected on the screens of motion picture houses throughout the world today with undimmed success.

Aside from *The Battleship Potyomkin* the greatest achievement of the Soviet film industry in the early years of the revolution was the Pudovkin film *Mother*. The ensuing cinematic works of Pudovkin have placed his fame as the greatest of directors on a firm foundation.

The name of Dzigi Vertov is associated with the founding of the Soviet documentary film, and with the solution of a series of basic problems in editing, cutting and trick-photography.

The Fifth International Motion Picture Festival took place in Moscow in 1967, but hardly anyone remembers the First International Motion Picture Festival held in Moscow during February and March of 1935. The first prize of the Festival was then awarded the Leningrad Motion Picture Studio for the films *Chapayev* (directed by S. and G. Vasilyev), *The Youth of Maxim* (directed by G. Kozintsev and L. Tauberg), and *The Peasants* (directed by F. Ermler). The second prize was awarded the French film *The Last Billionaire*, and the third prize went to Walt Disney for his masterpieces in the field of animated cartoons.

"The Soviet cinema," Henri Barbusse, a famous French writer, declared at the time, "immediately rose above all others, thanks to its great artistic and social realism. It revealed all the richness of a great new idea."

By a special decision of the Central Executive Committee

of the U.S.S.R. on September 6, 1936, the title of People's Artist of the Soviet Union was established for the most outstanding figures of the arts who distinguished themselves through their contributions to Soviet theater, music and cinema. On the same day, this title was bestowed on the thirteen most talented masters of the stage, namely K. Stanislavsky, V. I. Nemirovich-Danchenko, V. I. Kachalov, I. M. Moskvin, E. P. Korchagina-Aleksandrovskaya, M. M. Blyumental-Tamarina, A. V. Nezhdanova, B. V. Shchukin, M. I. Litvinenko-Volgemut, P. K. Saksagansky, A. A. Vasadze, A. A. Khorava and Kulesh Baiseitova.

Today this title is held by Dmitri Shostakovich, Aram Khachaturian, Svyatoslav Richter, David Oistrakh, Galina Ulanova, Maya Plisetskaya, Vakhtan-Chebykiani, Igor Moiseyev, Mikhail Romm, Roman Karmen, Sergey Bondarchuk and many, many other masters of Soviet culture.

Within a relatively brief historical period, the country, which quite recently had lived in darkness, beset with illiteracy, was transformed into a leader in the sphere of progressive culture, science and technology.

In 1966, the number of schools of general education in the Soviet Union was 214,000, embracing a student body upward of forty-eight million. In 1914–1915 Russia had a total of 105 institutions of higher learning, and the student body numbered 127,000. In 1966 there were in the U.S.S.R. 756 universities, with a student body of 3,861,000. In 1965, some five million specialists with higher education were actively engaged in all branches of the national economy, while those with a secondary education numbered seven million. In 1914 Russia had a total of 10,000 scientific workers, while the Soviet Union has raised that number to more than 660,000 today.

All of these indisputable achievements in building the new economy, in establishing new relations in the village, and in creating a new culture afford convincing proof of the fact that the first and foremost function of the dictatorship of the proletariat is not the unwanted recourse to force but that of giving guidance in terms of organization and constructive effort.

The Birth of a New Man. To be sure, one of the greatest achievements of the Soviet state was the shaping of a new man in the process of socialist construction.

What is it that distinguishes this man? Above all it is his attitude to work. This attitude came to the fore even during the years of hardship that attended the civil war. The Communist Subbotniks, or volunteer work days, were a reflection of this new, constructive attitude to work, an immense creative expression of the creative initiative of the masses and of their dedication to work. They appeared in the spring of 1919, when the Republic was going through the trying days of an offensive launched by the armies of Kolchak. On the night of April 12, which was a Saturday (*Subbota* in Russian, hence the name Subbotniks), fifteen Communists of the Moscow-Sortirovochnaya line on the Moscow-Kazan railroad repaired three locomotives within ten hours, working as volunteers without pay.

On May 10, 1919, the first mass Communist Subbotnik took place. As many as 205 railroad workers participated in it, all of them members of the Moscow-Kazan railroad. In May, Subbotniks were organized on the Aleksandrov, Nikolayev, Ryazan-Ural, Moscow-Vindau and the Kursk railroads. Following in the wake of the railroad workers, the workers of the plants and factories of Moscow and other cities joined the movement. It spread to a wide stratum of non-party workers.

Lenin pointed out the great importance of the Subbotniks in struggling against hunger and devastation, in supporting the fighting front, and in tightening the bond between the working class and the peasantry. He stated in his writings that nothing contributed so much to raising the prestige of the Communist Party and enhancing the respect evinced by it among the masses of non-party workers and peasants, as the Subbotniks. When they became regular occurrences, the workers realized that members of the Communist Party assumed greater responsibilities than non-party workers.

Lenin ascribed great significance to the organization and broadening of the scope of the Subbotnik movement, and predicted a further growth of the great initiative, a steady emergence of ever-new forms in the working activities of the masses. Calling for a solicitous attitude towards the earliest sproutings of communism, he wrote that tending these sproutings is the general and primary duty of all. "Communism," wrote Lenin, "begins when the rank-and-file workers display an enthusiastic concern that is undaunted by arduous toil to increase the productivity of labor, and husband every pood of grain, coal, iron and other products, which do not accrue to the workers personally or to their 'close' kith and kin, but to their 'distant' kith and kin, *i.e.*, to society as a whole."

On May 1, 1920, an All-Russian Subbotnik took place. Lenin took part in the Subbotnik by working on the grounds of the Kremlin. In Moscow, the participants in the Subbotnik numbered 425,000, in Petrograd 165,000, while hundreds of thousands participated in the Subbotniks in other cities.

During the years when the national economy was being established, and new industry was being created, during the years of the Second World War, Subbotniks were undertaken on a broad scale, making great contributions to the accomplishment of important tasks.

Even today, whenever a hitch develops anywhere along a construction line, when it is essential to hasten its tempo, or when something needs to be accomplished for the improvement of services in a locality, and the like, Subbotniks are organized. During my student years I helped in the building of a stadium at Luzhniki. I remember the sheds, warehouses and the little houses which we cleared away to make room for the handsome stadium. Whenever I am on the way to a football game or to a concert, I remember with pride that this magnificent building contains some fraction of my labor.

At the Kiev subway station, going up on the escalator, I jealously examine the polished trim of the escalator at the extreme left, because sometime in the past I was the first one to polish it.

In the distant Uzbek city of Namangan, the Secretary of the Municipal Party Committee always speaks with a show of emotion about the Namangan Park where each school, each section, has an area set aside where flowers are planted and trees are tended. Nowhere have I seen a profusion of flowers such as one sees in Namangan. They carpet the entire four-kilometer stretch leading into the city, they are to be seen in the park, and at every house and yard.

The Soviet man is unreservedly dedicated to work. However, this is not fanaticism, nor self-abnegation, but a genuine need and desire on his part to have people realize his usefulness.

In the early years of the October Revolution, in Saratov, one of the cities along the Volga, there lived a man with the common Russian name of Korolyov. He was known as Sergei Aleksandrovich. He was a familiar figure in the city and every resident of Saratov knew the house where he lived and worked. Korolyov invited to his home both strangers and acquaintances. He wrote the following in the local newspaper:

"I would appreciate it if institutions and individuals would be good enough to call on me at any time. S. Korolyov."

He was at the head of a special commission for aid to starving children. He had just reached the age of thirty-eight that year. He had even participated in the Revolution of 1905, as a member of a fighting squad. The tsarist authorities seized him and cast him into prison. He was later exiled to Siberia, but escaped. Up to the October Revolution Sergei Korolyov worked as a stevedore and a locksmith, but pursued his education untiringly, studying German, French and English. Shortly after the October Revolution, Korolyov was elected People's Judge. In his party enrollment application, which has been preserved, one of the questions posed is: "How many hours of service do you put in?" The answer given—twenty hours.

S. A. Korolyov died at the end of the 1920's from tuberculosis. But he continues to live in the hearts and minds of the people to whom he gave his utmost.

In 1929 a girl in the village of Starobeshevo which lies on the Don, was one of the first women tractor drivers. The name of Pasha Angelina became a watchword for the Komsomol girls of the early five-year plans. Angelina brigades sprang up wherever machines and mechanical devices had to be mastered, and women began acquiring new technical skills on a par with men.

An old comrade of Pasha Angelina, the writer Panfyorov, had this to say about her in his writings: "Pasha was not just the common run of tractor driver. She had a natural talent. The conditions of life under the Soviets afforded her the rich soil in which her endowments could blossom with lush abundance. . . . Work in behalf of the people's well-being was the central meaning of her life. Till the very end, while stricken with illness, Pasha would not let go of the steering wheel of her tractor."

Some years have passed since she died. Recently a memorial museum was inaugurated to celebrate the memory of this twice-decorated Hero of Socialist Labor, Praskovya Angelina. Both the native population and the visitors to this Don village never lose interest in the life of the first woman tractor driver.

It was the new attitude towards work that made it possible to achieve what appeared to be a utopian dream. A former worker in the Moscow automobile plant, A. Kryazhevsky, recalls how, carried away with the work performed by the brigade of blacksmith Ushkalov, an American engineer exclaimed:

"Mister Ushkalov, you're a marvel!"

And in fact, on that day Ushkalov performed what one might refer to as an average, habitual to him, miracle of speed, coordination and flexibility in the handling of his work. The description of it, as given by A. Kryazhevsky, reads as follows:

. . . No sooner was the blinding ingot snatched out of the furnace, than it came to rest on the hammer. Fleeting blows, a turn, and behold! the soft and round billet brings forth an elbow-shaped, curved shaft. It is snatched, lands on the trimmer, and appears to be floating through the air to the mandrel, dropping into the bay like a small stick of fire-wood.

The Americans, approaching the heavy hammer where the elbow-shaped shaft was being swaged, asked the chief engineer:

"How many shafts per shift?"

"One thousand," the chief engineer replied.

Smiling broadly, the Americans shook their heads dubiously. One of them said:

"America holds the world record: four hundred shafts per shift."

"And our blacksmith Ushkalov will still deliver a thousand shafts at the end of his shift! He has already five hundred of them now. . . ."

The Americans remained to the end of the shift. Ushkalov and his men did not reduce their tempo. In the flaming reflections of the furnace, it appeared at times that these were not blacksmiths, but some nimble and lithe devils who were handling the hammer. Soon nearly all the workers in the shop congregated around them.

There goes the factory whistle! The last shaft crashed into the bay. And the supervisor of the shop, Ivan Likhachyov, announced triumphantly:

"One thousand and thirteen!"

Thunderous applause followed, everyone cheering the heroes, sweated, livid-faced, and of course, quite tired.

One of the Americans then called out:

"Mister Ushkalov, you're a marvel!"

These marvels transformed the Moscow automobile shop, which on November 7, 1924, turned out its first ten clumsy (by present-day standards) low-speed trucks, into the giant automotive works which bears the name of its first supervisor, Ivan Likhachyov.

In 1967, the Likhachyov plant (ZIL) marked its fiftieth anniversary. Over a period of fifty years ZIL has produced many millions of automobiles, which are now being marketed in forty-one countries.

The director of the plant, Hero of Socialist Labor P. D. Borodin, comments in these words on the enterprise's five-year plan:

The tasks which we are pledged to fulfill according to the five-year plan place on us a great responsibility. One can do it justice only by enlisting the endeavors of the entire working force. Within that span of years we are to increase the output of automobiles one and a half times, and nearly double the output of engines. It is essential to build huge plant subsidiaries in Ryazan and Roslavl in the Smolensk Region and in Mtsensk in the Oryol Region. Lastly, there is the greatest of all tasks, namely the inclusion in our production program of two new powerful trucks—the ZIL-131 and the ZIL-133.

Competition helps in the successful accomplishment of these tasks. Up to 85 per cent of the ZIL workers participate in the competition for the title of Shock-worker of Communist Labor.

Our plant, the banner of which is adorned by two Orders of Lenin and the Order of the Red Banner of Labor, will multiply the number of distinctions which have already been won by it: We shall spare no effort to cause our trademark to gain an ever rising acceptance not only in our country but throughout the world. . . .

Here are the biographies of two ordinary workers. Their story was related in the newspaper *Izvestia* in January 1967, giving thereby due prominence to the one-millionth tractor to come off the assembly line of the Kharkov plant.

Valentin Byublink entered the plant as an ordinary worker. He worked at the bench while attending the school for young workers and later graduated from the institute. Having earned his diploma he returned to the plant, and for many years he has been chief engineer there.

Ivan Smirnov began his working career in the building of the Kharkov tractor plant, working later in the capacity of tool-maker. He continued his studies. At the present time he is director of a laboratory, and holder of the Lenin Prize. Incidentally, a whole dynasty of Smirnovs is working at the plant: There is Vasily, at the drill of the instrument shop, and Konstantin is employed as electrician in the thermal section. The latter is Ivan Smirnov's brother. His son, Vladimir, works there in the capacity of design engineer, while his niece Lyudmila and nephew Vladimir are employed as technicians. An entire Smirnov dynasty of workers grew up in the plant, and theirs is not a singular case.

In the report of the Central Committee of the C.P.S.U. to the Twenty-third Congress of the Party, its Secretary General, Leonid Brezhnev, stressed the part played by such vanguard workers, the blazers of new paths in production, referring to them as "people of the future." They work in a manner that will come to prevail among all people under communism. The example they set is a model to be emulated.

The torch of mutual help is being passed from generation to generation.

When in 1966 tragedy struck in Tashkent, everyone in the entire country came to the aid of the capital of Uzbekistan.

Following the first earth tremor on April 26 the formidable forces of nature returned to the assault more than seven hundred times; several force seven shocks were recorded. The city suffered considerable damage. Sixty-eight thousand families lost their homes. Some 35 per cent of housing was destroyed, as well as nearly 700 trade centers and catering establishments, more than 80 administrative buildings, upward of 180 schools and some 250 industrial buildings and the like.

The magnificent moral qualities of the Soviet people were displayed in their collective spirit, comradeship, brotherliness and mutual help. A fund was set up for the purpose of furnishing aid to Tashkent. Everyone able to do so made some contribution to it. Thus, for example, in that year a special issue of *Zarya Vostoka* magazine was published, and in it appeared articles by the foremost Soviet writers. All writers' fees went into a reconstruction fund for the city.

Alongside the institute where I work a white flag with a red cross flies above the building of a boarding school. This is where the children of Tashkent are living. Many people voluntarily opened their homes to the people who had become homeless.

Pouring into Tashkent came residents of Moscow, Leningrad, Kiev and Minsk. Soon, everywhere one looked one saw turret cranes. In 1966, on the eve of the October celebrations the tents on Shakhrisyabskaya and Shirokaya Streets were cleared away—the last remaining tents of the stricken city. By 1970, 5,650,000 square meters more of housing will have been constructed, as well as schools for 94,000 children, kindergartens and day nurseries to accommodate 45,000 younger children, and hospitals with a total of nine thousand beds.

I arrived by plane in Tashkent on the night of April 14, 1967. On that day another severe tremor had been recorded in the city. However, this in no way diverted the normal current of life. In fact, one could not hear any talk about the earthquake. At night the city slept peacefully, without panic, and only the old charwomen at the airfield grumbled about the crowding in the airfield's waiting rooms making it difficult to clean up on account of the passengers who were all around. In the morning children could be seen moving briskly in the direction of the school and the students hastened to their studies.

When Sunday came I first realized at the Pakhtakor stadium how strong is the infatuation of a real football devotee. One cannot find more single-minded and rabid football fans than the people of Tashkent. Life heals the wounds and fraternal help is making it possible to construct a new, most beautiful Tashkent.

On July 18, 1966, came the thirtieth anniversary of the outbreak of the fascist war in Spain. Those were the days when the immortal battle cries of revolutionary Spain were heard once again. And it is understandable today when they ring out again wherever people stand up in defense of freedom and wage a determined fight against all attempts on their freedom and independence. Once again, just as in those distant days, the people of the Soviet Union, as befits true internationalists, are aiding the peoples' struggles for freedom.

On October 12, 1936, a group of the most prominent representatives of the French intelligentsia, among them Romain Rolland, Paul Langevin, Jean Richard Bloch, Jean Cassou, Argou, Léon Moussinac, Francisque Jourdain, Le Corbusier, Charles Vildrac and others, addressed a letter to Litvinov, Peoples' Commissar for Foreign Affairs of the Soviet Union. The letter stated: "On two important occasions, when the destiny of two nations—Abyssinia and Spain—was being decided in Geneva and in London, the voice of the Soviet Union was raised as the voice of world conscience."

The well-known Soviet journalist Ilya Ehrenburg wrote when recalling those days:

Today mention of "1937" makes Soviet people alert but those who have been in Spain and who have witnessed the self-sacrificing heroism of its people, having arrived there from different countries as part of the International Brigade and as Soviet military personnel, without pretensions and with heart and soul devoted to the ideal of freedom, find in this date a unique significance. Nothing can be either gilded or smeared black indiscriminately. In 1937, the Soviet Union helped Spain to every possible extent, sending food, planes, and volunteers. It is a glorious page in our history.

The heroic deeds of the Soviet people are attested by the many, many graves in Spain itself, and the unmarked graves of those who gave their lives subsequently—G. M. Shtern, Yan Berzin, V. E. Gorev, V. A. Antonov-Ovseyenko, D. G. Pavlov, Loti (Lvovich). There are also the memories of the survivors—Malinovsky, Kuznetsov, Voronov, Mamsurov, Batov and Meretskov.

The birth of the man of a new morality, of the man of a new world—this is one of the greatest achievements of the October Revolution. More than one generation of people alien to the mores and prejudices of the old world have grown to manhood in the Soviet Union; now there are generations of revolutionaries and fighters. This is the principal guarantee serving as a pledge and earnest of the fact that the conquests of the October Revolution and its great traditions will continue to exist and grow.

Rights and Obligations.

Article 1. The Union of Soviet Socialist Republics is a socialist state of workers and peasants.

Article 2. The political foundation of the U.S.S.R. is the Soviets of Working People's Deputies, which grew and became strong as a result of the overthrow of the power of the landlords and capitalists and the attainment of the dictatorship of the proletariat.

Article 3. All power in the U.S.S.R. is vested in the working people of town and country as represented by the Soviets of Working People's Deputies.

These are the opening words of the fundamental law of the Soviet State—the Constitution of the U.S.S.R. It was adopted on December 5, 1936, at the Extraordinary Eighth Congress of the Soviets of the U.S.S.R. The Congress adopted a decision whereby that day became a national holiday—the Day of the Constitution of the U.S.S.R.

The fundamental law provides that the economic foundation of the U.S.S.R. is the socialist system of economy and the socialist ownership of the instruments and means of production, firmly established as a result of the abolition of the capitalist system of economy, the private ownership of the instruments and means of production, and the exploitation of man by man. The socialist principle of distribution: "From each according to his ability, to each according to his work" has ensured the interest of the members of society in the results of their work and served as a powerful impetus towards an increased productivity of labor.

All exploiting classes have been eliminated in the U.S.S.R., and the class composition of the population has changed. In the course of the struggle for socialism, radical changes have been brought about in the working class, the peasantry and the intelligentsia. The Soviet people have been fused into cohesive socio-political and ideological unity. New socialist nations emerged in the Soviet Union. Their friendship has grown stronger, and their fraternal cooperation is firmly established within the framework of a united socialist state.

By virtue of the Soviet system, some peoples—the Kazakhs, the Turkmens, the Tadzhiks, the peoples of the North, of Dagestan and others—made their transition directly to socialism, bypassing the capitalist stage of development.

The Constitution introduced the most far-reaching improvements into the organization of the state with a view of the all-around development of Soviet democracy and genuine internationalism in the relations between the peoples of the Soviet Union. It liquidated all residual restrictions in the elections to the Soviets*; and it substituted direct elections for

---

* Previously (on the basis of the 1924 Constitution) elections were not entirely equal for all strata of the population. They were conducted by means of an open vote and in a series of stages. These restrictions were imposed at a time when the exploiting classes and the private

those previously conducted in a series of stages. Universal, direct and equal elections by secret ballot were instituted for all Soviets of Working People's Deputies. All citizens of the Soviet Union were given an equal right to elect and be elected to the Soviets.

At the first elections, in December 1937, a total of 1,143 Deputies was elected to both Chambers—the Soviet of the Union, which is elected on the basis of electoral districts, at the ratio of one Deputy per three hundred thousand persons; and the Soviet of Nationalities, which is elected on the basis of the Union Republics and Autonomous Republics, Autonomous Regions and National Areas, providing for the election of twenty-five Deputies from each Union Republic, eleven Deputies from each Autonomous Republic, five Deputies from each Autonomous Region and one Deputy from each National Area. The country nominated the finest of the finest:

Valery Chkalov: the finest flier of those years, who shortly before the elections (in June 1937) made a non-stop flight from Moscow to the U.S.A. in a plane which had been designed by A. N. Tupolev, the ANT 25.

Alexei Tolstoy: the world-famed writer.

I. M. Moskvin: People's Artist of the U.S.S.R.

This list could be extended further and further, since the Supreme Soviet that convened included many workers, peasants, Heroes of the Soviet Union, scientists, artists and poets.

Article 122 of the Constitution provided as follows:

Women in the U.S.S.R. are accorded equal rights with men in all spheres of economic, government, cultural, political and other public activity.

The possibility of exercising these rights is ensured by women being accorded an equal right with men to work, payment for work, rest and

---

ownership of the means of production (particularly in the village) still prevailed. At the time some inequalities were in effect as regards the electoral rights of the workers and peasants. The urban population, for example, elected one delegate to the All-Union Congress of the Soviets for each 25,000 residents, and the village population one for each 125,000 residents.

leisure, social insurance and education. These rights are further ensured by state protection of the interest of mother and child, state aid to mothers of large families and unmarried mothers, maternity leave with full pay, and the provision of a wide network of maternity homes, nurseries and kindergartens.

A total of 189 women were elected to the first Supreme Soviet.

The Constitution of the U.S.S.R. is distinguished by a deep-seated internationalism. It proclaims as an immutable law the equality of Soviet citizens, regardless of race and nationality, in all spheres of economic, state, cultural and socio-political life. It is notable for a consistent and steadfast promotion of democracy, free of hedging and restrictions, free of any differentiation such as that between the passive and the active citizen, and the sorts of qualifications that are typical of other constitutions.

The Constitution of the U.S.S.R. established not only equal rights for all citizens regardless of nationality, race, or sex, but also political freedoms, namely freedom of conscience, of speech, of the press, of assembly, along with freedom to unite in social organizations, personal inviolability, as well as the inviolability of the home, and other basic rights.

No official documents contain provisions as to whether a person observes any specific religion or whether he is an atheist. This feature must be especially stressed since it is one of the conditions ensuring freedom of conscience in the U.S.S.R. In the Soviet Constitution, with a view to ensuring freedom of conscience, the church is separated from the state and the school from the church. Accordingly, the organs of the state do not interfere in the internal activities of religious organizations. Religious organizations, on the other hand, do not interfere in any matters relating to the state.

Cognizant of the fact that a segment of the population is made up of believers, the Soviet state allows church associations freedom to function without impediments so they may find it feasible to cater to religious needs. These associations are allowed the use of church buildings without compensation, and means are provided for the training of ministers, for the publication of religious literature, and for the production of objects of worship. The rights of believers are protected by laws. Any infringements on the sentiments of the believers and any discrimination is punishable by law.

All that has been stated in the foregoing is widely known to be true. Foreign church delegations that come to the Soviet Union concede that the church is unhampered and independent.

However, some organs of the foreign press from time to time come out with slander and misinterpretations, publishing all kinds of libel concerning the status of religion in the U.S.S.R. For example, the April 4, 1966, issue of the newspaper *Parisien Libéré* reported to its readers out of sheer sensationalism that new legislative measures had been enacted in the R.S.F.S.R. (Russian Soviet Federative Socialist Republic) to the detriment of the church, and followed it up with a snap conclusion to the effect that "a new attack is being launched against the Christian faiths" in the U.S.S.R.

The Chairman of the Council on Religious Matters attached to the Council of Ministers of the U.S.S.R., Vladimir Kuroyedov, dealt specifically with this question in the newspaper *Izvestia* in August of 1966. Because this issue interests many people, we shall cite here in detail the reply given by V. A. Kuroyedov:

Early in 1966 the Presidium of the Supreme Soviet of the R.S.F.S.R. adopted two Decrees and Decisions relating to legislation which has a bearing on religious worship. Similar Decrees and Decisions have also been adopted by the Presidiums of the Supreme Soviets of other Union Republics. By studying these documents (they are published in the *Journal of the Supreme Soviet of the R.S.F.S.R.*, No. 12, March 24, 1966), any unbiased person will realize that any "attack on the church, and on the rights of believers" is out of the question here.

These Decrees and Decisions have been adopted for the purpose of systematizing the laws concerning religious worship which are already in effect. Systematization, which is concerned primarily with violations of the law of separation of church and state, and school and church, is carried out with the following intention: Firstly with a view to introducing new legislation defining just what constitutes violations of the aforementioned laws, punishable as criminal offenses. Formerly, the Criminal Code of the R.S.F.S.R. (Article 142) lacked such concrete definition, and in this connection one must particularly emphasize the fact that the scope of criminal liability has been considerably narrowed. Moreover, for specific types of violations, administrative liability has been introduced in lieu of criminal liability. . . .

In fact, persons who have violated the law of separation of church and state for the first time receive mitigated judgments. However, persons brought to court more than once for such breaches of the law, and whose activity is aimed at perpetuating the violation, are liable to more strict punishment.

All of this shows that the new legislative bills do not in any manner infringe on the rights of believers. All the more so, since the Decision of the Presidium of the Supreme Soviet of the R.S.F.S.R. declares: "Discrimination against believers is punishable as a crime. Specifically this relates to instances where an issue is involved such as 'Rejection of citizens seeking employment, or refusal of admission to an educational institution, dismissal from a job or expulsion from an educational institution, denial to citizens of privileges and advantages to which they are entitled under the laws, and any other curtailment of the rights of the citizens, based on their attitude to religion.' "

It is not by mere chance that believers as well as the clergy have correctly interpreted these acts of the Union Republics, and approved them.

It must be stated to the credit of some religious publications abroad that they have objectively interpreted the new Soviet legislative acts on religion and the church. As influential a church organ as the *Bulletin of the World Council of Churches*, in its issue of May 26, 1966, wrote that "Early in April various press agencies published reports from Moscow, according to which a decree of the Supreme Soviet of Russia (R.S.F.S.R.) had introduced restrictions on religious freedom. A study of the text which in fact contained three decrees showed that these decrees by and large confirm, elucidate and in some instances introduce greater flexibility in the existing laws. Contrary to what had been said in the press, none of these decrees banned voluntary donations for church needs; none recognized as lawful any discrimination against people in connection with their religious beliefs."

Some violations of the law which formerly had been punishable by imprisonment were now punished by a fine of fifty rubles, which showed the mitigating character of the new decrees.

Thus, no matter how hard the *Parisien Libéré* may have sought to defame the policy of the Soviet government on the score of religion, it missed the mark completely. The new legislative acts on religion and church activities do not constitute any assault on religion or any breach of the principle of freedom of conscience in the U.S.S.R.

To be sure, freedom of conscience in the Soviet Union does not mean that the activities of religious organizations must not be subject to any limitations whatsoever, or that they may conduct themselves as they please without regard to the laws and the system prevailing in the country.

Every country has its special laws on religion and churches that define the limits of the activities of religious associations. Naturally, our country has its own laws relating to religion and churches as well. Central to these laws is the Decree of the Soviet government "On the Separation of the Church from the State, and the School from the Church," promulgated on January 23, 1918, and signed by V. I. Lenin.

The principal requirement of the law concerning religious organizations is that their activities are to be confined to catering to the religious needs of the believers, while doing nothing to disturb the social order and without permitting any encroachments on the rights and persons of the citizens. The law forbids using the assemblies of the faithful for the purpose of delivering speeches against the interests of Soviet society, instigating the members of the congregation to refuse fulfillment of civic duties or to decline participation in the social and political life of the country. It is against Soviet laws, and regarded as an infringement of the law, to indulge in any barbaric rites which are injurious to health, or to have recourse to deceptive acts for the purpose of arousing superstition.

Soviet laws provide that all religious organizations, before undertaking any of their activities, shall register with the state authorities. This is done in the interest of both the members of the congregation and the state. Registration bears witness to the fact that the religious congregation has been granted official permission to conduct its activities in compliance with the laws; at the same time the state authorities assume the obligation to protect the rights of the members of the given religious community. A religious congregation can be denied registration only if the teaching of the faith and the performance of the rites involve breaches of the law or encroachments on the persons or rights of citizens.

It is not out of place to state here that a majority of the clergy in the U.S.S.R. abide by the laws on religious worship and uphold the Soviet government's activities regarding domestic and foreign policy. One cannot in this connection pass over in silence the contribution which the Russian Orthodox Church headed by Patriarch Aleksey, as well as other churches in the Soviet Union, has made to struggle for peace, against the threat of a new world war, and for the strengthening of the ties of friendship between nations.

The Constitution of the U.S.S.R. has likewise secured the socio-economic rights of Soviet citizens, including the right to work, the right to rest, to education, and the right to maintenance in old age, or in case of sickness or disability.

The guaranteed right to work means that the Soviet people do not know what unemployment is. Numerous professional and technical schools are training highly skilled workers. The village experiences an increasing demand for mechanical technicians, teachers, doctors, and generally people with every type of skill.

To gain a clearer understanding of what the right to rest means and what part the government and the trade unions play in organizing the worker's rest, let us look into some of the facts reported on June 6, 1967, at a conference of the Moscow City Committee of the Party, the Executive Committee of the Moscow Soviet, the Moscow City Council of Trade Unions and the Moscow City Committee of the Young Communist League. Dealing with the subject of summer vacations, the Chairman of the Moscow City Trade-Union Council, Krestyaninov, cited specifically the following facts: Thirty-five million rubles were allocated from the social insurance budget for health resort care of the workers of the capital. A total of 800,000 people were sent by the trade unions to rest homes and sanatoria, and the majority of these received free accommodations. Some 331,000 residents of Moscow were able to participate in tours about the country on tourist ships and trains, and rest at suburban tourist centers and tourist homes. This figure showed an increase of fifty thousand participants over the previous year. Five million people took boat excursions in the summer of 1967. The plants and institutions of the capital now have 208 sanatoria, boarding houses, rest homes and dispensaries of their own. They also operate sixty tourist centers. In 1967 twenty-nine health resorts and suburban centers of rest were opened.

The conference dealt with Sunday holidays and with the question of rest at the end of a working day. Also touched on were questions concerning the observance of holidays in honor of the October jubilee, the improvement of the work of the clubs, homes and houses of culture, sports centers and stadiums, facilities available to vacationers in parks, and the better organization of leisure for residents of small townships. In short, nothing was omitted, not even the complaints of the residents of Moscow about such matters as a shortage of buses to transport people to recreation spots frequented by large crowds; jammed suburban trains, an inadequate number of summer snack bars and cafés, and the insufficiency of places dispensing refreshments. All of these matters came in for discussion by the delegates to the conference, and ways and means were explored for remedying all conditions which interfered with the true enjoyment of leisure by the residents of the capital. This is but a trifling example to demonstrate what procedure is followed in effecting the guarantees of rest granted under the Constitution.

One point should be stressed regarding the right to education: All forms of education in the U.S.S.R. are available to all, since they are free. At present, in excess of forty-eight million persons are obtaining educations in schools of general education, nearly four million in technical schools, and 4.1 million in institutions of higher learning. Some 75 per cent of those who in 1966 graduated from the eighth scholastic year are continuing their education in secondary schools and in specialized secondary educational institutions.

How much solicitude and concern is given in our country to old age can be judged, if by nothing else, by the fact that in Moscow alone twenty sanatoria for the aged have been established to accommodate the retired residents of that city.

"In the home, which we speak of as the pensioner's sanatorium," says ninety-seven-year-old N. A. Kapustyanskaya, "everything is available to us: medical care, excellent food and all possible comforts. Once a week we are shown a movie and attend a concert."

"The pensioner's sanatorium," to be sure, is the most suitable name they might have given to these homes with their bright and neat bedrooms, verandahs, halls, drawing-rooms, libraries and clubs.

There is in the Russian language a word used in tsarist times, but now forgotten: "charity." The word tells us that concern is being shown for paupers, cripples, sick people and orphans. Assumptions that the word makes were included in the Social Charity Act of former days: ". . . The inmates of the poorhouse shall receive sustenance of bread and water . . ." Old age was officially held up to contempt. In the Russian Empire old people lived on the dole.

Moreover, over a period of ninety years (!)—until 1917— the tsarist laws were graced with retirement rules according to which the treasury paid to officials a long-service pension of up to twelve thousand rubles a year.

And at the same time:

At the Utkinsk factory owned by Count Stenbok-Fermor

the worker Demid Vekshin was killed. In fact, three of his sons were also killed there. Vekshin's widow was granted a pension—1 ruble and 72 kopeks a year.

On the fifth day of the Soviet accession to power, that is on October 30, 1917, the workers' and peasants' government announced that it was immediately proceeding to enact decrees on full social insurance. On December 31, 1918, Lenin signed a set of regulations concerning social security for working people—the greatest enactment by the government at the time.

The adoption of the Law of 1956 concerning state pensions made it possible to increase considerably the benefits of the lower retirement categories and to scale down unjustifiably high pensions. The law extended the rights of the working people in receiving pensions. In the Russian Federation, the contingent of pensioners who are entitled to retirement pay under this law increased by 5,600,000 people, attaining a figure in excess of 15,000,000. In 1967, the sum of eleven billion rubles was to be spent in the U.S.S.R. for retirement insurance.

The adoption of the Pension and Allowances Law for the benefit of members of kolkhozes, has made it possible to claim that universal social insurance prevails in the U.S.S.R. Within a period of two years since the law has come into effect, nine million members of collective farms have received pensions.

The Twenty-third Congress of the Communist Party of the Soviet Union (C.P.S.U.) laid down plans for further improvements of the pension scheme. Measures contemplated include an increase in the minimum amounts under the old-age pension system allowed to factory and office workers and collective farm members, making provision for old age pensions to start at the age of fifty in the case of some categories of women's employment and in cases where the work performed within some industrial branches is more strenuous. Efforts are now under way towards their enactment, along with other provisions for better social benefits.

As one can obviously see, the Constitution does not confine

itself to the formal enunciation of the basic rights of the citizens, but it in fact shifts the center of gravity to matters of guarantees and the means for realizing these rights. The realization of the rights of the citizens, as the Constitution of the U.S.S.R. emphasizes, is predicated on the securing of the interests of the working people and the consolidation of the socialist system.

The same aims are pursued also in the duties incumbent on the citizens of the U.S.S.R., namely the observance of the laws, the maintenance of labor discipline, an honest performance of public duties, a respect for the rules of socialist society, the safeguarding and consolidating of socialist property, and honest fulfillment of the debt of honor, namely the obligation to perform military duty in the armed forces of the Soviet state.

The rights and duties of the citizens of the Soviet Union reflect the principles of socialist democracy.

Equality and Sovereignty. It is always difficult to write about everything near and dear. This is universally acknowledged. It is difficult to find words; there is fear of insincerity or affectation in the very display of sincerity. What could possibly be nearer and dearer than one's native land, its boundless spaces and its wonderful people?

When I visited Armenia for the first time, I was struck by the attitude people displayed towards each other. "Brother!" (*akhper*) that is the way I was addressed in the streets of Yerevan, when I turned to a passerby for information.

"Brother!" that is what I heard in Idzhivan and in Dilizhan, Echmiadzin and Leninakan. "Brother!"—strangers addressed me and I was proud of it, and happy.

My mother is Armenian. At my grandfather's and grandmother's home we spoke only Armenian. Grandfather read to us books in the Armenian language and both my younger sister and I became familiar from early childhood with the rich cultural treasures of that people.

My paternal grandfather was a Russian and my grandmother was a Finn. The earliest verse we listened to and memorized in our childhood was the poetry of the great Russian poet, Alexander Pushkin:

> Wise Oleg to the war now fares forth again,
> The Hazars have awaked his ire;
> For rapine and raid Hazar hamlet and plain
> Is subjected to falchion and fire.

The name of the poem was "The Lay of Oleg the Wise." The verses held one spellbound not only because they were melodic and beautiful. They also brought us close to history and inspired in us a sort of awed feeling for the distant age and the motherland.

Am I a Russian or an Armenian? What am I fondest of, the austere mountains of Armenia or the boundless fields of Russia? I never put this question to myself, not because I shied from falling into a reverie, but because I feel myself all the richer knowing that all of this is mine, native and near to me; I find myself feeling alike when I arrive in the Baltic Republics and in Central Asia or strolling down the streets of Tbilisi and Minsk, and I turn nostalgic when I leave behind Kiev the uncommonly beautiful. All of this belongs to me. I am a citizen of this country where all people are equally privileged to address each other with the word "Brother!"

The union of the fraternal republics emerged back in the years of the civil war. The struggle against the interventionists and the domestic counterrevolution called for the fusion of the endeavors of all nations. They showed the same solidarity in the diplomatic sphere, mindful of the fact that only unity would give them the strength to rebuff any combined assault by powers seeking to put an end to the governing system at whose helm stood the workers and peasants. The unity of all the sovereign national republics that were founded after the October Revolution was dictated both by the need for rapid economic growth and by a need to restore the war-shattered economy of the land, two goals which defied attainment unless mutual encouragement and support prevailed.

Fraternal aid and support between friends opened the avenue to a happy life and to a national renaissance in my native Armenia. When in the autumn of 1920 a proclamation of the Revolutionary Committee of Armenia announced the birth of the Soviet Socialist Republic, it received the support of Soviet Russia. It helped in February-July 1921 to put an end to anti-Soviet mutinies. Thanks to the diplomatic efforts of the government of Soviet Russia, the Turkish armies were withdrawn from the District of Alexandropol.

At a time when the Russian Republic itself was beset with troubles, its head, V. I. Lenin, then Chairman of the Council of People's Commissars, signed in December 1920 a decision of the Council of the R.S.F.S.R. to allot three billion rubles to Soviet Armenia for the restoration of her national economy. In 1921 trainloads of grain and sugar, manufactured goods, medicines, kerosene and petroleum arrived in Armenia. The workers of Moscow and Petrograd and of other industrial centers of the R.S.F.S.R. gave inestimable aid to the workers of Armenia during those difficult years. The textile workers of Ivanovo-Voznesensk sent to Armenia a gift of 850 looms and 180,000 spindles which served to establish the Leninakan mill —the first-born of the Republic's textile industry. Aid came from the peoples of the Soviet Ukraine, Azerbaidzhan and other fraternal republics.

The tasks of defending sovereignty, of overcoming the dislocation of the economy, and of building socialism persistently demanded the closest possible pooling of the economic, political and military resources of the Soviet republics and of their diplomatic actions. And in fact, such pooling did take place in December 1922.

The Union of Soviet Socialist Republics (U.S.S.R.), the new multinational state, came into being as a consequence of the nations moving into a voluntary union enjoying equal rights.

The First Congress of the Union of Soviet Socialist Republics took place in Moscow on December 3, 1922. Unfortunately, Lenin, to whom the principal merit of having elaborated the guidelines of the new union of the states belonged, was ill and could not attend. However, he was elected its honorary chairman. The Congress adopted a declaration for the establishment of the U.S.S.R. and a Union Agreement.

First to acquire membership in the U.S.S.R. were the Russian Federative Socialist Republic, the Ukrainian Soviet Socialist Republic, the Byelorussian Soviet Socialist Republic and the Transcaucasian Soviet Federative Socialist Republic (the Z.S.F.S.R., which included Azerbaidzhan, Armenia and Georgia). The Congress elected the supreme legislative body—the Central Executive Committee of the U.S.S.R. Lenin became the first chairman of the Union Government, the Council of People's Commisars of the U.S.S.R.

Next to join the Union were the Uzbek and the Turkmen Republics on October 27, 1924; the Tadzhik S.S.R. on December 5, 1929, which had been an Autonomous Republic in the Uzbek S.S.R. until then; the Kazakh S.S.R. and the Kirghiz S.S.R. on December 5, 1936, which were transformed from their earlier status as Autonomous Republics of the Russian Federation. The Transcaucasian Federation was dissolved on December 5, 1936, and the republics which had constituted it entered individually into the U.S.S.R. On August 2, 1940, the Moldavian S.S.R. was constituted. In the same month the Supreme Soviet of the U.S.S.R. approved the applications of the Lithuanian, Latvian and Estonian Republics (which had established Soviet power) and they were accepted as component parts of the U.S.S.R.

Today fifteen republics make up the U.S.S.R. They all enjoy equality of rights and sovereign status, except in matters which have been voluntarily transferred to the All-Union organs of power.

The area of the U.S.S.R. embraces 22.4 million square kilometers (8.65 million square miles). Its population is 234.4 million. The capital is Moscow.

The U.S.S.R. occupies one-sixth of the land surface of the globe. The Soviet state stretches over a distance of 10,000 kilometers (6,200 miles) from west to east, and over a distance of more than 4,500 kilometers (2,800 miles) from north to south. In terms of territorial dimensions, the U.S.S.R. occupies first place in the world, being three times as large as the territory of the U.S.A. and four times as large as the territory of all European states combined. The overall length of its boundaries is in excess of 60,000 kilometers (37,300 miles), of which 43,000 kilometers (26,700 miles) border the sea and 17,000 kilometers (10,600 miles) are on dry land. The U.S.S.R. borders on twelve countries, namely Norway, Finland, Poland, Czechoslovakia, Hungary, Rumania, Turkey, Iran, Afghanistan, China, Mongolia and Korea.

The geography of the U.S.S.R. is very highly diversified. Immense plains and lowlands alternate with plateaus and towering mountains whose peaks rise to a height of some 7.5 kilometers (4.7 miles), and nearly a third of the territory is covered with forests. In terms of the surface area of its forest and black-soil steppes, the U.S.S.R. holds first place in the world. Its earth contains every kind of exploitable ore to be found anywhere in the world. In terms of oil, iron, manganese, and apatite deposits, as well as turf and in terms of reserves of water power the U.S.S.R. holds first place in the world; it holds second place with respect to coal deposits. There are very large deposits of fuel-bearing shales and natural gas, platinum, precious metals, antimony, mercury, lead, bauxites, chromium, potassium salts, sodium chloride and sodium sulphate, phosphates, sulphur, graphite, mica and a variety of building materials.

In terms of population, the U.S.S.R. holds third place in the world, being second only to China and India. The U.S.S.R. is a multinational state. More than one hundred nations, ethnic groups and nationalities live within its boundaries.

During the period of fifty years of Soviet power, all the nations of the country have, in their development, made great strides in progress and education. Taking any of the Soviet republics as an example, it can be shown what truly impressive progress has been made by the socialist nations.

Soviet Armenia has changed during that period beyond recognition. The transformations achieved in that country of cattle-breeders and tillers could not be fairly described in any way other than as a social and economic miracle. Present-day Armenia is a country of flourishing non-ferrous metals industry and large-scale chemicals manufacturing, of precision machine building and instrument making, of radio electronics and automating devices.

Armenia possesses large industrial combines, first-rate shops and factories, as well as giant thermoelectric and hydroelectric stations. The Armenian Republic produces today five times the number of metal-cutting lathes produced in all of prerevolutionary Russia. More than 150 types of manufactured products are today being exported from Armenia to seventy countries throughout the world. In recent years alone, the enterprises of the country have participated in one hundred international expositions.

Today more than half of the population of Armenia has completed secondary and higher education. This republic with a small population of almost two million has more than 60,000 engineers and technicians, and more than nine thousand scientists. The Republic has more than 31,000 college students.

High in the mountains of Armenia the Razdansky mining and chemical combine, the largest in the country, is under construction. The idea of this interesting and important project was born in the Armenian Chemical Institute. It was there also that the plans for this new giant undertaking were worked out. The scientists and builders of Armenia received considerable assistance from the Designing Institutes of Leningrad. The machine-tool industry, as well as the instrument-producing and automotive industries developing in Armenia, is receiving assistance from the design and scientific research institutes of Moscow, and from the machine-tool plant of Odessa. The specialists of Leningrad, Kharkov, Rostov and Kiev have drawn up for the Republic plans for several large electric power stations.

The construction of large industrial enterprises and hydrotechnical works in the Armenian Republic has assumed a genuinely international aspect. Taking part are people who represent forty nationalities of the Soviet Union. Ivan Nuzhny, a Ukrainian, an Honored Builder of the Armenian S.S.R., became famous during the construction of a unique forty-eight-kilometer long bypass tunnel through which the Arpa River will flow to the high mountain lake of Sevan. The power-shovel mechanic Nikolai Kostin, Deputy to the Supreme Soviet of the Armenian S.S.R., distinguished himself in the construction of the Yerevan and the Razdan thermoelectric stations. The builders of Armenia are thoroughly familiar with such master skilled laborers as the mine-shaft drifter Guram Pakadze, a Georgian, and the insulator Mamed Mamedov, a citizen of Azerbaidzhan. At the same time, the Armenians are taking an active hand in the construction of enterprises in the R.S.F.S.R., in Kazakhstan, in Georgia and in Azerbaidzhan.

The fraternal bond between nations has also contributed much to the flourishing of science in the Republic. The works of Armenian astrophysicists and mathematicians, mechanical engineers and chemists, physicists and geologists, archaeologists and linguists have received worldwide recognition. Among the most prominent scientists of the Republic, there are more than a few whose scientific outlook has been shaped in the universities and polytechnics of Moscow, Leningrad, Kharkov, Odessa, Tartu and Kazan.

The ties between the Armenian people and the Russian people, as well as the Ukrainian, Azerbaidzhan, Georgian and other peoples, are centuries old. During the years of Soviet power these ties have grown even closer and more beneficial. And if Armenia has become, as she is today, the home of the remarkable canvases of Martiros Saryan and his numerous disciples, of the captivating music of Aram Khachaturian, Arno Babadzhanyan, Eduard Mizoyan and other marvelous composers; if today Armenian literature and art have earned wide recognition; there is in it not a small share of that life-giving beginning which has enriched the culture of the peoples of Armenia in the process of their intimate contact with the peoples of the Soviet Union. Similar examples of great progress in the fields of economy, culture and science could be cited from the life of each of the republics.

The friendship of the peoples of the U.S.S.R. is an embodiment of their ideological and material unity, of the creative cooperation based on equality, and of the fraternal mutual assistance between the Soviet Socialist Republics.

6 THE UNEXPLORED PATHS OF HISTORY

Trailblazing has always been an arduous task: Everything is new, unexplored and every step is a step into the unknown. In his *Notes of a Publicist*, Lenin has given a graphic comparison between the road pursued by the young Soviet state and a difficult ascent along a mountain which rises to great heights, with sharp twists and unexplored fastnesses. "There is no carriage, no road, in a word nothing, absolutely nothing that has been explored previously!"

The unexplored and difficult road of discoverers fell to the lot of the Soviet people. "Russia is the first country to which history has assigned the role of the initiator of the Socialist revolution," wrote Lenin, "and that is why so many struggles and sufferings have fallen to our lot."

Forces hostile to socialism not only foretold the inescapable downfall of the first Soviet Republic but they also did everything in their power to thwart and destroy it. The civil war and the intervention, the unprecedented profusion of lies against the Bolsheviks, the attempt at its diplomatic and economic isolation; these are but a small fraction of the trials which were visited on the new system.

A Page of the Country's History. It cannot be said that it was all smooth and unruffled sailing in this huge, new socialist experiment undertaken by the first workers' and peasants' state in the world. There is a page in the biography of the Soviet Union which is generally referred to as the period of the cult of personality. It is bound up with the name of Joseph Stalin.

As has been stated in the theses of the Central Committee of the C.P.S.U. entitled *The Fiftieth Anniversary of the Great October Socialist Revolution:*

> In pursuing its course towards the further development of socialist democracy, the Twentieth Party Congress resolutely condemned Stalin's personality cult, which was expressed in the glorification of the role of one man, in departures from the Leninist principle of collective leadership, and in unwarranted reprisals and other violations of socialist legality which inflicted harm on our society. These distortions, for all their gravity, did not alter the nature of socialist society, nor did they shake the pillars of socialism. The Party and the people had abiding faith in communism, they worked with enthusiasm to implement the Leninist ideals, overcoming difficulties, temporary setbacks and mistakes.
>
> The Party carried out measures to overcome the effects of the personality cult in every sphere of Party, state and ideological work, and to secure the observance of the Leninist rules and principles of Party life. The powers of the Union Republics, territories and regions in deciding on economic and cultural matters and the rights of executives at enterprises were extended.

Severe Trials. More than a quarter of a century has elapsed since the day when the people of the Soviet Union experienced their gravest trial, the most terrifying of all visitations: the invasion on June 22, 1941, by the armies of German fascism of the land of the Soviets along a wide front from the Barents Sea to the Black Sea.

Time rushes along with amazing swiftness when you have gone beyond the age of thirty. Nevertheless, this is not what gives you a new sense and perception of the world. It stems rather from the diversity of things which have accumulated, stored and deposited inside of you in the course of the years. You gaze at your own photos in short pants and disjointed recollections charged with the unforgotten joys and sorrows of numerous meetings and partings suddenly flash before you, in a single moment, underlining the passage of time.

My contemporaries and I have reached the same age as our fathers were when, shedding their peaceful pursuits and leaving behind loved ones and children, they donned the uniforms of soldiers. Many, like my own father, fell on the battlefields of the great war against the Nazis, a war which clearly manifested the unbending strength of character of the Soviet people.

Hitler's army hurled itself in a treacherous attack on the Soviet Union. The beginning of the war proved uncommonly trying to the Soviet Union.

The Communist Party mobilized the people of the Soviet Union for the Great Patriotic War against these fascist aggressors. The Party did not conceal the hardships of war with such a strong and insidious enemy. The Council of People's Commissars and the Central Committee of the Communist Party told the Soviet people frankly that "in the war which has been thrust on us by fascist Germany, the issue is one of life or death for the Soviet State, of whether the peoples of the Soviet Union shall be free or fall into slavery."

The appeal of the Party read in part:

"Now everything depends on our ability to organize rapidly and to act without losing a single minute's time, or missing a single opportunity in the struggle against the enemy."

This appeal became the watchword of the front and the rear.

On June 30, 1941, the emergency organ was formed in whose hands rested the conduct of the war, the State Defense Committee, under the chairmanship of J. V. Stalin. One-third of the members and candidate members of the Central Committee, 120 secretaries of the Central Committees of the Communist Parties of the Union Republics, and Regional and

Territorial Committees were assigned to political work in the army. In the days of the heaviest fighting more than 100,000 Communists and Komsomol members were dispatched by the Party to the front as political fighters.

The summer and autumn of 1941 was a time of the fiercest encounters on the battlefield between the Soviet armies and the onrushing Nazis, and also a time of the greatest heroism. The frontier guards repelled with honor the savage onslaught of the enemy. In the defense of Brest, Liepai, Sevastopol and Odessa, in the battle of Smolensk, on the approaches to Leningrad and in the South, day in, day out and hour after hour, the main striking force of the Hitler war machine was time and again beaten down as battle followed battle.

The first month of the Patriotic War gave the world examples of the collective heroism of the people of the Soviet Union as they stood up in defense of their motherland. The names of the fliers V. Talalikhin and N. Gastello, of the seaman E. Nikonov, of Generals L. Dovator and I. Panfilov, of the political instructor V. Klochkov, of Sergeant V. Basilevsky, of the young partisan girls Z. Kosmodemyanskaya and L. Chaikina, and the names of many, many glorious sons and daughters of the Soviet people, will remain forever inscribed in the pages of history.

Toward the fall of 1941 it became apparent that Hitler's plans of a *blitzkrieg* against the Soviet Union were developing into a fiasco, even though his army was standing on the approaches to Moscow. He boasted that on November 7 he would be reviewing a parade in Red Square. The fact is that his parade never took place, and instead there was the usual parade of the Armed Forces of the Soviet Union on the day celebrating the birth of the Proletarian State.

Semyon Budyonny, a twice-decorated hero of the Soviet Union, recalls:

During the long years of my service in the army, I have participated in many military parades. There were times when I had to command and also receive the triumphal marches of the armies. Each one of them left indelible traces in my memory. But the parade the memories of which I want to share today was a special parade, a truly legendary event. It remains in the hearts of all whose steps carried them before the Lenin Mausoleum, with battle arms in their hands—it will live in the hearts of the coming generations. That military parade on the Red Square in Moscow took place November 7, 1941, to celebrate the twenty-fourth anniversary of the Great October Revolution.

The enemy was then standing at the very walls of the Soviet capital. Hitler had boastfully declared that on that day he would be in Moscow congratulating his troops on their victory. The enemy was strong but he failed to achieve his deadly purposes. There was a parade on that day, but it was *our* parade, a parade of the fighting men who went into mortal combat with the accursed enemy of mankind—German fascism. To me, an old soldier, was given a great happiness that day: At the instructions of the Central Committee of the Party and of the Soviet Government I would pass that historic parade in review.

At the end of October I was on the Western front. Heavy fighting was in progress there against the Nazis, who were bearing down on us. Our units stubbornly contested every step of advance into our native land. The enemy paid a heavy price for the slightest gain. One time there at the forward defense perimeter, I was tracked down by a courier from headquarters. He told me that Moscow was calling me to the 'phone. At the other end of the telephone line was the Chairman of the State Defense Committee, J. V. Stalin. He instructed me to hurry to Moscow and informed me that I had an important mission to perform.

The next day I was at the General Headquarters. As he greeted me, Stalin said:

"We are getting ready to stage a military parade in Moscow on the 7th of November. What do you say?

"Of course we shall stage the parade," Stalin repeated as though taking counsel with himself. "You and I, Semyon Mikhailovich, will share the responsibility of reviewing the parade: you will inspect and greet the troops and I will deliver a brief address. Agreed?"

"I will be pleased to carry out these instructions."

"Fine. Get together with Artemyev and consider what precautions must be taken in the event of enemy provocations, particularly from the air, and make sure that this is a truly huge parade of the troops of the Moscow garrison."

On the day of the celebration, the 7th of November, I rose at five in the morning and walked out into the street. It was broad daylight and freezing. "In such weather they are apt to break through . . ." I thought. But the matter had been decided and I began to prepare. Fortunately a blizzard came down at six o'clock, a blizzard of such intensity that immediately the snow covered the squares of the Kremlin with heavy drifts. The columns of troops, drawing to the middle of the road, waded in snow up to the knee.

A strange thing happened to me as I was riding out into Red Square on a dashing prancer. The way was barred by a snowdrift at the Spassky Gate. The trained horse reared up and cleared it with a single leap, as though it were a training hurdle. Then snowdrift followed snowdrift. The excited horse took the next snowdrift as well, but slipped on the stone block of the pavement and came near pitching me out of the saddle. I reined in the horse with difficulty, and there ahead was another snowdrift, and I cleared that one. And so, at a gallop I rode out into the expanse of the snow-covered Red Square. I received the report of the parade marshal, Lieutenant-General P. Artemyev, and with him I inspected the troops in parade trim.

The rank-and-file fighters were lined up in columns. But at that moment they appeared to me like legendary heroes. The Red Army men responded warmly to the greetings. "Hurrah," the shouts were reverberating through the Red Square, martial and resounding like a vow.

Having inspected the troops, I rode up to the Mausoleum. Stalin walked up to the microphone and as was his habit, speaking softly and with a hardness that was even for him out of the ordinary, he delivered a speech, the last words of which ran with a parting admonition of the Party to the fighters who were moving out directly from the Red Square to the front.

. . . The military parade of the 7th of November, 1941, on Moscow's Red Square aroused a mighty patriotic tide throughout the country. The collectives of factories and shops, collective farms and state farms pledged increased production, which was indispensable for the front. The Red Army men in the trenches vowed to keep the enemy out of Moscow.

Not only the people of the Soviet Union but also people abroad realized how great was our confidence and determination to defend Moscow and to rout the insidious enemy. As the British *News Chronicle* put it at that time, the holding in Moscow of a traditional parade, at a time when fierce battles were being fought on the approaches to the city, furnished a splendid example of courage and bravery.

People also became aware of another thing, namely the weakness of Hitler's command. The Germans were at a distance of some thirty kilometers from the Red Square, but even so they were unable to hinder the parade. They were faced with an iron curtain of the brave defenders of the city.

On December 6 the Red Army launched a counterattack. On the snow-laden fields of the outskirts of Moscow was buried the myth of the invincibility of Hitler's Germany. The crushing defeat inflicted on the Nazi army divisions at the approaches to Moscow became the turning point of the war.

The Great Patriotic War was an event of world-historic importance. While the war was being waged there emerged the anti-Hitler coalition of the U.S.S.R., the U.S.A., Great Britain and France. Concurrently, the nations of Europe were evolving a resistance movement to fascism.

Responding to Mikhail Kalinin's birthday greetings, Franklin Roosevelt wrote on February 11, 1942, that the resoluteness and success with which the peoples of the Soviet Union were hurling back the aggressor hordes inspired other nations fighting to preserve their independence.

The anti-Hitler coalition encountered difficulties in its formation. The Second Front did not materialize in 1942, although Great Britain and the U.S.A. had every opportunity to make it do so. Driven back from Moscow, Hitler's armies surged against the capital from the north, at Rzhev. The enemy had already seized the Baltic Republics, Byelorussia and a considerable part of the Ukraine. Leningrad fought valiantly, caught in the vise of the blockade. After 250 days of heroic defense, the Red Army abandoned Sevastopol!

Such was the situation on the fronts of the Great Patriotic War towards the summer of 1942. The enemy concentrated 266 divisions on the Soviet-German front, about one and a half times the number that operated in 1941. The spearhead of the thrust was pointed towards the Volga.

The summer of 1942 was a hard one. Choked with dust, the Soviet armies retreated along the steppes of the Don, under ceaseless bombing, moving towards the Volga. The heroic defense of Stalingrad had begun.

For a period of more than two months battles raged on the approaches to the city, and in September they flared up in the city proper. It appeared to the enemy that the final hour was imminent. The whole world watched the outcome of this battle. Squeezed against the banks of the Volga, against its waters, contesting every house, every floor and every ledge, the fighters of the Stalingrad front exhibited an inflexible fortitude. They gained time. During the very days and nights when, beyond the Volga, mighty reserves of the Soviet Army were drawing close, arms were being forged in the Urals and in Siberia and the plan of offensive operations was being readied at the General Headquarters.

Having withstood the savage onslaught of the enemy and having drained the strength of his armies in fierce battles, Soviet troops went over to the counteroffensive on November 19, 1942. As early as November 23, 330,000 enemy men and officers and large masses of enemy equipment were completely encircled in the Stalingrad region. Neither the hysterical appeals of Hitler not to surrender nor the abortive attempt of the Manstein armored columns to break through to Stalingrad were of any avail. The enemy was doomed.

On December 13, 1942, the Soviet Information Bureau reported:

Over the period when our armies launched their offensive at Stalingrad, that is from November 19 to December 11, the following equipment was seized from the enemy: 105 planes, 1,510 tanks, 2,234 weapons of all calibers, 1,714 mortars, 28 anti-aircraft installations, more than 2,000 machine guns, 4,196,000 shells, more than 20,000,000 cartridges, 7,306 motor vehicles, 1,385 motorcycles, 62 radio stations, 522 kilometers of telephone cable and other stores.

By the end of December 11 the number of prisoners had grown by 6,400 men. The total number of war prisoners taken during the Stalingrad offensive came to 72,400 enemy men and officers.

In the battles waged from November 19 to December 11, our fighting men destroyed 1,386 motor vehicles, 632 aircraft, including 353 transport planes, 548 tanks, 934 weapons of all calibers, and 1,946 machine guns. During the same period the enemy lost at Stalingrad 94,000 men and officers.

The victory was ensured by the men, officers and the political workers at the front. It was forged at the benches by the wives of the fighters at the front; 52 per cent of all industrial personnel was composed of women. In this victory the farmers, the scientists, the men in the field of literature and art all invested their labor. Towards the middle of 1942 the entire national economy had been placed on a war footing. In the autumn, the residents of Tambov initiated a nationwide patriotic movement for collecting means to arm the Soviet forces. For the period of the war, the voluntary contributions of the people of the Soviet Union totaled 94.5 billion rubles.

Letters from the front are documents of the heroic war days. They cannot be read without emotion.

Dear Mother:

We cannot see each other now. The time to meet will be when our country experiences that profound joy—the destruction of the fascist hordes. . . .

Be patient, Mother: What a great honor, what pride it gives one to be a fighter in the Red Army. Our beloved people's army will gain a victory. Your daughter is a fighter in that Army. Have no fear about me. I shall live up to this honorable title. I shall give all of my strength, knowledge, and willpower to master whatever is demanded of me. We are ready to lay down our all for the motherland in recompense for our brief, but happy life, for a great and bright future. Call us and lead us, our motherland, our own! We shall follow you anywhere. We are ready to die for you with the same love we bear you in our lives.

Dear Mother:

Expect my return home only when victory has been won. When you hear that victory has been won come out to meet me. With the warmest greetings of a Red Army fighter,

I am your daughter A. Vasilenko

. . . Do not thumb, dear Mom, the wax-stained pages of ancient tomes, do not go to see grandpa Arkhip Nafdenov and do not read with him any miracles in our astonishing deeds. Listen to me: We are vanquishing death not because we are invincible—we are vanquishing it because we are fighting not only for our own lives; in the midst of the battle our thoughts go out to the life of the little Uzbek boy, the Georgian woman, the old Russian. We go into the battlefield in defense of the holy of holies—our motherland. When I utter that word I want to go down on my knees.

Dear Mother:

I am ready to lay down my life quietly in battle for the life of my motherland and I shall not falter even at the thought that you will remain all alone, without a son.

I kiss you with all my heart,

Your son Kazmin

The rout of the Nazi army at Stalingrad signaled the start of the mighty offensive surge of the Red Army. The Soviet fighters struck at the Hitlerites at Leningrad and Voronezh, and in the south they occupied positions along the lines of the Severny Donets and the Miuss Rivers. A full-scale expulsion of the invaders from Soviet soil had begun.

The rulers of Hitler's Germany would not resign themselves to this state of affairs. They concentrated an enormous force in the Kursk Region in the summer of 1943. The enemy concentration there numbered about 900,000 men and officers, some 2,700 tanks, in excess of 2,000 aircraft and up to 10,000 pieces of ordnance.

Early in July a fierce engagement of forces took place here. The Nazi command hurled into battle the new heavy Tiger tanks and self-propelled assault guns, the Ferdinands, with a heavier armor plating. After checking the enemy drive and bleeding them white, the Red Army launched an offensive; Oryol, Kursk and Belgorod were liberated. For the first time a salute boomed out over Moscow in honor of the victorious army.

The attack was launched by Soviet armies deployed along a front of about 1,200 miles. The Red Army now held the strategic initiative firmly in its hands. It liberated the Donbass, and swept the enemy completely out of the portion of the Ukraine lying along the left bank. Kiev, the capital of the Ukraine, was liberated on the eve of the twenty-sixth anniversary of the October Revolution on November 6. More than two thousand soldiers, officers and generals were distinguished with the title of Hero of the Soviet Union for courage and bravery in crossing the Dnieper River. Towards the end of 1943 more than half of the Soviet soil that had been overrun by the Nazis was liberated. The struggles of the partisans behind the enemy lines played a tremendous part in the successful outcome of the 1943 military operations.

As the saying went at the time, "the voice that was raised at Oryol was echoed in Rome." Mussolini's regime collapsed. In

September 1943 Italy was first to break away from the Axis power bloc formed by Germany and her satellites, marking the beginning of its disintegration.

The thrust of the Red Army's offensive was irresistible. It was routing the Nazis along the entire line running from the Black to the Barents Sea, giving them no respite. The Soviet fighters broke the ring which Hitler had thrown around Leningrad and liberated it from the fascist blockade. The enemy was driven out of the Crimea and Odessa. In the course of its headlong offensive the Red Army liberated Minsk, Vilnius, Kishinyov, Riga, Tallinn and Petrozavodsk.

The state frontiers of the Soviet Union were entirely recovered along their whole extent. The war entered its terminal phase. The whole world realized that with its own forces the Soviet Union had the capability of entirely routing Nazi Germany and of liberating Europe from the fascist yoke. This prompted the ruling circles of the anti-Hitlerite coalition— Great Britain and the United States—to open a second front. In June 1944 their armies disembarked in France. However, even after this the fate of the war, as before, continued to be decided on the Soviet-German front, which had tied down two-thirds of the enemy's fighting force.

Under the blows of the Red Army the satellites of Nazi Germany began to defect one after another. The peoples of Poland, Hungary, Rumania, Czechoslovakia, Bulgaria and Yugoslavia intensified their blows against the fascist invaders to liberate their native soil from the enemy's grip. In their struggle against the fascist tyranny, the laboring masses of Europe leaned on the aid of the Red Army.

The aid that came from the rear sustained the mighty, unrelenting offensive of the Soviet armies along all sectors of the front. In every month in 1944 the defense industry produced five times as many tanks as at the outbreak of the war. In the output of tanks, aircraft and artillery, the Soviet Union topped the Germans in 1944, despite the fact that nearly all of Europe was still producing for them. The war potential of the

Soviet Union exceeded that of Nazi Germany. This was the greatest victory of the war economy of the Soviet Union.

Early in 1945 the Red Army launched the final phase of its offensive along the entire 720-mile front from the Baltic to the Carpathian Mountains. This offensive had been planned to start at the end of January but Hitler's armies pushed the Anglo-American armies in the Ardennes to the brink of catastrophe and the Prime Minister of Great Britain, Churchill, made an appeal for help. Responding to this request from the Allies, the Soviet Army launched a powerful offensive in the middle of January.

The hour of retribution struck. On April 16, 1945, the Berlin operation commenced. For ten days battles raged in the streets of Berlin. Early in the morning of May 1, 1945, the banner of victory was hoisted over the Reichstag. On May 8, Nazi Germany was forced to agree to an unconditional surrender. May 9 became a national holiday, a holiday celebrating the great victory over the strongest and most vicious of enemies.

Here are some of the many inscriptions that were painted on the walls and columns of the fascist Reichstag in Berlin in May of 1945:

> WE DEFENDED ODESSA AND STALINGRAD
> AND WE ARE NOW IN BERLIN!
>
> WE HAIL FROM THE VOLGA . . .
>
> AND WE HAIL FROM MOSCOW!
>
> FROM LENINGRAD TO THIS SPOT CAME MAJORS
> ANDREYEV, ORKHIMENKO, MIKHAILIN,
> WE CAME HERE TO MAKE SURE THAT
> GERMANY WOULD NOT COME TO US.
>
> I WILL NOW BE PAYING A VISIT OF COURSE
> TO MY LITTLE NATIVE VILLAGE, AND GO TO
> SEE MY MOTHER . . .

"The Red Army and the Russian people started Hitler's forces on the road to their ultimate defeat and have earned the lasting admiration of the people of the United States," wrote Roosevelt, President of the United States, in his message to the Government of the Soviet Union.

Winston Churchill said: "The Red Army celebrates its twenty-seventh anniversary amid triumph which has won the unstinted applause of its Allies and has sealed the doom of German militarism. Future generations will acknowledge their debt to the Red Army as do we who have lived to witness these proud achievements."

The Danish Minister of Foreign Affairs, Christmas Möller, announced over the radio:

"All nations are giving thanks today to the Soviet Union for its enormous contribution to the rout of the bitterest enemy of all mankind. The peace-loving Russian people rose up against the invader and all the peoples of the occupied countries immediately understood how one must battle against the German invaders."

Delivering a speech over the radio on the day of victory, Josip Broz Tito declared as follows:

"On the day of the great victory over the common enemy the thoughts of all of our peoples turn with thanks to the glorious, unconquerable liberator, the Red Army. The thoughts of all of our peoples are turned with gratitude to the heroic peoples of the Soviet Union who have made the greatest sacrifices in this superhuman struggle."

But as yet there was no peace in the world. The war was still raging in the Pacific Ocean. On August 8, 1945, loyal to its Allied commitments, the Soviet Union entered the war against militarist Japan. Battered by crushing blows dealt by the Soviet Army, the Kwantung Army, which numbered in excess of one million men, was routed, gave up resistance and surrendered. On September 2, 1945, Japan signed the act of unconditional surrender.

Through its victory in the Great Patriotic War, the Soviet people made an enormous contribution to the delivery of mankind from the peril of fascist enslavement, and it gave convincing proof of the power and viability of its state.

The victory over fascism belongs to all of mankind, who have an obligation to defend it.

The Inextinguishable Fire of Eternal Glory. A remarkable holiday was born during May of 1945. On May 9 of every year the Soviet Union celebrates the Day of Victory over Nazi Germany. Millions of heroic men and women laid down their lives to bring that day closer, for the sake of freedom and happiness, for the sake of the future. Large are the numbers of those who do not know where the graves of their near and dear ones are to be found. Nor do I know where to find the grave of my father, who lost his life at Moscow in December 1941. When the remains of the Unknown Soldier were laid to their eternal rest at the Kremlin wall in 1966, my mother, like many mothers and wives of those who died in the war, wept as she watched the interment. My five-year-old niece Anechka, my sister's daughter, fell silent as she watched the interment, and she asked:

"Why are you crying, granny?"

And the grandmother, not realizing that she might cause pain to her beloved grandchild, replied:

"They are burying your grandpa, Anya. . . ."

It was the first time in twenty-five years that I had seen my mother shedding tears for her husband.

The burial site of the Unknown Soldier is overlaid with gray stone. At the center of it is a huge square block made up of slabs of red granite. In the middle appears a large bronze star against a background of black marble. The shape is identical with that of the gold star that decorates the chests of Heroes of the Soviet Union.

The well-known Soviet writer, Lenin Prize holder Sergey Smirnov, who has done much to immortalize the memory of the glorious exploits of Soviet men and women in the Great War, writes as follows:

I had occasion to be among those who composed the inscription that was carved out on the Tomb of the Unknown Soldier. This is the way it came about. Four writers—K. Simonov, S. Mikhalkov, M. Lukonin and myself—were invited to attend a session of the Moscow City Committee of the Party. We conferred a long time, making suggestions, and rejecting the best inscriptions to be found on tombstones both here and abroad. In the end we adopted the inscription submitted by Mikhalkov: "His name is unknown but his deed is immortal." In the general discussion these words were approved with but a slight amendment. The final text read: "YOUR NAME IS UNKNOWN, YOUR DEED IS IMMORTAL!"

This inscription makes one think again, not only of the heroes who have laid down their lives, but also of the veterans and of those who have fought and survived. The number of the latter keeps on dwindling as the years go by.

Rising to the left of the main headstone is a wall of crimson quartzite with the inscription: *To those who died for the Motherland. 1941–1945.* To the right, on a tall granite wall, rise six blocks of marble. Enclosed inside them is soil gathered from heroic cities where every inch of the ground was saturated with the blood of Soviet soldiers. The people of Leningrad brought it here from the Piskarev cemetery, which is the resting place of the victims of the most formidable blockade of that great city; the people of Volgograd, from the famed Mamayev Burial Mound; the people of Odessa, from what was once the city's defense line; the people of Kiev, from the place that once served as the command post of General Vatutin; delegates from Sevastopol, from the heroic Malakhov Burial Mound; the people of Brest, from the foot of the legendary fortress; and soil was brought also from the fraternal graves of Darnitsa and Lukyanovska.

On May 8, 1967, the people again gathered at the Kremlin wall before the Monument of the Unknown Soldier. The vast Manezhnaya Square was crowded with people from Moscow and delegates of all the fraternal republics, representatives of the heroic cities, leaders of the Communist Party, officials of the Soviet government and prominent military leaders.

Hero of the Soviet Union Alexei Maresyev, the world-renowned war pilot who continued to engage the fascist enemy in the air even after the amputation of both feet, walked up to the armored carrier and, borrowing the flame which had been carried from the Field of Mars in Leningrad, the resting place of the dead of the Great February and October Revolutions and of the Civil War, lit the torch. This flame, which symbolizes the spiritual union of generations of Soviet people, was delivered in armored carriers to Manezhnaya Square, along with the urn of soil gathered from the Piskarev Memorial Cemetery. They traveled a distance of 390 miles from Leningrad to Moscow through many towns and villages. And everywhere the people stood at silent attention paying a tribute of respect to the heroes, honoring the immortality of their deeds.

Eternal Flame! It proclaimed to each and every person: "No one is forgotten and nothing is forgotten!"

Millions of names of unknown heroes of the past have been rediscovered by members of Komsomol, to whom the life of the older generation stands as a model and prototype of bravery and heroism.

The noble enterprise, brought to life by Sergei Smirnov, took on a broader scope and brimmed over into a widespread and meaningful quest. The children are now engaged not only in a search for heroes of the Patriotic War, but also for heroes of the October Revolution, of the Civil War and of the early years of Soviet power.

Letters pour into Moscow television studios from all ends of the Soviet Union, addressed to the Central Headquarters of the All-Union Search. The letters are from the pens of both children and adults. They tell something of the life of kith and kin, of the results they have garnered on walking tours to distant parts along trails covered with glory won in battles, and they send in interesting documents and pictures. These letters bring out the deeper meaning that lies behind such outwardly simple words as "the heirs of a generation."

The meaning is to be found in the indelible remembrance of people who have laid down their lives for the sake of the future, and also in their deeds, actions and accomplishments.

"YOUR NAME IS UNKNOWN, YOUR DEED IS IMMORTAL," reads the inscription carved into the marble.

PART III

U.S.S.R.:

MONTREAL 1967

7 A MODEL OF SOCIALISM

. . . War has tricked us. It is not true that hatred adds anything to the exaltation of the race.

Why should we hate one another? We all live in the same cause, are borne through life on the same planet, form the crew of the same ship. Civilizations may, indeed, compete to bring forth new syntheses, but it is monstrous that they should devour one another.

These are the words of the great French humanist, writer and pilot, Antoine de Saint-Exupéry. The theme of his well-known book *Wind, Sand and Stars*, Man and His World, became the theme of EXPO 67, the International Exposition of 1967 which opened on April 27 in Montreal.

The festive ceremony of its inauguration lasted the entire day, from morning till late into the night, when brilliant fireworks flared out over the city. Music, a 21-gun salute, the tolling of the bells of the two hundred Montreal churches, the whistles and horns of the ships, cutters and barges anchored in the city's harbor, the roar of old-fashioned biplanes and modern jet fighter planes circling above the EXPO area, the guard of honor, the torch that came from the capital of Canada, and speeches—the celebration resounded with all of these. The Commissioner-General of the Exposition, Pierre Dupuy, and Jean Drapeau, Mayor of Montreal, along with other officials, spoke before the assembled celebrants at the Place des Nations of the township of EXPO 67.

The Prime Minister of Canada, Lester Pearson, said:

EXPO stands as a monument to the glory of man; it is an impressive assemblage of his finest deeds and ideas. It is a stirring tale about the world which belongs to all nations. It is a heartening manifestation of man's faith in the future and his abilities to conquer nature. The Exposition shows what nations are capable of accomplishing if they cooperate with each other. The theme of the Exposition, Man and His World, harmonizes well with the spirit of our times. And it is not a mere chance that in the number of participating countries EXPO has broken all records.*

In conclusion, the Prime Minister of Canada expressed the hope that EXPO 67 would serve as another reminder of the fact that nations must live in peace and cooperation.

The Governor General of Canada, D. R. Michener, officially opened the Exposition. The flags of all nations participating in EXPO 67 were hoisted. To the strains of the hymn of the U.S.S.R., the flags of all fifteen of the Union Republics along with the state flag of the U.S.S.R. rose against the sky before the Soviet pavilion. In the year that celebrated the fiftieth anniversary of the Great October Socialist Revolution this silver-gray pavilion, which occupied an area of 3.7 acres, made it possible for people to understand the victories of 1917 and to retrace the road traveled by the peoples of the U.S.S.R. in half a century.

In an interview held on the eve of the Montreal exposition,

---

* At the Brussels Exposition of 1958, 40 countries participated, and in New York in 1965 there were only 13 countries, while in Montreal the number of participants reached 62. Moreover, participating in EXPO 67 were also the Canadian provinces, three U.S. States, international organizations and trading companies.

the chairman of the organizing committee in charge of the preparatory work for the U.S.S.R. section at the exposition, the Deputy Chairman of the Council of Ministers of the U.S.S.R., I. T. Novikov, outlined the aims of the Soviet Union in its participation in EXPO 67 as follows:

As is well known, the International Exposition of Canada has been organized to celebrate the 100th anniversary of its Confederation and the 325 years of the existence of Montreal. However, 1967 is a year of Jubilee not only in Canada. It is also a Jubilee year for the Soviet Union. It marks the fiftieth anniversary of the Great October Socialist Revolution, half a century of the existence of the first state of workers and peasants in the world. Thus, by its participation in the exposition, the U.S.S.R. is endeavoring to show all of its accomplishments during that period.

Man and His World is the theme of EXPO 67. Reflecting this theme in every respect, our exposition will show the fundamental features of the Soviet system, its economy and its culture. While stressing the socialist nature of the Soviet state, the exposition of the U.S.S.R. remains entirely within the framework of the idea "Everything for Man, everything for the Sake of Man."

B. A. Borisov, Commissioner General of the Soviet section of the International Exposition, delivered a speech at the gala opening of the Soviet pavilion on April 28, 1967.

"Everything you find on display in our pavilion," he declared, "has been created by the hands, minds and efforts of the toilers of all the republics of the multinational Soviet state.

"The people of the Soviet Union have come here to the International Exposition in order to demonstrate again their unalterable devotion to the ideas of peace, friendship and cooperation among nations."

Having expressed to the government of Canada his thanks for the hospitality which had been extended, B. A. Borisov, acting on instructions of the Soviet government, declared the pavilion of the Union of Soviet Socialist Republics at the International Exposition of 1967 officially open.

Thousands of people filled every floor. The *Moscow News*

in English and French was distributed to the guests. The opening issue contained the following message from the President of the Presidium of the Supreme Soviet of the U.S.S.R., N. V. Podgorny:

RESPECTED GUESTS OF THE SOVIET PAVILION:

It gives me great pleasure to welcome you on behalf of the Soviet people, on behalf of the Presidium of the Supreme Soviet of the U.S.S.R., on behalf of the Government of the Soviet Union and on my own behalf, to the Pavilion of the Union of Soviet Socialist Republics in this International Exposition. We trust that you will find your visit to us pleasant and interesting. If you are a resident of Canada, may we be permitted to convey through you our gratitude to the Canadian people who have extended to us their hospitality and who have contributed in great measure to the successful accomplishment of EXPO 67.

This is a year of special significance to our country. In the month of November the Soviet Union will celebrate the fiftieth anniversary of the Great October Socialist Revolution, which set free the spiritual and physical powers of the Soviet people and set it on the road towards the building of a new society. Certainly, the exposition could not possibly reflect all of the events, all of the heroic exploits, which make up the history of the Soviet Union during the past half century. Our aim is to give you an inkling of at least some facets of the full-blooded life of our multinational family inhabiting fifteen Union Republics of the Soviet Land; about the work we do and the culture we create, about the way we rest and learn; about the things the Soviet people bring to pass today and the plans they have for the future.

When we Soviet people are asked about the wellsprings of the indisputably enormous achievements of our state, we do not throw a veil over the social and political causes which helped us within a span of three decades of peaceful labor—bearing in mind that twenty years have been consumed by the wars which have been forced on our country—turn the U.S.S.R. into a mighty world power. We are hopeful that these causes will be better understood in Canada, on the whole of the American continent and in all other countries. We are certain that other peoples as well have much important work to do in their own households. EXPO 67 is the clearest proof of what mankind is able to achieve if allowed to live in peace.

Peaceful coexistence and business-like cooperation between countries with different social systems, and not military contests between them, should govern the nature of international relations in our times. And, of course, the world being what it is, and the links in the chain of events being closely knit, all attempts to interfere in the internal affairs of other countries are in blatant contradiction with the principles of

Red Square, Moscow. Roads to outer space start here.

Wheat harvesting on a state farm in Kazakhstan.

A crop of melons in Uzbekistan.

Timber—a traditional Russian export.

Snow removal in Eastern Siberia.

Caspian Sea fishermen.

Young chemical workers at a nitric fertilizer plant in Georgia.

Minsk-made tractors—known in many countries.

Valentina Tereshkova (right) shown soon after landing from outer space.

The pennon delivered to the moon on February 3, 1966, by the Soviet automatic station Luna-9.

President Kennedy with Cosmonauts John Glenn and Herman Titov.

The Kirghiz Academy of Sciences in Frunze, Kirghizia.

The Presidium of the U.S.S.R. Academy of Sciences in the Lenin Prospekt, Moscow.

Moscow University.

Students attending a lecture.

A concert in a shop. Moscow.

A folk art festival at the
Komsomol Stadium in Tallinn, Estonia.

INSET:
Karine Kazarian,
a solo dancer of the
Armenian Dance Ensemble.

Maya Plisetskaya in *Swan Lake*.

Svyatoslav Richter.

Aram Khachaturian.

The Protopopovs, Olympic figure-skating champions.

Innokenti Smoktunovsky as Hamlet.

In the Pushkin Art Museum, Moscow.

Youth and beauty.

Children from all over the world arrive at the Artek camp for holidays.

"Everything for the sake of Man; everything for Man's good."

Expo 67, Montreal.
At the entrance to the Soviet Pavilion.

LOWER LEFT:
In the space section.

LOWER RIGHT:
A Moskovich car in Montreal.

peaceful coexistence of states with different social systems. The founder
of the Soviet State, V. I. Lenin, repeatedly stated that our ideal is to
put an end to wars, plunder and violence, and to establish peace among
nations. The U.S.S.R. follows these behests with firm dedication.

We are pleased to note that Soviet-Canadian relations have made
further progress in recent years. Not only the economic ties have been
expanded, but also the exchange of scientific, technical and cultural attainments. We welcome this development and we are of the opinion
that the expansion and deepening of this kind of fruitful cooperation
serves the interests of our peoples and the interests of improving the
situation the world over.

We want to thank each one of you for having come here to see what
we are doing and how we are doing it, what our dreams are and what
brings us joy. There is a popular saying to the effect that it is well if
there are enough reminiscences to carry over till next we meet. Allow
me to express to you our best wishes and the hope that you will enter-
tain the most pleasant reminiscences of what the Soviet Exposition has
brought to your attention.

> N. PODGORNY,
> President of the Presidium of the
> Supreme Soviet of the U.S.S.R.

The first visitors to the Soviet pavilion turned out to be an
American student, Ruth Thurston, and her countryman
Wayne Elliot, a chemical engineer (from Massachusetts).
When asked why they had decided to begin viewing the Expo-
sition with the Soviet pavilion, they replied:

"We were very anxious to meet the Russians, to have a look
at them and to get to know more about the Soviet Union."

"The Soviet Pavilion promises to be the main attraction of
the entire Exposition," declared the Montreal paper *La
Presse*. "No sooner do you approach the pavilion than you are
impressed by its huge dimensions, reflecting the geography of
the country; after all Russia comes near to being a continent."
Alluding to the wealth of the Soviet exhibit, the paper came
to the notable conclusion that "The Russian pavilion is an
exposition by itself."

The Canadian corporation did not stint in advertising the
Soviet pavilion. They distributed a color poster in the United
States that was reproduced in *Life* and *Holiday* as well as

other American magazines with large distributions. The advertisement showed a photograph of the Russian pavilion against the background of a red flag. In the upper part it read in big letters: "Look what the Russians are building, just forty miles from the U.S.A. As an American, you should look into it."

The text below the photo read:

You're invited to step in, and take a look at life in the Soviet Union. Meet the people, see what they do for a living in Vladivostok or Minsk, and how they have fun.

What kind of ideas do the Russians have, about education, medicine, housing, industrial development, space exploration? You'll find out here. In the great Lunar Hall, they'll treat you to an eerie expedition to the moon. On the way, you'll discover what the feeling of weightlessness is like. . . .

And on the lighter side of things, you can see what the Moscow Miss is wearing, at a fashion parade. Browse through nearby stores that sell the identical items you'd find in shops in Leningrad or Kiev. Drop into the 600-seat cinema and watch a Russian movie. And wind up in one of the restaurants, where you can take your pick of specialties from every part of the country.

". . . I have no doubt that the Russian exposition will enjoy an enormous success," said the Commissioner General of EXPO 67 when visiting the pavilion of the U.S.S.R.

The Soviet pavilion evoked high praise from the American Senators who visited it. Among them were the U.S. Senate majority leader, Mike Mansfield, as well as Senators Stennis and Aiken.

What was it that attracted people to the Soviet pavilion? What was the story told by the six thousand items?

Forty Miles from the United States. Russia, which once displayed commercial samovars for worldwide viewing, now put on display space ships, electronic and optical products, atomic reactors and the end-products of the most complex chemical processes. This alone afforded sufficient evidence of what strides forward the Soviet people had taken in the development of science and technology within half a century.

However, this was only one facet of the matter. In the report of the Commissioner General of the Russian section of the Paris World Exposition that had opened at the turn of this century, specific mention was made of "the first Russian telegraphic equipment demonstrating that time and again the Russians were the first great inventors." Now it is hardly possible to think of the telegraph as a miracle. Nothing surprising in this! Only a few decades were needed for us to cease being wonder-struck by electric light, the telephone, the television set, jet planes, atomic reactors, and space ships—in short, no dearth of objects can be enumerated, each one of which bears incontrovertible witness to the enormous potential of human genius. Displayed in profusion at Montreal were the economic and social conquests of the Soviet people. Many of the visitors were amazed at the revelation of a new world brimming over with daring and creative plans. No wonder, therefore, that the visitor's book of the Soviet pavilion had so many candid congratulatory messages addressed to the Soviet Union and its peoples, and wishes for even greater attainments.

Before the entrance to the Soviet pavilion stood an eleven-meter sculpture, "The Hammer and Sickle." On one of the faces of this silvery composition one could read the inscription "All for the sake of man, for the benefit of man," one more restatement and avowal of the theme of EXPO 67, "Man and His World."

A short distance from the entrance to the pavilion, large stands carried reproductions of the founding documents in the history of the land of socialism, from Lenin's Decree on Peace to extracts from the Constitution.

Ascending the escalator to the first floor, visitors entered the main hall, which covered an area of 7,532 square yards. There in front of them loomed up a bas-relief of Lenin. That was where the visitors set out on their journey into the life of the Soviet people, a journey into the world of socialism.

A large electrified wall map of the U.S.S.R., covered with photographic inserts showing landscapes, sites under construction, buildings, and national shrines, gave the first impression of the country that held first place in the world in terms of prospected deposits of coal, iron ore, manganese, copper, nickel, and tungsten. Here on display were also precious stones, specimens of rare and precious metals, and semi-precious stones from the Urals used in the jeweller's craft and for decorative and industrial purposes.

Sixteen screens were fitted into the illuminated map. Documentaries, slides and photos showed scenes from the life of the peoples of the U.S.S.R. Taped commentaries afforded the necessary information. An extensive series of large slides, which were also accompanied by commentaries, were arrayed along the middle of the principal hall. Their theme was "The People of the Soviet Union." A number of picture stories depicted such subjects as "The Dynasty of Metallurgists of the Urals—the three Buzhin brothers"; "The Inventors of the Quantum Generator, academicians A. M. Prokhorov and N. G. Basov"; and "The Islambeks, a Family of Physicians in Uzbekistan."

An illuminated electrification network showed how far the Soviet Union had gone in the realization of the plans conceived by Lenin, plans which seemed fantastic even to so brilliant a creator of fantasy as H. G. Wells. From the huge model of an atomic reactor surging impulses flashed across the entire floor and appeared finally on the huge illuminated chart as a sea of flaming spots with a cascade of Siberian hydroelectric stations standing out in their midst.

The dioramas and models on the first floor were devoted to the achievements of the industries of the U.S.S.R. in oil, coal, chemistry, metallurgy, power engineering, machine building, instrument-making and optics. Shown here were the most recent techniques in the smelting of metals, coal mining and oil recovery, as well as functioning models. For instance, there were models of the Temp coal combine, the largest blast furnace in the world, of the Apatity chemical combine, of the famous town of Neftyanye Kamni, and of the maritime industries in the Caspian Sea not far from Baku, the capital of Azerbaidzhan.

Power engineering was represented with models of all atomic power stations, beginning with the first such station in Obninsk and continuing with the huge thermoelectric stations. There was a model of the Krasnoyarsk electrical station, which is the largest in the world, with a power output of five million kilowatts, as well as models of the 500-megawatt hydrogenerator and of the vertical hydroturbine for the Krasnoyarsk hydroelectric station.

A number of exhibits showed the scope of the work carried on by Soviet scientists. In 1967 more than 666,000 scientific workers, one-fourth of all scientists in the world, were working in 4,651 Soviet scientific research institutes.

The "Atoms for Peace" section enjoyed great popularity. It illustrated graphically the way atomic energy was used in industry, medicine and agriculture, and what progress nuclear physics was making in the Soviet Union. Among the exhibits were large illuminated models of Serpukhov, a town on the outskirts of Moscow, near which a gigantic synchrophasotrone was being built.

Soviet scientists furnished a unique exhibit concerning thermonuclear research and its prospects, the study of the properties of high-temperature plasma. It included a working UN-6 unit inside of which plasma was heated by a shock wave, and models of the Soviet research plants Tokomak-4 and Ogra-2. In the center of the exhibit was a model of a thermonuclear reactor, the prototype of a future inexhaustible source of power using water as fuel.

Lodged on stands in the pavilion were functioning optical quantum generators produced by Soviet industry. Among them were some that generated light rays used to work super-hard metals, to perform operations on the retina of the eye and to measure great distances. Here one was able to become acquainted with an instrument that made it feasible to determine the distance to the moon with a precision of within 394 feet, namely the gas quantum generator, the ray of which carries telephone conversations.

The international pavilion "Man the Explorer" displayed

objects connected with the conquest of the Arctic and Antarctic regions. The variety and scope of these explorations appeared on an electrically illuminated chart, which represented the drift chart of fifteen Soviet North Pole stations, an atlas of the Antarctic, and a functioning diorama of the aurora borealis.

In the section devoted to agriculture, as well as in the international technological pavilions, an account was given of the tremendous changes which had taken place in the Russian village during the past half century.

The displays showed the development of agriculture during the latest Five-Year Plan. There one found information concerning the extent of the mean annual increase in the output of agricultural products, particularly that of grain, the technological means to be made available to collective farms, and what resources the government and the collective farms plan to invest in the development of agriculture.

There was also a comprehensive display of materials relating to karakul sheep breeding farms. During the years of Soviet power the stock of sheep increased by a multiple of four. In terms of beauty and quality the Soviet karakul cannot be matched.

The Soviet Union, which in 1967 held first place in the world in terms of raw cotton yields, also had on display the finest quality cotton plants. Diagrams illustrated the achievements of the Kuibyshev state farm in the Tadzhik S.S.R. On this state farm the area under grain crops was in excess of four thousand hectares, and the yield was 32 hundredweights per hectare.

No other country in the world possesses such huge stands of forest as does the Soviet Union, where the area covered by all timberland comes to 3,058 million acres. Photopanoramas of the taiga, and of mixed and mountain forests gave an inkling of the boundless timber resources of the Soviet country. Special stands dealt with the planting of field-protecting forest belts. Visitors viewing the photopanorama of the forest belts of the Kamennaya Steppe learned that some 1,976,000 acres of forest belt had been planted in the Soviet Union.

In recent years magnificent projects have been implemented in the Soviet Union in the sphere of irrigation and in the draining of soils that retain excessive moisture. Shown at the exposition were the principal irrigated areas, among them the Golodnaya Steppe and the areas along the Kara Kum Canal. Appearing in scale models were the Syr-Darya, the Kairak-Kum, Farkhad and Chardaryin Reservoirs, the South-Golodnaya Steppe and North-Golodnaya Steppe Canals, basins, the contours of existing and projected irrigation areas, water mains and pumping stations.

Also interesting was the section devoted to education. Its exhibits afforded information on the organization of the country's educational system and disclosed the fact that in the Soviet Union all persons are guaranteed the right to an education regardless of sex, religion and nationality; and that education is free and conducted in the native language. Within a period of fifty years the number of people receiving an education has increased in excess of five times. In 1966 a total of 214,000 schools were operating in the country in the field of general education alone. While the student body in tsarist Russia amounted to 181,000, the number runs at present to 7,520,-000. Special exhibits were devoted to the themes of "Preschool Education" and "The General Education School," with photos showing lessons in mathematics, physics, chemistry, biology and draftsmanship, and the work carried on by secondary, evening and correspondence schools. In addition, the organization of aesthetic and physical education, children's recreation in Pioneer camps and specialized childrens sanatoria were shown.

Two figures eloquently demonstrated the scope which education had reached in the Soviet Union: In 1917 the number of teachers was 280,000, while in 1967 their number reached 2.5 million.

The exhibits devoted to building and architecture showed the principles and methods of urban construction, as well as the measures taken to solve the country's housing problem. Within the period of the last five years 393 million square meters in housing accommodations have been built in towns, workers' settlements and state farms. The scale of housing construction will be expanded still further during the current five-year plan. In Moscow alone, approximately 28 million square meters of dwelling space will be constructed during the current five-year-plan period.

". . . Towns and communities must constitute a rational and comprehensive organization of industrial areas, residential areas, public and cultural institutions, communal services, transport, engineering equipment and power sources, ensuring the best possible conditions for labor, life and leisure. . . ." This is how the program of the Communist Party of the Soviet Union defines the trend in urban construction.

On exhibit were scale models of new towns, as for example, those of transpolar towns, since construction in a zone of hard frosts and snow storms is of particular interest to the Canadians, who are a people of the north.

A special 956-square-yard section of the Soviet pavilion was devoted to public health. Colored photos, slides, and illuminated electrical charts showed the organization of public health services in the Soviet Union.

Prerevolutionary Russia: Three doctors to every 20,000 persons. These statistical data revealed a great deal, for example, that hundreds of peasants of tsarist Russia came into contact with a doctor only once in a lifetime, and that was only on the occasion of the draft. And here was another fact: The Soviet Union now has nearly one half of all doctors in Europe. A span of fifty years stretches between these facts.

At the turn of this century the well-known writer V. Veresayev, author of The Doctor's Notebook (he was a graduate physician and a practitioner for many years), remarked indignantly, "Medicine is the science of healing only the rich and the free. In its relation to all others it is merely a theoretical science dealing with the question as to how one could heal them if they were rich and free."

The chief aim of the public health section of the Soviet pavilion was to show that no matter where the Soviet citizen lives, no matter where he works, he is at all times assured of free and qualified medical aid. This is one of the principal achievements of the Soviet state.

Placed close to the stands were small screens which afforded the visitor an opportunity to view three-minute color films dubbed in English and in French.

Large color slides gave an account of mother and child care and of the methods which are followed in bringing up the young generation so that they develop both physically and mentally in a balanced way.

The exhibit showed the comprehensive medical services that are provided for the workers of industrial enterprises and in the villages, and information was furnished concerning the most fundamental phase of Soviet public health service, namely preventive medicine. The public health services work in close touch with the community as a whole.

In 1967 the Soviet Union held first place in the world both in terms of absolute number of physicians, and of the ratio of physicians to the population.

Cited below are some comparative data according to countries:

	NUMBER OF PHYSICIANS (IN 1000)	NUMBER OF PHYSICIANS PER 10,000 POPULATION
U.S.S.R.	555	23.9
U.S.A.	351.8	18.4
GREAT BRITAIN	79.1	14.7
FRANCE	75.2	15.4
INDIA	83.3	1.9

Some 28,000 physicians are being trained at the present time annually in the U.S.S.R. Two-hundred-twenty thousand students are now pursuing their medical studies in 87 higher medical institutes.

In 1913 (the last prewar year in tsarist Russia) 16 higher medical institutes graduated 900 physicians in Russia.

In the Republics of Central Asia alone more than 50,000 physicians are engaged in medical practice, which is twice as many as in all tsarist Russia.

The number of physicians per 10,000 population as far back as 1959 had shown the following increase as compared with 1913: in Turkmenia by 34 times, in Uzbekistan by 42 times, in Kazakhstan by 42 times, in Kirghizia by 66 times and in Tadzhikistan by 112 times.

A special section of the exhibit acquainted visitors with the achievements of Soviet medicine in the treatment of cardiovascular diseases. Seven large models displayed an array of modern radiological equipment employed in diagnostics and in the treatment of various diseases. Films projected on screens flanking the stand showed original methods employed in surgical interventions developed by Soviet specialists.

The application to medicine of the achievements of modern science, of the most delicate analytical techniques, and the most recent drugs is by no means inexpensive. Moreover, the trend towards all-around treatment that characterizes present-day medicine, which requires several times more numerous service staff and equipment, on occasion boosts the cost of treatment to three- and four-digit figures.

Ever greater amounts are expended in the U.S.S.R. for medical aid. A noted Soviet surgeon, academician B. V. Petrovsky, cited in a press interview operations performed in his clinic with the assistance of fourteen highly qualified specialists. Of course, this involves a great expenditure.

But how much?

Here is a statement concerning one such operation:

Patient's name: VLADIMIR SOROKIN.
Diagnosis: Mitral rheumatic heart disease 2nd and 3rd stage circulatory disturbance.
Total number of days confined to bed: 64.
Of the above number, 25 preoperative days in bed.
Postoperatively: 39 days in bed, or bed-days.

The cost of the patient's care during the exploratory period was as follows: 25 days in bed, at 6.81 rubles per day, or 170.25 rubles.

Cost of the operation:
a) Salaries   131.90 rubles
b) Surcharge on salaries   5.9 per cent
c) Medicines during operation   400.21
d) Amortization of equipment   150.00
e) Amortization of linens   38.00

The cost of the patient's postoperative maintenance: 39 bed-days at 6.81 rubles, or 265.59, plus blood, 240.15, plus plasma, 95.15, or 601.99 rubles.

Overall, the treatment of the patient, V. M. Sorokin, as an in-patient came to 1,429.35 rubles.

According to the medical certificate, payment was made in the amount of 223.30 for a period of three months.

Total expenditure: 1,715.65.

During all the days that Vladimir Sorokin, a 25-year-old worker in the Serpukhov ready-to-wear plant, spent in the hospital, both he and his family were concerned about only one thing, namely the successful outcome of the treatment. The question concerning expenditures on medical aid had been resolved in advance, since in Vladimir's case, as in the case of any Soviet citizen, the physicians will leave nothing undone regardless of cost, inasmuch as the state pays the bill for the treatment.

The exhibit traced the development of medical technology, including various instruments and apparatus for use in diagnostics and treatment and for scientific research. Moreover, most of these were shown in actual use.

Particular interest was elicited by the display showing the full range of the newest surgical instruments employed in the Soviet Union. There was a reanimating apparatus and instruments used for the suturing of vessels that have become known throughout the world. Special cases housed articles employed in the pharmaceutical industry, which exports its products to 53 countries.

The concluding stand was devoted to a display showing what the Soviet Union had contributed in the field of safeguarding public health over a period of fifty years. The average life span of the population has been extended during that period to twice its former term. General mortality has been reduced four times, and infant mortality ten times.

Thus, the best traditions of medicine in the U.S.S.R. and the aspirations of progressive people were developed and realized after the state assumed the responsibility and concern for the health of the people.

The theme of the rich and diversified exhibit of the second floor of the pavilion of the Soviet Union was the conquest of space. Shown here were the achievements of Soviet scientists from the days of Tsiolkovsky down to our own day. The visitors lingered long before the spaceships, examining the Luniks.

The exhibit showed graphically that space probes are today directly connected with terrestrial events. This was evidenced, for example, by the models of the explorer satellite Cosmos-112, which was equipped with meteorological instruments, and the communications satellite Molnia-I which threw a radio and television bridge through space between Moscow and Vladivostok. Other exhibits gave an account of the exploration of the Earth's immediate vicinity.

A replica of the Vostok ship with the last stage of the carrier rocket afforded a view of the apparatus on which Soviet man took his first step into space by performing an orbital flight around the Earth.

By the way, the visitors to the pavilion also had the opportunity of simulating such a flight. Anyone so minded could take a ten-minute "trip" into space on a "ship" that was shaped like a gigantic lens. The visitor took his place in a ship's chair, the lights went out, and—takeoff. As he looked out through the portholes he could see gleaming stars, the flashing of meteorites, and down below Earth receded while out there ahead the Moon grew larger. The polyscreens and special apparatus created the illusion of a cosmic flight.

The first lunar capsule made by Soviet scientists and special panoramas of the Moon and Venus were there as well. Once in the "Lunar Chamber," the visitors saw, for instance, as though close to them, the surface of the Moon, the stars and the Earth, as they would appear to the eye of people standing on the Moon.

The Soviet Union is one of the greatest maritime powers. An illuminated electrical map of the world had traced out on it the routes of the Soviet merchant fleet, which links the U.S.S.R. with eight hundred ports in 92 countries. The map also detailed the scientific and ichthyological research conducted by the Soviet Union in the world's oceans.

The roar of the engines of the passenger super-aircraft Ty-144 could be heard in one of the open spaces of the pavilion. This aircraft is able to carry more than 120 passengers from Moscow to Montreal in three and a half hours. There was always a large crowd, particularly of young people, grouped around the 39-foot-long working model of this super-airliner.

While on the upper platforms of the Soviet pavilion the themes were the earth, aviation and space, there was the lapping of the sea down below. Here one could see in a tank with bluish water the lazy beating of the fins of authentic sturgeon from the Volga. They were brought here by the fliers of Aeroflot from far-away Astrakhan. Crowds of visitors riveted their eyes, from the handrails around the tank, on the life of the living "factories of black caviar."

A great deal of interest is now being shown in the exploration of seas and oceans. Such exploration makes it feasible to solve the problems both of feeding future generations and of the shortage of fresh water, which is already besetting many countries. Interesting in this connection was the Soviet Union's model of an atomic reactor situated near Mangishlak, on the shore of the Caspian Sea. A portion of the electric power produced by this reactor is employed there for the desalinization of sea water.

Which of the thousands and thousands of exhibits in the Soviet pavilion attracted the greatest interest? Let us hear what the *Chicago Daily News* had to say:

It is hardly possible to answer this in one word. The exposition was so big and so varied—from children's ingenuous drawings to the most sophisticated space vehicles, from sensitive devices for detecting cancer tumors to ancient icons, from rich carpets to power station models. Some 10,000 exhibits gave the visitor a view of the Soviet Union today and a glimpse of its coming tomorrow.

The principal surprise that visitors experienced on touring the national pavilion of the U.S.S.R. was their extraordinary impression of a country only a few decades ago poor and backward having become an advanced industrial power.

All for the Sake of Man, For the Benefit of Man. People are strong when united. People are strong when they work for the benefit of humanity. People are strong when they realize that they have open to them all the avenues leading to the full realization of their capabilities, and for the embodiment of their creative ideas.

The map of France made of precious stones exhibited by Russia at the Paris World Exposition in 1900 was interesting as a specimen of the masterful skill of Russian craftsmen. It was rich only in terms of the materials that went into its making. The map of the Soviet Union in the pavilion of the U.S.S.R. was excellent not only in terms of its form but also in terms of its content.

The map of Estonia was forged out of copper, a layer of velvety sand represented the desert, and against this background the map of Turkmenia was fashioned out of organic glass with appliqués showing the growth of the principal branches of the Republic's national economy. In the map of Armenia the cities were marked off against a background of natural landscape, as were also the locations of mineral deposits, industrial projects, power lines, transportation routes, irrigated land areas, new construction projects and monuments of ancient Armenian architecture. Maps, maps—maps of all the Republics, revealing in concrete terms the theme of the Soviet pavilion, which was "All for the Sake of Man, For the Benefit of Man."

At the Paris Exposition, Central Asia was represented by the cloaks of the Emir of Bukhara, and by paintings depicting exotic landscapes. In Montreal, however, the Exposition told the story of the achievements of the Central Asian Soviet Republics, of cotton and oil, of the gold deposits, and of the construction of the largest gas pipeline in the world connecting Central Asia with the central regions of the country.

Central Asia boasts the longest artificial river in the world, the Kara Kum Canal. This Canal, which now measures 1,460 kilometers, will eventually be nearly identical in length, for example, with the St. Lawrence River, on the islands of which the International Exposition in Montreal was situated. The waters will come pouring into regions where life is unknown. This made it necessary to carry out a number of projects seventeen times greater in scope than the earthworks carried out on the site of the Panama Canal. This is understandable, because when completed the Kara Kum Canal will irrigate an area equal to that of all irrigated lands in Tunisia, Algeria and Morocco. The navigable portion of the Kara Kum Canal from the River Amu-Darya to Ashkhabad exceeds the overall length of the Suez, Panama, Kiel, Volga-Don, White Sea-Baltic Canals and the Moscow-Volga Canal.

"All for the sake of man!"—and that means not only the new industrial face of Soviet Russia. It also means the memory of what was its past and its history. This is the reason why, when speaking of the Kara Kum Canal, one must never fail to underscore the fact that its use for navigation opens up new prospects for tourism. Of great interest to tourists is the opportunity it affords of becoming acquainted with the monuments of the ancient culture of the East, such as the castle that goes back to the era of early feudalism (eleventh to twelfth centuries) and the majestic mausoleum of Sultan Sandzhar in the vicinity of Mara Mountain, the Mosque of Astan-Baba (twelfth to fourteenth centuries), and lastly the excavations of the period of the Parthian tsars in the vicinity of Ashkhabad.

At the world exposition in Paris, 1900, tsarist Russia introduced the Russian North to the world by displaying only a few animal skins, as though it had no human population. In the pavilion of the U.S.S.R., on the other hand, the population was represented by accounts of geologists, of people who are engaged in the cutting of the Yakut diamonds, and by the model of Aikhal, the northern city under a glass roof which is due to be built above the Arctic Circle. In the exhibit of the country's minerals a prominent place was given to the nearly 1,500-pound block of mica found on the spurs of the Aldan Uplands, in the Timpton mine. The Montreal exposition also featured specimens of the work of the world-famous Yakut bone carvers, such as that of the Honored Artist of the Yakut Autonomous Soviet Socialist Republic (Y.A.S.S.R.), S. Nesterov, People's Artist of Yakutia A. Fyoedorov, and People's Artist of the R.S.F.S.R. and of the Y.A.S.S.R., T. Ammosov.

In the Russian pavilion at the Paris Exposition one could not find even as much as a mention of the Ukraine or Byelorussia. A reference to the Donets Coal Basin was confined to the story of the then newly established industrial center. Today both the Ukraine and Byelorussia stand on a par with the most highly developed countries of the world. They are also members of the United Nations.

In the Ukraine more than 2,400 large-scale industrial enterprises have been constructed in recent years alone. New branches of industry, such as aircraft, the automotive industry, the instrument-making industry, radio electronics, the chemical industry, the gas industry and many others have been developed and are growing rapidly. In terms of production of cast iron, steel, rolled iron, and in terms of output of natural gas and iron ore, and the output of Diesel locomotives for standard-gauge railroad lines, the Ukraine holds first place in Europe. In terms of coal mining, iron ore yields, and the casting of pig iron and steel on a per capita basis, she has outdistanced even the United States of America.

The Ukrainian S.S.R. stands out in the international market by virtue of her exports of over a thousand different types of items to 81 countries.

Among the exhibits of the pavilion of the Soviet Union in Montreal the Donbass, or pearl of the Ukraine, drew special attention. A large-scale diorama of the Donbass gave an account of the giant strides with which the country's oldest coal basin had forged ahead through the years of Soviet power.

In the section dealing with "Power and Electrification" there was a large photo-montage of the engine room of the recently completed Dnieper thermal power station, the largest in the U.S.S.R. The Ukraine possesses a widespread electric power network.

The section dealing with the ferrous metals industry had an exhibit designed by the associates of the E.O. Paton Institute of Electrical Welding in Kiev of an electrical-slag smelting plant. There was also a model of the world's largest furnace, under construction in Krivoy Rog, which is to have an annual output of as much pig iron as the aggregate smelted annually in Turkey, Denmark and Norway combined.

The Ukrainian S.S.R. is not only a republic with a mighty industrial complex but it is also the largest grain and animal produce center and one of the principal sugar beet regions.

The honor of representing the agriculture of the country at EXPO 67 fell to the collective farm named after the Twenty-second Congress of the C.P.S.U. in the village of Shlyakho-vaya, which is headed by Hero of Socialist Labor V. M. Kavun. This diversified agricultural enterprise has been achieving high yields in grain and industrial crops and produces a considerable output of livestock. Here every hectare of soil yields more than 550 rubles of income.

An illuminated electrical model in Montreal showed the modern village community of Shlyakhovaya. Here one found a palace of culture, clubs, schools, children's institutions, dining halls, shops and public services. In recent years alone more than five hundred families moved into new houses there. The members of the collective farm have personal automobiles, motorcycles and refrigerators. There is an aggregate of more than forty thousand books in the public libraries of Shlyakhovaya.

The achievements of the people of the Ukraine in the sphere of culture were richly illustrated at the Montreal exposition. While 70 per cent of the people of the Ukraine were illiterate prior to the October Revolution the goal now being pursued is to ensure a complete secondary education to the entire younger generation. In the Ukraine, out of every 100 workers, 54 have a higher or secondary education. Every third person is involved in obtaining an education. The exhibit of the Kiev State University, which bears the name of Taras Shevchenko, gave an account of the organization of training for highly qualified specialists in the Republic. Special stands were devoted to the development of professional, technological and general education in the Ukrainian S.S.R.

Visitors to the Soviet pavilion learned that in the Ukrainian S.S.R. there are some 26,000 clubs, houses and palaces of culture, 27,000 film projectors and tens of thousands of libraries in operation. Some 2.5 million people participate in amateur artistic circles.

Many collectives of Byelorussian industrial enterprises also sent their exhibits to EXPO 67, among them the Minsk instrument-making enterprises, clock and porcelain works, the Borisov Dzerzhinsky Glassworks and the Neman glassworks, the Orsha flax combine and dozens of enterprises of the light and food-stuffs industries, of the building materials industry and the studios of the artistic fund of the Byelorussian S.S.R.

The achievements of the peoples of the Soviet Union could not but attract the attention of their countrymen who for one reason or another live abroad. On May 20, 1967, the Day of Soviet Armenia was celebrated in the Soviet pavilion in Montreal. For the occasion a delegation of the Republic arrived, headed by the Chairman of the Council of Ministers of the Armenian S.S.R., B. A. Muradyan.

Fate dealt with the Armenian people in such a way that thousands of its sons and daughters lived beyond the borders of sunny Aiyastan, the native land of the Armenians. There are even some ten thousand of them today in Montreal.

Many of them, bearing bread and salt and wearing their national costumes, went out to meet the delegation of Soviet Armenia at the Montreal airport. The local Armenian colony formed an eight-man commission for the purpose of assuring the active participation of the Armenians residing in Canada in all of the events organized in connection with the celebration of Armenia's National Day.

The meeting on May 17 in which more than 800 Armenians living abroad participated was most interesting. With solemn attention they listened to the address of B. A. Muradyan who spoke of the rebirth of the ancient Armenian people and how it was increasing its material and spiritual wealth.

A 128-man delegation of American Armenians who had arrived that very day also attended the meeting. The editor of the newspaper *Lraper,* Vagan Gazaryan (U.S.A.), declared on behalf of his companions that they had come there for the express purpose of seeing the pavilion of the Soviet Union. Addressing his countrymen, the composer Ambartsumyan Berberyan (U.S.A.) declared that the time had come to break all links with those who bring injury to the common cause of the Armenian people, that one must not be a spectator from afar but contribute to every new advance of the native land.

One of the members of the action committee of the Canadian Armenians proposed to his countrymen that along with their friends and relatives they participate in the inaugural festivities of the Day of Soviet Armenia and in the solemn ceremony of the hoisting of its State colors.

It appeared as if all the Armenians arrived simultaneously at the Soviet pavilion on May 20. The management of the exposition had to issue to them one thousand special passes. After the playing of the state hymn of the Armenian S.S.R. there were loud cheers: "Long live Soviet Armenia! Long live the Motherland!"

On that occasion the Soviet pavilion assumed a very special appearance. All around stood the exhibits telling of the life, the work and creative genius of the people of Armenia. Melodious Armenian airs could be heard and films from the Yerevan studios were shown in the motion picture hall, while models displayed to the guests the colorful national costumes of Armenia.

The Chairman of the Council of Ministers of the Republic, B. A. Muradyan, addressed the guests, giving them a warm welcome.

The visitors extended a particular welcome to the artists, among whom appeared such world-famed personalities as the singer Goar Gasparyan, the performer of national dances Flora Topchan, and the Komitas Quartet. A real hit of the National Day program was the televised quiz game "Do you know Armenia?" Absolutely correct answers were given by 69 people. The jury was in a predicament, and the viewers had to be enlisted in making a fair distribution of the prizes. A six-year-old Montreal youngster, Karapet Sukasyan, was entrusted with drawing the lots, and the first prize, a gold watch stamped "Made in Armenia" was given to Miss Anaid Chamuryan, a twenty-five-year-old resident of Montreal who had come to Canada from Egypt five years before.

"This is an unforgettable event in my life," said the prize-winner, "I am very happy. The first thing I will do is to write a letter to my friend in Yerevan and I will tell her that this watch will always give me Yerevanian time. . . ."

The first National Day was celebrated by Soviet Estonia on May 6. On May 14 Turkmenia Day was celebrated, on May 20 Armenian S.S.R. Day, on May 28 Tadzhik Day and so on. The National Day of the U.S.S.R. was celebrated on August 15.

While at the Paris Exposition of 1900 Russia was represented by people in uniform, in 1967, at the Montreal exposition, it was represented by all the peoples of the Soviet Union.

Azerbaidzhan chefs were represented in Montreal by Kuli Melikov who had been awarded the Order of Lenin. For a period of nearly forty years he had been working in public catering establishments. Only once, when the Motherland had to be defended from the Nazi invaders, did he leave his work, to take up arms. His valorous deeds in battle brought him four decorations. In 1967 Melikov received a gold medal at the Exhibition of U.S.S.R. National Economic Achievement. This native of Baku was also rewarded for the high craftsmanship he demonstrated at the contest of the best culinary artists which took place in 1966 in Moscow.

One of the guides of the Soviet pavilion at the world exposition in Montreal was twenty-year-old Khamida Khalmatova, a fourth-year student at the Foreign Languages Department of the Ferghana Pedagogical Institute. She is of Kirghiz nationality, but has full mastery of the Uzbek, Tadzhik, Russian and English languages. Her parents are members of the Pobeda collective farm in the Uch-Kurgan District. There are ten children in the family and Khamida is the third among them. Her elder brother Rakhmon Khalmatov is working as dispatcher in the mines, while the second brother, Sharif, is a driver.

Soviet people carefully cherish their national traditions and the treasures of native culture. The exhibits of the Soviet pavilion displayed works of the decorative and applied arts and of the national crafts of all the constituent republics.

Baltic amber, Georgian metal embossing, wood carving, laces and carpeting, all of this had a strong appeal for the visitor. Most admired were the master craftsmen who did their work right there in the pavilion. A large crowd gathered around the woodcarver from Bogorodsk, the woman painter from Khokhloma and the lace-maker from the Vologda Artel.

The Vologda lace-maker's deft, careful hands and her keen eye were more than a match for the complexity of the tracery of frost painted on a January window, for the marvelous delicacy of glistening snowflakes and for the majestic simplicity and mistiness of the northern landscape.

The lace-maker displayed a tablecloth, light in weight, and tenderly white like the foam of the sea. Shining out of the tablecloth was a radiant sun, while scattered through the scenery were young spruce which parted company like a bevy of tiny friends and among them frozen in trepidation were round-eyed deer with upturned horns tilted in watchful poses.

Alongside the former was another tablecloth, one that could be boldly described as the height of lace-making. It was the handiwork of another lace-maker, Victoria Elfina. The enormous panorama, nearly ten feet in diameter, portrayed the austere beauty of the north. The entire pattern was conceived as a play of snowflakes. It was difficult to comprehend how human hands could ever manage to weave such an image of beauty!

The works of masters of painting with lacquers, from Palekh, Mstera and Fedoskino, were remarkable to behold.

Wood carving is a traditional form of Russian folk art. There were lathed and polished boxes made in Zagorsk and Kalinin, and simple but aesthetically devised chests, cigar and cigarette cases produced in the Kirov Region by master craftsmen who like no others are capable of identifying the quality of pieces of timber. The Daghestan village of Untsukul is famed for hardwood objects with metal inlays.

Such artistic crafts as the painting of Khokhloma, the fashioning of knives at Pavlovo and of wooden dolls at Maidan are centuries old. They have won a considerable number of citations and medals in international expositions, such as those of Paris and Brussels, London and Rio de Janeiro, Leipzig and Cairo. Khokhloma sends its handicraft wares into thirty countries throughout the world.

The exhibit showed the finest work of the bone carvers of Uelen, such as those of Tukkai, Emkul, Khukhutan, Vukvutagin and the artist Yanku. It included such works as "The Hunter and the Deer," "Dog's Harness," "The Walrus

Hunt," "Bear-Hunt with Spear" and others. Many of them have been awarded prizes and citations at expositions both in the Soviet Union and abroad. The works of artists such as Tukkai, Khukhutan and Vukvutagin have been purchased by the largest museums both within the country and abroad. Miniature works of art made out of walrus tusks are highly valued in the world market.

Well represented in Montreal were the jeweller's art, which has preserved the best traditions of the country, the deeply rooted folk art of embroidery, the majolica of Skopy and the paintings with cobalt, salts and gold, the handwoven products of Cherepovets, and the handicrafts of the Kholmogory, Tobol and Khotkovo bone carvers and much else.

The professional artist was represented here by paintings and works of sculpture. A bas-relief of Lenin by G. and I. Nerod seemed to be the center of the pavilion. Visitors were attracted by such canvases as "On the Snows," by Nissky, "The Expanse" by A. Deineka, "Portrait of Konenkov" by P. Korin, and "Hoisting the Flag" by G. Korzhev. Among the sculptures deserving of mention were "Portrait of a Partisan Girl" by V. Mukhina, "Fight to the Last Ditch" and "Portrait of Sholokhov" by E. Vuchetich, and "Portrait of Chekhov" by M. Anikushin. Gracing this section were stained-glass panels of crushed glass entitled "Motherland" and "Hymn to Labor" by the Lithuanian masters Stoshkus, Gabrauskas and Morkunas. These windows were unique in terms of their technical excellence.

It must be stated that the response to the works of art on display in the Soviet pavilion was quite consistent. The visitors were unanimous in their comments, and they did not stint such terms as "most beautiful," "We welcome the Russians," "unusual," etc. Many people observed with pleasure the realism of Soviet fine art, and its optimistic life-affirming tone.

A special place was assigned to the exhibit of books. The object of this section was to show the diversity of multinational literature published in the Soviet Union. For this purpose the books that came for the Montreal exposition embraced all the Union Republics as well as special, artistically produced children's books and other editions. In order that visitors might have an opportunity to become acquainted with the first emergence of book-printing in Russia, unique Russian volumes by Ivan Fyodorov antedating the eighteenth century were displayed in the hall, along with replicas of the Gospels from the eleventh to the fourteenth centuries.

The total number of titles displayed there by the central publishing houses and those of the various republics came to about 800. Among them were books and albums, sets of reproductions and prints, picture postcards and booklets.

The exhibit displayed a wide array of fiction. There were collected works of the classics, of Soviet writers and writers of the national republics of the Soviet Union, and numerous single-volume editions illustrated with consummate art.

Here one could find side by side the works of Pushkin, Tolstoy, Chekhov, Gorky, Mayakovsky, Yesenin, Sholokhov, Simonov, Lavrenev, Rylsky, Gonchar, Aitamatov, Mezhelaitis, Ovanesyan and others.

Samples of children's literature were also displayed on the stands. Naturally, the children's book section included the *Tales* of Pushkin, the *Fables* of Krylov and other works. The attention of the visitor was attracted by the anthology *The Children of the World* which was a compilation of stories by a number of writers for children of twenty-five different countries, along with toy books containing stories, pop-up books, and a large volume of children's folklore designed by the artist Y. Vasnetsov.

Art, theater and music lovers also found a good deal of interest at the Soviet book exhibit.

Visitors were introduced to the history and monuments of Soviet culture in such books as *Vladimir, Bogolyubovo, Suzdal* by N. Voronin, the most outstanding researcher and expert on the architecture of these ancient towns; in the album entitled *Old Russian Paintings* which gave an account of the most recent discoveries in this sphere; in the album *Kizhi* with poetic photos of the unique cathedrals built by the masters of Russian architecture; and other works.

Remarkable collections of works of art were shown in the albums *The Tretyakov State Gallery, The Russian Museum, The Hermitage* and *The Pushkin State Art Museum.* Albums and books such as *Maya Plisetskaya, Arkady Raikin, The Ber-yozka Ensemble,* and *The National Dance Company of the U.S.S.R.* told the stories of the collectives and prominent figures in the theater arts whose fame reaches far beyond the borders of the Soviet Union.

About one-third of the exhibit was devoted to scientific, technical and school books.

It is interesting to note that this was the first time in the history of such expositions that an international pavilion was set up for fine arts exhibits. Museums of thirty different countries sent their paintings to the Exposition. Fourteen works of art taken from museums in the Soviet Union were highly successful with the visitors. The paintings "Lenin in the Smolny Institute" by Brodsky and "The Defense of Petrograd" by Deineka attracted much interest. There was always a large crowd surrounding them. Visitors lingered long before them exchanging views and expressing their frank approval. Great praise was lavished on two sculptures, "The Paving Block—Weapon of the Proletariat," by Shcadr and "The First Swallows," by Mikenas, which stood in the International Park of Sculpture, out in the open. Rarely seen icons were another focal point. Among them the icon "The Birth of Christ," belonging to the school of Andreu Rublev and on loan from the Tretyakov Gallery, stood out most prominently.

An International Festival of the Arts was held while the exposition was in progress. Representatives of many countries participated in this Festival, among them the Vienna Opera, La Scala of Milan, the French Grand-Opera Ballet, the Stockholm and Hamburg Operas, and symphony orchestras from Great Britain, the U.S.A., France and Czechoslovakia.

The Soviet Union was represented at this Festival by a

number of ensembles. Early in August the ensemble of the Bolshoi Theater offered to the public its spectacles *Boris Godunov, The Legend of the City of Kitezh, War and Peace, The Queen of Spades,* and *Prince Igor.* The singers Vishnevskaya, Milashkina, Petrov, Andzhaparidze, Ognivtsev and others appeared in these performances. At the same time six concerts were given in Toronto by the Bolshoi Ballet Ensemble.

A gala concert was given on August 15 to celebrate the Day of the Soviet Union. Participating in it were artists of the Union Republics also. Soviet artists performed in the programs given to celebrate the Day of the Ukraine, the Day of Byelorussia, and the Day of the R.S.F.S.R.

The International Competition of Vocalists, one of the programs given under the aegis of EXPO 67, ended in Montreal on June 2. The winner of this competition was Yuri Mazurok of the Soviet Union.

Ranking second in the competition was the Rumanian singer Marina Krilovich, and third, an American, Gwendolyn Killibrew.

The soloists of Leningrad's Kirov Opera and Ballet Theater, Vladimir Atlantov and Galina Kovaleva came out in fourth and seventh place, respectively.

On a screen in the Soviet pavilion visitors could view the films that had become classics of the cinema, such as *Potyomkin, Mother, Earth* and others. Current cinema in the Soviet Union was represented by scores of the best films produced most recently. Among them were *War and Peace, Everyday Fascism, The Soldier's Father, Nobody Wanted to Die, The Quick and the Dead, Ballad of a Soldier, The Shades of Forgotten Ancestors* and others.

The Soviet cinema also participated in the work of the international pavilions. The Science pavilion housed the displays of the scientific achievements of all countries in every part of the world. Shown here were Soviet pictures about the cosmos, the polar regions and the discovery of the secrets of the ocean. A special pavilion was built, known as the "Pavilion of Youth." Here also Soviet films were shown. They included works of cinematic art produced by directors up to thirty years of age, and films concerning the life of Soviet young people. "Labyrinth" was the name given to the cinema pavilion. On a special multiple screen, where films of different countries were shown, special films about Soviet cosmonauts, hydrofoils, the Pioneer camp Artek, Russian ballet, and the world-famous clown Oleg Popov could be seen.

Among other exhibits, visitors to the Soviet pavilion also had the opportunity to see Russian fashions in clothes. The fashion show of the designers of the Leningrad Fashion House was accompanied by a color film which showed Russian architecture of the North, of the ancient Kizhi, of Solovky and white-stoned Novgorod. Against this background, the models displayed clothes sprinkled with the flavor of old Russia's national costumes. Designers adorned smart evening gowns with embroidery featuring pearls and bugle beads. One of the fashions on display was called the "Russian Wooden Doll." It consisted of a woolen topcoat and a bright cashmere dress, graced with a kerchief.

The people of Russia have long been noted for their hospitality and lavish table. At the Paris world exposition of 1900, to be sure, this trait of their character was reflected only in the displays of the wine and liquor pavilion and in the tavern that stood in the courtyard of the Central Russian pavilion.

The Soviet Moskva restaurant, with a capacity of 1,100, including a café and a bar, threw open its doors to visitors of the Montreal Exposition on opening day. In the comfortable premises appointed in genuine Russian style, the people of Montreal and the large numbers of visitors to the Exposition had an opportunity to treat themselves to the favorite and most popular dishes of the peoples of the Soviet Union.

Seventeen chefs, acknowledged necromancers of the pot and griddle, performed veritable culinary miracles under the direction of the master chef, Grigory Yermilin.

On May 20 a special gala event was held to celebrate Moskva's one hundred thousandth guest. The finger of fate pointed at Eric Kahn, who had come there with his wife from New Jersey. The chief pastry cook, Afanasy Polyakov, brought a very special cake to the table at which the couple was seated.

"You are a magician!" Kahn said to him. "I am sure that if you open one of the bottles, a genie will leap out of it." It seemed, in fact, that the touch of the miraculous was very much in evidence on this occasion. Eric Kahn turned out to be also a pastry cook by profession. Having partaken of Russian dishes, he asked to have a look at the way his Russian colleagues went about their work. All of the equipment in the restaurant had been brought from the Soviet Union. The kitchenware bore the trademarks of Kiev, Moscow, Ashkhabad and Leningrad. The rare spices had been shipped from the republics. The pastry cooks brought along with them even the beechwood boards on which were distributed batches of dough for cakes, pastry and doughnuts. The beechwood boards have the same effect on the dough as oak has on brandy; that is, they give it aroma.

From Genoa to Montreal. There was a time when fables about bears taking their strolls down the streets of Moscow were current among western "specialists" in Russian affairs. This sort of treatment of the Soviet Union dates back to the very first day of the victorious October Revolution in 1917.

"No country in the world has in its government a Minister of Foreign Affairs so insane as to consider talking with the Council of People's Commissars . . ."

"They will scornfully ignore all the declarations of the new government . . ."

"The conclusion of peace with Germany and 'Smolny Socialism' will transform Russia into a weak, enfeebled country which will in actual fact come under the domination of Deutsche Bank and Morgan . . ."

These were statements made by the Mensheviks and the Right-S.R.'s. The official press of the Entente without exception echoed these statements. A British newspaper declared categorically on November 8, 1917:

"Lenin's followers, be their existence long-lived or short lived, are flagrant enemies of the Entente. . . . We can have no dealings with them."

President Poincaré of France made the following notation in his diary on November 8:

"I came out in favor of an understanding with the Allies not to recognize the new government . . ."

The press of the neutral countries, making a pretense of "objectivity" and "restraint" in their judgment of what was occurring in Russia, pointed out that "orderly governments find it difficult to enter into relations with governments of, so to say, a volcanic nature."

On November 8, 1917, the Soviet government called on all belligerent countries to proceed to immediate negotiations for an armistice and the inauguration of peace talks. However, the ambassadors of the Entente, convened on November 9 by American Ambassador Francis, dean of the diplomatic corps in Russia, expressing the positions of their respective governments, adopted a decision not to reply to the Soviet note.

The unwillingness to establish contacts with the new government went to ludicrous lengths. The British Ambassador, George Buchanan, preferred to walk rather than ask the Soviet government to furnish him a routine pass that would put a car at his disposal. He feared that this might be tantamount to a "de facto recognition" by Britain of the Soviet of People's Commissars.

On the civil war fronts, soldiers of the revolution, battling at times with but one rifle for every three men, buried forever all the hopes entertained by the foreign monopolies that regarded Russia as their own preserve of restoring the old order. Both the domestic and the international counterrevolution counted heavily in their struggle against Soviet power on hunger, typhus and economic disarray. The parliaments of the leading capitalist countries rubber-stamped resolutions banning trade with the newly founded Soviet Union. In their opinion, an economic blockade was bound to accomplish what neither the White generals nor the crack troops of the interventionists were able to do.

Four years of severe trials and struggle demonstrated to the whole world the viability of the young republic. The political leaders of the West who realized that without the participation of Soviet Russia the economic rebirth of Europe was practically impossible were forced to take this into account. The capitalist world was forced to recognize the land of the Soviets. Later events confirmed Lenin's prediction made in 1921, when he wrote: "There is a force, more powerful than the wishes, will and the decision of any of the governments or classes that are hostile to us. That force is world general economic relations, which compel them to make contact with us."

Representatives of Soviet Russia participated for the first time in an international conference that opened on April 10, 1922, in the Italian city of Genoa. The delegations of the capitalist countries sought to form a solid bloc for the purpose of a de facto nullification of the conquests of the October Revolution by means of "general demands."

The Soviet delegation in Genoa adopted a firm position based on principles. A clear-cut program was formulated and its fundamental ideas became the foundation of Soviet foreign policy. Equal cooperation of states with differing social and economic systems, unconditional recognition of the socialist system of ownership, a workable plan for the restoration of the economy in keeping with the interests of all countries, a demand for the calling of a World Congress in which world labor organizations would participate to deal with the question of the establishment of universal peace—this is what the representatives of the Soviet Union proposed, in contrast with the proposals of the bourgeois governments.

The Soviet proposals met with a hostile reception. It was then that people throughout the world heard from the rostrum of the conference the truth about the land of the victorious proletariat. The young Soviet republic came into the international arena, defending and asserting the right of all nations to freedom, equality and the peaceful pursuit of work. The curtain of silence, lies and vilification was torn away! This is the historical significance of Genoa.

The firm position adopted by Soviet Russia caused consternation in the ranks of the capitalist governments that had but recently presented a solid front. As early as April 16, 1922, a treaty was signed in Rapallo, near Genoa, between Soviet Russia and Germany. Both sides renounced all mutual claims that had arisen in consequence of the war. Germany did not insist on the return of the nationalized enterprises. At the same time diplomatic relations were restored between the two countries and they accorded each other most-favored-nation treatment in their trade relations.

This exploded like a bombshell about the heads of the bourgeois governments participating in the Genoa Conference. It became apparent that the economic and political blockade of the Soviet country had been broken. The Treaty of Rapallo opened the path to subsequent treaties and agreements with other capitalist countries.

A period of forty-five years has since elapsed. The Soviet Union now holds fifth place among the largest trading powers of the world, trading with some one hundred countries in every part of the world, and of these it maintains long-term trade agreements with seventy-three countries.

The development of trade relations with the countries of the socialist camp has been most successful, and the latter accounts for some 70 per cent of the total foreign trade of the Soviet Union. Trade agreements concluded with them in 1966 provided for reciprocal commodity deliveries for a term of five years. A further expansion of this trade turnover is anticipated.

Beyond the borders of the socialist system, the largest trading partners of the U.S.S.R. are India and the United Arab Republic. Trade with other countries of the "Third World" is also gaining rapidly. Thus, from 1955 to 1965, the foreign trade of the U.S.S.R. with the developing countries of Asia, Africa and Latin America increased more than sixfold.

Trade has expanded with Finland, Great Britain, France, Japan, Italy, Sweden and other industrially developed capitalist countries. Sober-thinking representatives of the business circles of other countries seek a broadening of trade and economic ties with the U.S.S.R.

Here is an account, for example, of trade relations with Finland, one of the steady partners of the Soviet Union:

On February 10, 1967, in Moscow, the Minister for Foreign Trade of the U.S.S.R., N. S. Patolichev and the Minister of Foreign Affairs of Finland, A. Karjalainen, signed an agreement establishing a Permanent Intergovernmental Soviet-Finnish Commission on Economic Cooperation.

The conclusion of this agreement by the governments of the U.S.S.R. and Finland was based on the successful and diversified development of economic ties between the two countries, a desire to strengthen these ties further and a mutual wish to utilize to an even greater extent the economic possibilities of cooperation arising out of the structural peculiarities of the economies and the geographical position of the two countries.

In addition to trade relations predicated on long-term agreements concluded for periods of five years, other forms of economic intercourse are also developing, such as the construction of a metallurgical combine in Finland with the technological cooperation of the U.S.S.R., the construction by Finnish firms of a hydroelectric power station on the borderlands of the U.S.S.R., cooperation in the field of power production, railroad transportation, the reconstruction of the Saimaa Canal, and barter transactions in regions situated along the border.

To ignore the Soviet Union as a trade partner means first and foremost to bring injury to oneself. Many capitalist governments have already reached this sober conclusion. Nevertheless, many "hotheads" in the West keep forgetting this and seek to practice a policy of discrimination against the Soviet Union. It is not too difficult to establish the undesirable effects of such attempts; one need but recall the NATO embargo on the export of large-diameter pipe to the U.S.S.R. The fact is not only, as *The New York Times* was able to ascertain, that the Soviet Union boosted its own domestic production of such pipes with a diameter of 40 inches from only a slight quantity in 1961 to 600 thousand tons in 1965, and at the present time is not by any means dependent on the supply of pipes from abroad. Another point is also evident, namely that today it is not possible to halt the development of economic ties between states with different social and economic systems. In 1966 the NATO Council was forced to revise its decision, which once again demonstrated to the whole world the hopelessness of a policy of economic isolation directed against the U.S.S.R.

In the exports of tsarist Russia, the proportion of agricultural products came to about 70 per cent, while at present 90 per cent of Soviet exports represent industrial goods, including industrial raw materials. This includes jet and turbojet aircraft, helicopters, products of the optical and instrument-making industry, complex pharmaceutical preparations and many other items which bear evidence of the high technical level of Soviet industry.

At the World Exposition of 1900, the Russian section, in the nature of a national symbol, displayed a pyramid consisting of bast sandals in a profusion of styles, bast matting, mat-bags, garish prints, bast fiber, and other objects of that sort. However, in Montreal at EXPO 67, the displays took in models of space ships, of the atomic icebreaker *Lenin,* and of luniks. The Russian words "sputnik" and "lunik" have become firmly entrenched in the languages of peoples in different parts of the world.

Peace in the World. "Nations want to live in peace and they are entitled to it"—this is the message that rang out in the earliest diplomatic notes of the Soviet government. The call for peace was made by the first workers' and peasants' government in the world in the earliest hours of the existence of the Soviet government. Hence, the first legislative enactment was the Decree on Peace. The Soviet government abrogated all inequitable treaties of the tsarist regime, renounced all the rights and privileges it enjoyed in other countries and formulated a broad program of peaceful coexistence and economic cooperation with the capitalist states.

The struggle for peace, which from the very outset became the pivot of the policy pursued by the Soviet government, was imperative not only as a demand of the peoples who had been driven to the point of utter exhaustion and ravaged by the war, but also as a direct consequence of the new approach to the solution of domestic and international problems by the proletariat that had won victory in one country. It served as a patent confirmation of the idea that the struggle for peace was linked to the struggle for socialism.

By the very nature of socialism, a genuine peace policy is organically native to a socialist state. "An end to wars, peace among nations and the cessation of plunder and violence—this is our idea," repeated Lenin.

This in fact determined the basic stages of Soviet foreign policy. The foundation was laid with the promulgation of the Decree on Peace, the proclamation of entirely new principles of international policy, the struggles waged for the withdrawal of revolutionary Russia from the imperialist war and the nullification of "the humiliating and predatory" Brest-Litovsk peace treaty of 1918, which permitted the Soviet republic to have an indispensable "breathing spell"; the granting of independence to the outlying national regions of the former Russian empire and the establishment of good-neighborly relations with them; the proclamation by the Soviet state of the course of peaceful coexistence; the Genoa Conference of 1922 that broke the blockade imposed on Soviet Russia. Then followed the diplomatic recognition of the land of the Soviets in the mid-twenties by the Western powers. This started with France, whose government was then headed by the far-seeing statesman Edouard Herriot, was followed by Great Britain when the Labourites for the first time came to the helm of the government, and continued to the establishment of normal diplomatic relations with the United States of America, at the initiative of Franklin Delano Roosevelt, in 1938. The Soviet Union adhered to this policy during the period when it was ignored by the important international organizations. Among these was the League of Nations, which was founded following the First World War. The U.S.S.R. was admitted to this organization of pathetic memory, which was incapable of solving most of the problems which were debated there, on September 18, 1934. The policy of friendship with the countries of the East and the conclusion with them of the first equitable treaties in the history of the world (in February 1921 with Iran and Afghanistan, in March of the same year with Turkey, on May 31, 1924, with China and on April 15 with Japan)— all of this represented only some of the landmarks in Soviet foreign policy up to the outbreak of the Second World War.

The principal efforts of the Soviet government were bent on the solution of the problems in the sphere of disarmament. It made an important proposal in this field at the session of the Genoa Conference. Subsequently, at the Geneva Conference in 1927 the U.S.S.R. brought forward a draft of the first agreement on the universal demobilization of land, sea and airborne military forces. Though it had no diplomatic relations with Washington at that time, the Soviet Union gave its strong support to the proposals of the then Secretary of State of the United States, Mr. Kellogg, concerning the renunciation of war as an instrument of national policy. Although the Soviet Union was not invited to be a party to the Kellogg-Briand Pact, it sent its People's Commissar (Minister) for Foreign Affairs to Paris and gave its adherence to the Pact four days later, and was the first to ratify it.

The government of the U.S.S.R. sponsored a plan to establish a system of collective security, and proposed to its European neighbors the signing of agreements defining aggression, to be followed by the signing of non-aggression pacts. When the Soviet Union was accorded membership in the League of Nations, it used its voice in behalf of an active struggle against German militarism. The Soviet government fought untiringly against the aggression of fascist Germany and Italy during the Spanish Civil War. The Soviet Union countered with its policy of collective security all efforts of the ruling circles of Great Britain and France to ensure their own security by resort to a policy of appeasement towards the fascist powers.

From the moment when Hitler's Germany attacked the U.S.S.R., up to the end of the Second World War, Soviet foreign policy was aimed at strengthening and expanding the anti-Hitler coalition and at crushing the fascist invaders. The consistently peace-loving policy adopted by the Soviet Union at the meetings of the Allied Powers (the Teheran Conference of 1943, the Crimean Conference in Yalta in 1945 and the Potsdam Conference of 1945) prompted the adoption at these conferences of resolutions which furthered the victorious conclusion of the war and formulated the important principles of the postwar system.

To commemorate the sojourn of President Roosevelt of the United States at the Crimean Conference in Yalta in 1945, one of the streets of this wonderful Black Sea town was named after him. It was at Yalta, in fact, that a decision was adopted concerning the establishment of an international organization for the maintenance of peace and security, and on April 25, 1945, a conference of the United Nations was scheduled to take place in San Francisco for the purpose of drafting the Charter of this organization. It was also in Yalta that an understanding was reached as to the voting procedure in the U.N. Security Council. The principle then adopted was subsequently incorporated into the Charter of the United Nations. It established that all matters of substance shall require for their adoption a unanimous vote of the permanent members of the Council (the U.S.A., the U.S.S.R., Great Britain, France and China).

It was also at the Yalta Conference that the "Declaration on Liberated Europe" was framed and signed, providing for the harmonization of the policies of the three powers, namely the U.S.S.R., the U.S.A., and Great Britain, and their joint action in the solution of political and economic problems of liberated Europe in keeping with democratic principles. The question of the western boundaries of Poland was also resolved.

After the end of the Second World War the Soviet Union continued the stubborn struggle for the consolidation of peace and international security. However, now the Soviet Union was no longer taking a hand in this alone in the world arena. The struggle against the rule of force, the defeat of Nazi Germany and its allies, Italy and Japan, the growth of the international prestige and influence of the U.S.S.R. brought about a renewed upsurge of the revolutionary movement in the world and the emergence of a world system of socialism.

Relations of a new kind were established between the Soviet Union and the new socialist states, based on proletarian internationalism, friendship and mutual assistance. Cooperation among these free nations manifests itself in all spheres of economic, political and cultural life. At the same time close relations of mutual support among the countries of the socialist camp constitute an important factor in the maintenance of the universal peace and security of nations.

The main concern of the Soviet Union throughout the postwar period has been and continues to be to prevent the unleashing of a new war in Europe, and to paralyze the forces that are seeking revenge for the defeat they suffered in the Second World War. In West Germany there are open avowals of discontent with the outcome of the war, and demands are being made for a revision of the European boundaries which have come to prevail since the war. At the same time, they are scrambling to lay their hands on weapons of mass destruction.

The Soviet Union stands firmly determined to ensure peace in Europe and it bases its policy in European affairs on the proposition that the postwar boundaries must be respected in every case, and that includes the boundaries between the two sovereign states, the German Democratic Republic and the Federal Republic of Germany. The Warsaw Treaty of 1955, which rallied the efforts of the socialist countries to ensure European security, represents an important step in the direction of guaranteeing the inviolability of these boundaries. The problems of the consolidation of peace in Europe and the means for achieving it are fully outlined in the Bucharest Declaration of 1966 adopted by the European socialist states participating in the Warsaw Treaty Organization and in the Declaration of the Conference of European Communist and Workers' Parties in Karlovy Vary in the year 1967. Putting forward a whole series of constructive proposals on vital questions of European security, the U.S.S.R. and the other socialist countries have also adopted measures aiming at consolidating their military might and political unity, realizing that only this will check the revanchists in their attempts to bring about a revision of the boundaries established under the Potsdam Agreement in 1945.

The Soviet Union actively aids national liberation movements. The swift disintegration of the colonial system has become one of the fundamental features of contemporary history. A tempestuous liberation movement has spread through the continent of Africa. In 1960 alone seventeen new and independent states came into being in Africa. There are at present dozens of countries that have recently gained their independence. Supporting national liberation efforts, the U.S.S.R. moved a resolution at the fifteenth session of the General Assembly of the United Nations in September 1960 calling for the immediate, complete and final abolition of colonialism, and the granting of freedom and independence to all oppressed peoples. The resolution of the Soviet Union received the support of the overwhelming majority of states. On

December 14, 1960, the General Assembly of the U.N. adopted the Declaration on the Abolition of Colonialism. Its significance is all the more important since there are countries that are still seeking to retain the old or to impose new colonial orders.

A year earlier (September 1959) the Soviet Union submitted for the consideration of the United Nations Organization a draft resolution concerning universal and complete disarmament. To eliminate the danger of war it is essential to destroy all types of weapons, including rockets and nuclear types of armament, to remove military bases on the territories of other nations, and to do away with all war propaganda. This was in fact the purport of the Soviet proposal. The U.N. General Assembly adopted a resolution approving the idea of universal and complete disarmament and calling on all states to work for its realization.

In the summer of 1963, in Moscow, the signing of a treaty between the U.S.S.R., the U.S.A. and Great Britain, with the participation of other countries (more than one hundred states affixed their signatures), banning nuclear tests in the atmosphere, in space and under water took place.

In recent years the main efforts of the Soviet government were directed towards preventing the proliferation of nuclear weapons in any form, shape or manner.

The foreign policy actions of the U.S.S.R., personal contacts between the statesmen of the Soviet Union and those of other countries, the mounting influence and the international prestige of the Soviet state, have led to the total annihilation of the myth of the would-be aggressiveness of the Soviet Union. At present the U.S.S.R. maintains diplomatic relations with 97 states, holds charter membership in the United Nations Organization, and is one of the five permanent members of the U.N. Security Council. It participates in many large international organizations, among them the International Labor Organization (ILO), the International Telecommunications Union (ITU), the Universal Postal Union (UPU), the World Health Organization (WHO), the United Nations Educational, Scientific and Cultural Organization (UNESCO), the International Atomic Energy Agency (IAEA), the Interparliamentary Union (IPU), the Warsaw Treaty Organization of 1955, and the Council for Mutual Economic Assistance (CMEA). In actual fact no one believes any longer today that NATO and other aggressive blocs have been created for the purpose of "defense." John Galbraith, professor at Harvard University, one-time adviser to President Kennedy, and former ambassador to India, wrote recently in the Paris daily *Figaro Littéraire* that the administration was proceeding on the premises of the cold war and a Soviet military threat. Today no one believes this any more. The Pentagon has lost its best ally in Europe, namely fear.

France has withdrawn from NATO and is pursuing its own foreign policy. The present orientation of Franco-Soviet relations is in keeping with the traditional feelings of friendship between the peoples of the two countries, and is based on the understanding of the role of each one of them in the question of peace and European affairs.

At the end of June 1966, the President of the French Republic paid a visit to the Soviet Union. This visit and the discussions between L. I. Brezhnev, A. N. Kosygin, N. V. Podgorny and General De Gaulle, to quote the very phrasing of the Soviet-French declaration adopted on the occasion, "represent a fundamental contribution to the development of concord between the Soviet Union and France, between the Soviet and the French peoples."

At the conclusion of these discussions between the top leaders of the U.S.S.R. and the President of the French Republic, two important agreements were signed in addition to the Soviet-French Declaration, namely an Agreement on Scientific, Technological and Economic Cooperation, and an Agreement on Cooperation in the Peaceful Uses of Outer Space.

In the course of the previous year other agreements were also concluded between the Soviet Union and France. In December 1966 a Consular Convention was signed. An Inter-Governmental Maritime Agreement concluded in April 1967 was intended to further the growth of shipping communication between the Soviet Union and France. In May a protocol was signed expanding air communications between the two countries, each of them being granted the right to fly across the territory of the other party to the agreement. A new agreement on cooperation in the sphere of the peaceful uses of atomic energy was signed in the same month.

In the autumn of 1967 regular color telecasts were inaugurated between the Soviet Union and France. This is, literally speaking, a visible result of the joint efforts of Soviet and French scientists, engineers and workers.

The rapprochement between the Soviet Union and France is not aimed at any third parties. Bringing about a détente in the strained international relations, and the consolidation of peace, primarily in Europe—such as the clear and patent aims of this rapprochement, which was articulated in joint Soviet and French documents. This was also underscored in the joint Soviet and French communiqués on the outcome of the visit to Moscow of French Premier Georges Pompidou, who was accompanied by the Minister of Foreign Affairs, Maurice Couve de Murville. Their visit lasted from July 3 to July 8, 1967.

The talks between the leaders of the Soviet Union and the Premier of France were conducted in an atmosphere of cordiality. Both countries expressed their satisfaction with the good relations existing between the Soviet Union and France, and observed that these friendly relations and the mutual understanding that is developing between the two countries and their cooperation in all spheres were conducive to the furthering of means for the peaceful adjustment of the critical problems besetting the world.

Such problems have become numerous today. Above all else the situations in the Near East and in South-East Asia are gravely disturbing at this time.

Once again peace is being disrupted by the explosion of

shells, bombs and the whistle of bullets. The war in Viet Nam, Israel's aggression against Arab lands—all of this leaves little cause for peace of mind.

In our nuclear age the question of war and peace takes on a special significance. Humanity will never forgive the statesmen who at this critical juncture fail to show enough fortitude to align themselves with the forces struggling to curb aggressors. Millions of people view with gratitude and hope the just and consistent struggle for peace waged by the U.S.S.R. and the other socialist countries.

In the Soviet Union war propaganda is officially banned. The law on the defense of peace enacted by the Supreme Soviet of the U.S.S.R. on March 12, 1951, branded war propaganda of any sort as a very grave crime against humanity.

8 AN AGE OF COMPETENT MASTERS

In 1921 the great French writer Anatole France said: ". . . Russia is a country where even the impossible comes true. The Bolsheviks are now bringing the impossible to its ultimate conclusion."

A country where the impossible comes true! How well and meaningfully expressed!

Lord Bertrand Russell, the famed English philosopher, in turn said that it could be taken for granted that our era would go down in history as the era of Lenin and Einstein, who accomplished immense syntheses, the latter in the realm of thought and the former in the realm of action. The world's bourgeoisie saw in Lenin a destroyer, but it was not destruction that gave him prominence. Others could also destroy, but Russell doubted whether it was possible to find another person who had such skill in building.

Two different individuals and two different countries, but how unanimous in their appraisals of the essence of a new system, in which the creator is master of what he creates, thus becoming capable of achieving miracles and accomplishing the impossible.

Building: that is the hallmark of the people of the U.S.S.R. In the twenties and thirties they were building to overtake the advanced countries. They were building while denying themselves much of what any man would wish to enjoy, knowing as they did that this was indispensable. The war destroyed the fruit of much labor. The fascists reduced to rubble and plundered more than 1,710 towns, more than 70,000 villages, sacking tens of thousands of hospitals, schools, technical schools, higher educational institutions, research and development institutes, and libraries. The Nazi invaders sacked and pillaged 98,000 collective farms, 1,876 state farms and 2,890 machine-and-tractor stations. Agriculture suffered a loss of seven million horses, as well as seventeen million head of horned cattle. The aggregate losses in consequence of direct damage came to 679 billion rubles (in terms of 1941 official prices). As a whole, therefore, the material losses and expenditures of the Soviet people in the war came to 2 trillion 600 billion rubles.

No country ever suffered such losses in the entire history of mankind.

Once again building was started. Again people denied themselves in every possible way in order that they might heal the wounds and restore the economy of the country, to attain and surpass the prewar level of industrial and economic output.

Everywhere in the van of construction stood the Communists just as always before: as in the days of October 1917, as in the years of the civil war, as in the earliest projects, and as in the struggles against fascism.

The title of member of the Communist Party has never accorded any advantages, except the advantage of being first in the most difficult places. Lenin wrote that all those joining the Party must demonstrate the application of the principles of communism in deed. And the Communists, with their profound ideological convictions and with their brave example, fired the workers with enthusiasm for the realization of all the daring plans advanced by the Party. Twelve million eight hundred thousand members are now in its ranks.

The role of the Party grows as socialism advances. The law governing this process is determined by the magnitude and complexity of the tasks of transforming society, by the upsurge of the creative activity of the masses and the further development of the international ties of the working people.

Today the principal goal of Party activity is the theoretical substantiation and the practical organization of communist construction. The most important principle in Party guidance is an organic unity of science and politics. The Party takes the position that the interests of the people require that it give itself over to the pursuit of policy which will ensure a more rational utilization of the gigantic productive forces that have been released in the country, a speedier increase in the well-being of the workers, and a full utilization of the advantages afforded by the new social system. In this connection, in the sphere of the Party's theoretical activity it is particularly incumbent on it to perfect the concrete forms of economic relations and to define the tasks of the national economy, taking into account material, labor and financial resources, and the international situation.

The Communist Party has to its credit the theory and practice of the planned management of the economy of the U.S.S.R. This is a great contribution to mankind's historical experience and to the building of communism. The Party attaches particular significance to implementing stage by stage a new system of planning, which reflects the changed conditions in conducting the national economy. Economic reform, being consistently socialist in its essence, signifies a new approach to economic management.

The realization of the reform calls for considerable extra effort. Its success depends to a great extent on the correct combination of centralized leadership and greater economic independence on the part of the enterprises, moral and material incentives, skillful utilization of commodity, and monetary relations on the basis of socialism as well as the economic factors associated with them—profit, prices, credit and the like, which under conditions of socialism acquire a new social content. The effectiveness of the reform depends on the organizational and ideological-educational work invested in it.

The theoretical and practical activity of the Party in the field of economics is subordinated to the policy of continued development of the union of the working class and the peasantry. With this in view, a system of economic and political measures was worked out at the March Plenary Meeting of the Central Committee of the C.P.S.U. (1965) with the object of accelerating the output expansion rate of collective and state farms. The implementation of this policy, the proper utilization of the achievements of science and technology, of qualified cadres and of economics and moral incentives, ensure the indispensable conditions for the speedier growth of agriculture.

Concern for the peasantry and for the growth of agriculture aids the Soviet government in dealing with the problems of food supply for the country, of augmenting the productivity of labor and of raising the standard of living among the people.

During the year that followed the Twenty-third Party Congress, the growth in national income, gross output, agriculture, and the real income of the working people exceeded the mean annual quotas envisaged in the directives of the Twenty-third Party Congress for the five-year period. In terms of industrial output, the 1966 and 1967 plans were overfulfilled. The real per capita income of the population gained at a much faster rate than it did several years ago.

Construction continued to progress in 1967. Wherever you turned your gaze, you found turret cranes, which tourists from abroad have come to regard as the symbol of the Soviet Union.

New Era—New Ways. The new conditions under which

the economy operates, and the increased material responsibility of the working people for the results of their activities, along with other factors, have their effects on the current period, and shape new ways of managing the national economy.

In the endeavor to find production reserves, in the struggle for a rational organization of labor and in the practical awareness of the fact that the results of the work performed determine the material level of existence, there comes an awakening on the part of the working people of a responsible and pragmatic attitude towards the common good.

Profit has today become the common index reflecting the ability of any collective to manage its affairs. The object is not just to supply a higher output, but to manage affairs in such a manner that with a minimum of expenditure of labor and materials one may ensure a maximum output.

An economic justification of commitments assumed involves above all a sober estimate of reserves, a strict appraisal of capabilities, and the working out of a complex of organizational and technical measures. The scientific organization of work is a factor of great importance in this connection.

The scientific organization of labor (SOL) seeps down into all the pores of any industrial organism and to a great degree determines the results of the enterprise's efforts. The experience of advanced enterprises has demonstrated that quite often an improved organization of production and labor is no less effective than the purchase of costly equipment.

Each branch of industry has its own specific requirements in terms of the scientific organization of labor, and its own specific features concerning the introduction of SOL. In consequence of the reform, ministries have found it possible not only to establish a uniform technological policy but also to introduce such a policy in the sphere of the organization of labor. The first important steps have already been taken in that direction. Some ministries, particularly those concerned with the construction of machinery for the chemical, oil, food, machine-tool and instrument-making industries, have made major scientific research institutes responsible for the systematic guidance of SOL in given spheres and for the coordination of this work. Centers of this type make it feasible to combine the forces of scientists and production directors and to achieve a planned introduction of scientific organization of labor in the specific branch.

The ministry for the oil extracting industry and some others have set up special firms that work out projects and elaborate methods for the scientific organization of labor, under contract with the enterprises. This aspect of the undertaking was reported on by the director of the All-Union Scientific Research Institute for the Organization, Management and Economy of the Oil and Gas Industry, Doctor of Technological Science S. Yatrov.

Within the framework of the Institute there is a Center for the Scientific Organization of Labor and Industrial Management. The principal task of the Center is to furnish practical aid to enterprises and organizations of the oil industry in the improvement of the organization of labor and management. The work of the Center is organized along the following lines: An analysis of the state of the organization of labor and management directly within the enterprise; the elaboration of a plan and the making of recommendations with a view to improving the organization predicated on the concrete conditions prevailing on the job, as well as the technological and economic substantiation of the plan; its appraisal from the economic standpoint; the exposition of the thinking behind the plan to the satisfaction of the client; and last, the actual realization of the recommendations as a joint endeavor with the enterprise or organization.

Here are the earliest results: A total of seven agreements was concluded in 1966. For the work done the Center received 126,000 rubles. The annual economic gain as a result of the plans put into effect came to 2,905,000 rubles! The scope of this work grew markedly during 1967. Eleven contracts were concluded in the first half of the year for an amount exceeding 400,000 rubles. The clients are in nearly all the oil- and gas-bearing regions of the country.

Economic reform also exhibits new demands as regards socialist emulation. At the September Plenum of the Central Committee of the C.P.S.U. the discussion touched on the indispensability "of directing socialist emulation toward speedier introduction of new technology, scientific organization of labor, boosting the profitability of enterprises, qualitative improvement of production and the increased productivity of labor.

In 1967, the year that celebrated the fiftieth anniversary of the October Revolution, Socialist emulation assumed particularly broad sweep. There was hardly an enterprise in the country, nor a single brigade or shop, that did not contend for the distinction of exceeding the goals of the plan, of boosting production and improving its quality.

People's attitude toward economy has undergone a change. This is a paramount result of the activity of these enterprises that have been converted to the new system of economy. Members of collectives are showing increased interest in the outcome of their own work, and in that of the given section and shop, as well as of the plant as a whole. There has been a marked gain in the creative activity of workers, engineers, technicians and employees, while a fuller use is being made of labor, financial and material resources.

Among the new features of the economic life of the country, one must also note the serious attention being given to the quality of output. On April 7, 1967, at 10:50 A.M., the Board of the Committee on Standards, Measurements and Measuring Instruments of the Council of Ministers of the U.S.S.R. established a "State Quality Mark." It is affixed to certified industrial products of the Soviet Union and it is both uniform and mandatory in all branches of national economy. Since its establishment in April of 1967 many industrial enterprises of the Soviet Union received the right to use it. Products bearing

the state sign of quality can be seen among the exhibits of
EXPO 67.

Raising the yield of all types of crops and improving the
quality of output had become the paramount goals of agriculture. Here again clear-cut gains have been made. Suffice it to
say that in terms of cotton yield the Soviet Union holds first
place in the world.

Output gains are being made in the villages, and revenue is
on the increase in farming enterprises while the incomes of
the farmers are growing. A division of labor is taking place,
and professional skills are being enhanced.

Here is a story that Vanin, the head of the regional department of agriculture of the Penz Region, related in June 1967:

Two and a half years ago, the Economic Council of the region
drafted a specialization plan. The specific features and potential of
each farm as well as the wishes of the membership of the collectives
were taken into account. This resulted in the establishment of six
zones: a grain and beet-raising zone with considerable hog breeding; a
grain and beet-raising zone with stress on poultry raising; a hemp-
growing zone with meat and dairy cattle breeding; a truck gardening,
dairy and meat zone with a strong emphasis on potatoes and sunflow-
ers, and a meat and dairy zone with the main stress on the potato yield.

Each zone has its own specialty, inter-organizational cooperation in
grain growing, sugar-beet production, poultry raising, the fattening of
horned cattle, as well as hog raising and fattening. As a rule, the farms
of each zone specialize in from one to four commodities. In large state
farms there is also concentration and specialization in the offshoots of
cattle breeding and plant growing.

What has the accomplishment of these plans already given and what
is further expected to come of them? The farms of the first and second
zone are our chief suppliers of commodity grain. Their proportion in
the state purchases of grain grows from year to year and it will exceed
30 per cent at the end of the five-year period. A process of concentration of output is under way, and it can best be illustrated in terms of
beet raising. While in 1964 a total of 227 farms cultivated sugar beets,
there were 163 such farms last year and in 1970 there will be 143 state
farms and collective farms engaged in the pursuit. However, the quantity of beets will not decline, since they are being cultivated on a larger
scale in specialized farms, while mechanization and the skill of the
farmers are both increasing. This raises revenues in the branch. The
gain is also carried over to sugar mills, since the radius of the haulage

channels for raw materials is diminished and along with it there is also a reduction in the cost of supply.

There is a further consequence of specialization in the sphere of cattle breeding. Two years ago the produce of cattle breeding in most of the collective and state farms of the region showed a deficit. The organization of large cattle-fattening farms made the production of beef and pork profitable.

In 1966, nearly half of the cattle supplied to the state were fattened in specialized farms. Profits have accrued both to farms engaged in fattening and those engaged in breeding.

However, specialization also calls for cooperation in production. Not every state or collective farm today puts out the finished product. Many of them are engaged in supplying younger animals, seed, saplings and the like to other farms. And while formerly the director of a state farm, the chairman of a collective farm, or even the collective as a whole were not overly concerned about the way their neighbors went about doing their work, they have now learned to appreciate the fact that their success is a function of the common effort.

The advancement of agricultural science is also receiving serious attention. Handling agricultural production on a scientific basis and improving and perfecting its organization raise the productivity of labor, boost the yield of each acre of soil, and promote a steady increase in the efficiency and profitability of the different branches of the economy. This is precisely the goal that is being pursued through the growing link between science and production.

There was a time when willpower was regarded as one of the paramount qualities of a manager, along with persistence and executive ability. What the national economy now calls for is a manager and specialist with considerable knowledge, enterprise and far-sightedness. He must at all times see his enterprise in perspective, have a thorough knowledge of the nature and range of the problems of his branch, and have the ability to apply in practice all the valuable achievements of science. He should be capable of rallying the collective and firing it with enthusiasm for the common goal. It is a source of satisfaction to note that in all of the republics, in every region and territory there is an abundance of managers and specialists who exhibit these precious qualities to the fullest extent.

Today as never before all conditions are being created for the involvement of every single worker of the enterprise in the positive organizational activity that goes into the management

of production. In the Soviet Union the welding of the organizational and executive functions in the worker's production
activity is taking on two basic orientations: firstly, the workers
are taking an ever-increasing part in design and technological
activities, and their role as organizers of scientific and technological advance is gaining in importance. This participation as-
sumes the form of helping in rationalization and contributing
resourcefulness—the activity that the worker invests in the
public designing bureaus, in public institutes and on research
teams, etc. Secondly, an increasing role is being played by the
worker in the management of enterprises, in planning and rate-
setting, in the scientific organization of labor and in uncover-
ing inner production resources. All this enhances the role of
the worker as organizer of the socialist economy.

The necessity for the involvement of all toilers in the organizational process of the economy is dictated by the very nature
of socialist production relations and by the nature of socialist
democracy. Under socialism one could not and should not
have mere "bolt-tighteners" of a giant mechanism; instead,
every worker and every collective farmer must also act as a
production organizer to one degree or another.

People of the Future. "The good name of the Soviet
worker," wrote Ivan Leonov, a milling-machine operator at
the Kirov Plant in Leningrad, in *Pravda,* "is rooted in his
doing a job conscientiously, tenaciously, creatively, looking
with an eye of thrift at his materials and equipment. Your
good name is also rooted in a determination to fire the enthusiasm of the entire collective in combating all inadequacies.
You, the worker, are the master of your own factory." And the
pages of history do, in fact, confirm the truth of this assertion.

Perhaps the clearest example of the organizational activity
of Soviet workers is their participation in the formulation and
implementation of the plans of the scientific organization of
labor (SOL), which was mentioned earlier. This movement
has spread widely throughout many of the country's enterprises.

Professor L. N. Kogan in one of his papers cited the fact

that in the middle of 1965 more than two million SOL plans had been worked out in the plants and factories of the Sverdlov Region, which covered about 56,400 work sites, sections and shops and embraced working personnel numbering 45,-000. The financial saving resulting from the application of SOL methods came to 13.5 million rubles.

L. N. Kogan also cites figures to show what an active part the workers play in drawing up plans for SOL. In one Urals car-building plant (Nizhny Tagil), a total of seventy SOL plans have been put into effect and the financial return achieved thereby came to 333,000 rubles. Not a small share of the credit for this goes to the workers who took a hand in the drawing up and implementation of the plans.

By taking part in the formulation and implementation of SOL plans the workers actually have intimate contact with the tasks of technological improvement, with the sphere of improving the organization of labor and rate-setting, and with production management. The work they perform in public offices, in the drawing up of individual plans concerning the utilization of production reserves, and their participation in conferences on production demand of the Soviet worker both a high level of general education and a thorough knowledge of the economics of production. It is not by mere chance that in recent years, to take the Sverdlovsk Region alone, more than half a million workers have studied the principles of economics in study circles and seminars.

Active participation in the work of public bodies develops the worker's management capabilities and his habit of organizational activity. At the Sverdlovsk Pharmaceutical Plant, Professor L. N. Kogan posed the following questions to an assembly of 418 workers: "Are you prepared to manage your team or section?" and "Do you speak at the meetings of your collective, or team?" These were the answers received:

REGARD THEMSELVES PREPARED: 229	SPEAK: 257
REGARD THEMSELVES UNPREPARED: 126	DO NOT SPEAK: 124
NO ANSWER: 63	NO ANSWER: 37

The answers show that 55 per cent of the workers regarded themselves to be prepared for management of a team or section and that 60 per cent of the workers spoke at meetings where matters of production were the predominant subject under discussion.

The participation of hundreds and hundreds of thousands of workers in elective bodies of the Party, the government, the trade union and Komsomol bodies, in the activities of the Soviets (more than 23 million people take part in the avocational activities of the Soviets), in the numerous amateur organizations (sports, women's, amateur art activities, etc.) is of great value as a means of developing the worker's personality and in blending the functions of organizer and executive in his productive activity.

In 1967 more than two million people were deputies to the Supreme and local Soviets of the country, of which nearly 60 per cent are workers and collective farmers. A total of nearly 16.5 million working people were elected to the local Soviets alone over a period of ten terms. The electors, numbering 143,917,031, sent 1,517 deputies to the Supreme Soviet of the U.S.S.R. for a term commencing in 1966. A total of 698 workers and collective farmers was elected to the country's highest governing body. Of the deputies elected 425 were women. More than 70 per cent of those elected have a secondary and higher education. Among the deputies there were 1,141 Communists and 376 non-party people.*

Nearly one and a half million of those elected are deputies of village Soviets and Soviets of workers' settlements.

The changes that have taken place in the conditions of social and everyday life among the working people of the U.S.S.R. have also contributed to the enhancement of their general culture. Here it is important to stress that these

---

* For the sake of comparison we will cite here the figures showing the composition of the State Duma in tsarist Russia: 242 landowners, 49 representatives of the clergy, 36 merchants and industrialists and 84 lawyers and officials. There were only 16 workers and artisans.

changes are felt not only in large industrial centers, but in the village as well.

The cultural revolution in the U.S.S.R. and the intimate contact of the broadest masses with the spiritual culture of mankind have left not a single vestige of the fable now being disseminated by sociologists about the age-long antithesis between the culture of the minority, the highest stratum of society, the "elite," and the culture of the millions, or "mass culture." For the first time in history the culture of the masses has come to signify the intimate assimilation by the masses of the highest attainments of mankind's spiritual culture.

During the span of the prewar five-year plans, and particularly since the war, the rise in the educational level of the workers has assumed an ever mounting tempo. Even in 1964 as much as 44 per cent of the country's workers had an educational background of at least a partial secondary education. Every year sees the accession into the national economy of the U.S.S.R. of 160,000–170,000 young engineers, more than 300,000 technicians and hundreds of thousands of other highly skilled specialists. During the span of years from 1918 to 1966, the higher educational establishments have trained some seven million people, while the secondary vocational schools have trained in excess of eleven million specialists.

The spread of workers' education naturally leads to an increasing importance for the book in everyday life. The cultural revolution has had the effect of raising the Soviet Union to first rank in the world in terms of the number of libraries and their book funds. Suffice it to say that the United States has 17.5 times fewer public libraries than the U.S.S.R.

The newspapers and magazines are today an integral part of every household. The number of subscribers is increasing from year to year. This can be judged from the figures for subscriptions over a period of only three years in the town of Artemovsk, a mining center in the Middle Urals, whose population numbers 75,000. Here, in 1964, residents subscribed to 48,329 copies of newspapers and magazines, in 1965 to 68,336 copies, and in 1966 to 79,648 copies.

The Five-Year Plan called for an increase in the output of books by 25 per cent, of newspapers by 40 per cent, and by 1.5 times for magazines. The plan also provides for a marked expansion of the television network.

The working people are ever more attracted to art. Statistics have shown that workers and peasants see motion pictures no less than four times a month. While I was in the final stages of writing this book, an International Cinema Festival was taking place in Moscow. Daily, crowds besieged the motion picture houses where both competitive and non-competitive showings of films were taking place. The American film based on Bel Kaufman's book *Up the Down Staircase* was quite well received. The film, directed by Robert Mulligan and produced at the Warner Brothers studios, caught the fancy of Muskovites and they extended a warm reception to the young actress Sandy Dennis, who performed in the leading role. The viewer in the U.S.S.R. is properly and objectively conditioned. Many important figures in the cinema arts spoke of the Soviet viewer as a subtle connoisseur and expert.

Some ten million workers and peasants in the Soviet Union take part in amateur art activities. Recent years have witnessed an increase in the numbers of those participating in amateur activities, but also a change in quality. There has been a proliferation of people's theaters, cinema studios, conservatories, etc. These ensembles stand out not only by virtue of the greater dimensions that they have assumed, but also by an incomparably higher level of mastery of the crafts.

The concepts of "the common worker" and of "peasant" have acquired new content. Half a century ago, these words had a contemptuous ring to them when spoken by the "top ten thousand," and served as labels for lack of culture and development. Today, however, the workers and peasants who have come to the forefront of the peoples of Russia have changed the face of the country and turned it into a great world power. While transforming the entire life of the country, they have also undergone change themselves. At present, the terms "common worker" and "peasant" have a proud ring to them. They symbolize the vanguard of Soviet society, the people of the future.

When Figures Come to Life. The labor of millions of people brings the future closer and makes the impossible possible. No matter what the plans are, no matter how bold the dreams, they become a reality. Dry-as-dust diagrams, tables and graphs become animated. Figures reveal a great deal of what is behind them, and all comments are superfluous. A mosaic of the reports of the Soviet press during the jubilee year gives an idea of the time and sweep of construction and changes.

While the share of the Russian Empire is total world industrial production came to less than 3 per cent in 1917, and the proportion that the U.S.S.R. contributed in 1937 was less than 10 per cent, we find that it has now risen to nearly 20 per cent.

The national income of the U.S.S.R. exceeds 200 billion rubles. Some three-fourths of this is utilized for the satisfaction of the material and cultural needs of the population.

In 1966, some 73 million people were receiving an education from public funds. Forty-eight million of these were studying in schools of general education while 4.1 million attended higher educational institutions and 4 million were in secondary vocational institutions. The government pays out pensions to more than 32 million people. More than 8.5 million children are receiving preschool education. Over 18 million people benefit from care in sanatoriums, rest homes, boarding houses and pioneer camps; in all of these they receive medical treatment and enjoy rest. Public consumption funds now furnish about 700 rubles annually per family of workers, employees or members of collective farms.

Within the last fifteen years, the mean annual increase in industrial output exceeded 10 per cent. In a number of industrial branches, the Soviet Union is outstripping the U.S.A. in terms of absolute increase. We are increasing the output of oil by 13.7 million tons annually, while the increase in the United States amounts to 7.9 million. As regards the output of cement, our increase is at the rate of 4.1 million tons, while that of the United States comes to 1.8 million tons. In terms of output of electrical power, gas and a series of chemical substances, the absolute gain in the U.S.S.R. is still lower than the United States.

More than 40,000 large industrial enterprises were built, restored and put into operation from 1918 to 1966. They employ a total of 28 million workers, engineers and office workers.

Special attention is being given to the development of the economy of the eastern regions of the country. It should be noted here that the Urals Region has long since become the highest productive area of the country. Siberia and the Far East are also becoming regions of the most diversified industrial production.

By the early months of 1967, more than 15,000 of the most important mineral deposits had been located and prospected in the Soviet Union. More than 200 large mining enterprises are at work on these deposits.

A total of 74 deposits of minerals was discovered during 1966, not to mention numerous deposits of building materials, and subterranean waters. As an anniversary gift to celebrate the fiftieth anniversary of the October Revolution, geologists have presented 39 new deposits of oil and gas, among them 17 in Western Siberia. One must specifically mention here the Urengoi deposit of natural gas, opened in the north of the Tyumen Region, which is unique in terms of available reserves. According to preliminary data, the wealth of natural gas stored here totals about 1,300 billion cubic meters. Deposits of natural gas have also been discovered in the Komi A.S.S.R. Some hundreds of billions of cubic meters of first-class fuel from the Vuktylsky deposit will be supplying the centers of the European part of the country. The largest oil deposit, namely the Belozernoye, has been opened in the middle reaches of the Ob River. Its reserves are estimated at 400 million tons. Stored gases and oils have also been found in the Udmurt and Orenburg Regions, in Yakutia and the Ukraine, and in Turkmenia and Kazakhstan.

In the diamond territory of Yakutia, two new deposits of the precious mineral have been uncovered. One of the diamond-bearing fields, "Lucky Chance," does in fact justify its name. This is the largest stone in the diamond necklace of the North. Twelve years ago, it was discovered by a young geologist, Vladimir Shchukin, who is now the director of the Botobinsk Expedition, and a holder of the Lenin Prize. Twelve new gold-bearing fields have been found in Chukotka, Kolyma and Yakutia and deposits of gold-bearing ore have been discovered in Kazakhstan.

In the first half of 1967 two billion cubic meters of natural gas have been channeled through the Igrym-Serov pipe line. The main line now also connects with the Igrym deposit.

In the western Urals, two oil deposits have been discovered—the Kuzmin deposit to the west and the Padun deposit in the south of the region. Both wells have provided gusher oil from a depth of 1,750 meters. In the Perm Region, there are currently 55 deposits of coal. Over the five-year period the output of oil in the western Urals will be nearly doubled.

Of the 345–355 million tons of oil that the country will be extracting in 1970, nearly one-third, or 98–100 million tons, will be provided by the Tatar Autonomous Republic.

Russia's foresters have fulfilled their annual seeding and planting plan for 1967. New forests have been planted on a surface area of 1,712.7 thousand acres with such valuable timber varieties as pine, spruce and oak. Cedar groves have made their appearance in many forests of the European part of the R.S.F.S.R. New walnut plantations appeared on an area of 7.4 thousand acres, while 3.7 thousand acres are planted under orchards.

More than 20,000 high-tonnage trawlers, floating docks, and refrigerators under the flag of the Soviet Union are engaged in fishing in the seas and oceans of the world.

Exploration to determine the reserves of fresh water in the subsoil of the U.S.S.R. has been completed. Specialists of the All-Union Scientific Research Institute on Hydrogeology and Engineering Geology and of the Moscow University have compiled an atlas comprising maps and detailed topography of the country's underground water resources.

A powerful trench excavator has been mounted on the base of the S-100 tractor by the builders of the Gorky Polytechnical Institute. Tests conducted on experimental models of the machine in the northern areas of the country have established for it a high performance record. It digs a one-hundred-meter trench 60 centimeters wide and 1.20 meters deep in hard frozen soil within a period of one hour.

The semiconductor medical apparatus called Gipoterm was produced by the physicists and physicians of Azerbaidzhan. Within a matter of minutes, it is capable of cooling down the human organism to a temperature at which it is possible to perform the most complex operations —heart operations and operations on the large blood vessels. The Gipoterm is a compact apparatus simple to operate. Two models have been produced: a stationary unit, and a portable model for ambulances and ambulance aircraft.

A new turret crane, the MSK-10-20, has been produced at Sverdlovsk Mechanical Plant. It lifts a ten-ton load to a height of up to 46 meters, is suitable for work under any climatic conditions, and is capable of the widest use in the construction of industrial facilities and high-rise apartment buildings.

Five thousand cubic meters per hour is the output of the rotary excavator "RShR-5000" which advances on a track. It was designed by the engineers of the Lenin plant in Novokramatorsk. The apparatus is intended for the extraction of hard bituminous coals from an open-cut mine.

The Voronezh Radio Works has produced the four millionth transistorized radio under the "Suvenir" trademark.

The Poltava Elektromotor plant has produced its one millionth electric motor. The products of this plant are widely known in the country, as well as in thirty-seven foreign countries.

A large shipment of wrist watches bearing the trademarks "Zarya," "Luch," and "Polyot" has been made available to Japan by the All-Union Association Mashpriborintorg via the first commercial flight of the new Moscow-Tokyo Line.

An order for the production of dresses for England has been received by the Latvian ready-to-wear firm, Rigas Apgerbs, which is very popular in the Soviet Union as well as abroad.

International parcels containing ladies watches with the trademarks "Zaraya," "Vesna," and "Yunost" are ever more frequently being shipped by air mail to new addresses. The plant has sent its first shipment of attractive and high-precision chronometers to Japan. A large shipment of very diminutive watches bearing the trademark of "Mechta" has been made to France.

A cargo shipping line has been inaugurated between Leningrad and the Norwegian port of Tofte. Vessels, each with a carrying capacity of three thousand tons, will be making three voyages a month. The new cargo line has been organized for the purpose of supplying the pulp and paper combine in Tofte with raw material from the Soviet Union.

Forty years have elapsed since the date on which the Zemo-Avchalsk Hydroelectric Station (ZAGES) in Georgia was put into service. It is the second largest hydroelectric power station in the country, and was built according to the Lenin GOELRO Plan. Lenin gave enormous assistance to the building of the ZAGES. Eight million rubles in gold was alloted for the building of the station during the difficult days of 1922, at his behest.

One year ahead of schedule, construction had been completed on the first section of the Abdusamatsk Pumping Station, the largest in the Ferghana Valley. It has brought moisture to virgin lands that are now being placed under rice cultivation.

Ready for shipment from the Gomel Stud Farm for use on the country's race tracks are forty-nine two-year-olds of the Russian trotter breed. Russian trotters have of recent years captured numerous prizes in large contests.

The Taimyr fur center dispatched to Leningrad 2,400 first-quality polar fox skins. They were intended for the international auction.

The largest mink-breeding farm in the country today is the Ussurisk State Farm at Primorye. The basic mink colony here numbers 20,000 minks.

A 200-meter bridge over a mountain precipice is being built near the spa of Dzhermuk in Armenia. One of its metal structures, a 75-meter span, will be suspended over the turbulent Arpa River. The bridge will link the resort with a new residential complex.

The five hundred thousandth resident of Yaroslavl has been named Yaroslav by his parents, Gertrude and Vladimir Zavitkov. They have received a commemorative medal bearing the inscription "To one born in Yaroslavl—to the five hundred thousandth resident of the city, Zavitkov Yaroslav" and a welcome address by the Executive Committee of the city Soviet.

The output of a new factory being constructed in the capital of Tadzhikistan will be 3.2 million pairs of footwear annually. Once the enterprise is set in operation, the republic will double its output of footwear.

Surveyors have traced the path of the country's first super-high power line, which will carry 750,000 volts. The AC electrical bridge, running over a distance of 1,200 kilometers, will deliver power generated by means of coal from the Donets Basin through all of the Ukraine to Lvov.

Kuban polyhybrid-9 sugar beets weighing about one kilogram each were displayed at the Soviet Pavilion in Leipzig, where the Fifteenth World Agricultural Exposition took place. The new variety was developed by the scientists of the Pervomai Selection Stations of the Krasnodar Territory.

The workers of the Primorye State Farm, situated along the shore of the new lake which serves as a reservoir for the Krasnoyarsk Hydroelectric Station, harvest 25 centners of hay from each hectare of perennial herbs.

The Moscow-Paris Line is the fifth international airline and is serviced by the TU-114 airliners. Once a week, the giants make regular flights between the two capitals and carry on each flight up to 170 passengers.

Not so very long ago, the aviation experts of many countries were overwhelmed by a new Russian marvel, the gigantic Antheus aircraft which landed at Paris's Le Bourget airport. A placard inside the plane posted absolutely fantastic information concerning the ratings of the craft. One fact was particularly striking, and that was that the Antheus is able to lift into the sky and carry over a distance of thousands of kilometers more than 700 people!

Three paintings by Stanislav Babikov have been sent from Ashkhabad to Paris. The canvases, "Harvesting the Grape," "Stockade," and "Autumn in Ashkhabad," will be shown at the International Exposition of Young Artists.

More than a thousand drawings of Italian architects of the Renaissance period have been discovered in the storage rooms of the Hermitage Library. Scholars are calling attention to the unique historical value of these drawings, which afford views of large structures that have not survived to the present.

A copy of the *Gospels* published in Russia 412 years ago enriches the collection of Andrei Rublyov's ancient Russian arts museum. It was printed in 1555. This book is regarded as the first example of printing in Russia. The name of the printer of the *Gospels* is unknown, but experts believe that it was Marusha Nefedyev, whose name is mentioned in sixteenth-century chronicles.

The Bolshoi Theater has begun work on the opera ballet *The Snow Queen* by the composer M. Rauchberger. The work is based on themes by the Soviet writer Evgeny Shvarts. The director of the work is N. Nikiforov, the choreography by Asaf Messerer. Elena Ryabinkina will perform in the leading role.

The Bolshoi Theater completed its 191st season in the spring of 1967. As its final performance, it presented the *Nutcracker* on its own stage and *Swan Lake* at the Kremlin Palace of Congresses. On August 10, 1967, the Theater started performances of its opera spectacles at the World Exposition in Montreal.

Brief newspaper notices, a scant few lines of reportage, figures, names—thus, the life of the Soviet people is devoted to peaceful pursuits and to great endeavors.

What is of paramount importance to the U.S.S.R. is to fulfill to the utmost the plans it has mapped out for itself for the accomplishment of vast and far-flung construction projects. To do all of this, the country must have peace and, echoing the words of Anatole France, many people will then be able, on acquaintance with the Soviet Union, to exclaim:

"Russia is a country where the impossible comes true!"

9 THE PATH TO THE STARS

The great Austrian writer Stefan Zweig entitled his cycle of historical miniatures *Mankind's Starry Clock*. These stories depicted the triumph of man's spirit and mind. Now and then they overly magnify the role of the individual in history and his effect on the development of society. Nevertheless, taken as a whole, Zweig is correct. The highest achievements of mankind have been attained in moments that are with good reason called starry moments because they are brilliant and pure and exceedingly beautiful, like the distant stars, which mankind has always held in admiration down the generations.

Such, in fact, is the "starry clock" that ticked off the minutes of the distant October assault of 1917 when the workers and peasants of Russia took power into their own hands. Such are also the years during which the backward country took a colossal leap to the lofty peaks of industrialization, a time when all the achievements of science and technology were placed at the disposal of man. It was in fact during those years that Soviet man felt himself to be borne up on wings and capable of accomplishing anything he wished and anything he regarded as indispensable. It was precisely those years, the years of struggle, construction, study, creativity—years which saw the emergence of ever bolder plans and ever more effective undertakings—that prepared the true and authentic triumph of man's mind, the onset of the space age. It began on October 4, 1957.

I well remember the day. The sky of Moscow was cloudy and leaden. A drizzle was seeping down, but the voice of the finest announcer on Soviet radio, Isaak Levitan, reading the TASS statement, did something to make you forget that this was autumn.

". . . The first artificial earth satellite has become a reality thanks to the unflagging effort ardently pursued by the Scientific and Research Institutes and the Designing Bureaus." He was reading triumphantly and his voice stirred a kind of bittersweet agitation as it did in the years of the war against fascism when Levitan would read the Informbureau news from the fronts.

"On October 4, 1957," he continued, "the first satellite has been successfully launched in the U.S.S.R. According to preliminary information, the carrier rocket has imparted to the satellite the indispensable orbital speed of about eight thousand meters per second. At the present moment, the satellite is describing an elliptical orbit around the earth and its flight can be observed in the rays of the rising and setting sun with the aid of the most simple optical instruments [binoculars, telescope, etc.]."

In those days, one spoke of nothing else but the first emissary of the earth in space.

The very word "Sputnik" has become internationalized just as have the words "Soviet" and "Kolkhoz." All of the newspapers and radio stations in the world discussed this first flight into space, regarding it as a fantastic achievement of Russian scientists and engineers.

Man becomes quickly accustomed to technological marvels.

However, the exploits of the people who were the first to overcome the terrestrial force of gravity, who made the first sortie into the universe and presented to mankind a new and magnificent gift of an authentic "starry clock," will always stir the minds and the imaginations of our contemporaries and their descendants.

As the New York *World Telegram and Sun* put it at the time, the launching of the Russian Sputnik opened a new era.

The Opening of the Space Era. It was necessary for the Soviet people to accomplish all that they had during the period preceding it, in order to inaugurate the space age. Invested in this celebration of the achievements of Soviet science, technology and human prowess were the efforts of the first builders of the Magnitogorsk Metallurgical Plant and the Dnieper Hydroelectric Station, and of the members of the workers' faculty burrowing into the mysteries of science, the exploits of the heroes of the Great Patriotic War against fascism, the self-sacrificing spirit of the young cultivators of the virgin soil, and the endurance of the explorers of the Antarctic. The flourishing of Soviet science, the mighty power of Soviet industry, the moral duty and grandeur of the Soviet man, all of these helped to lay the basis for the space triumph of the U.S.S.R.

This was not a brilliantly dazzling burst of genius. It was a clear manifestation of a process which had unfolded and continued to advance along strictly defined guidelines.

Even when still engaged in the preparations for conquering power, the Bolshevik Party devoted considerable attention to questions of science and technology. It would seem that all the forces of the Party should have been swallowed up by the political struggle, the struggle for the winning of the masses, and during those stormy days, there simply shouldn't have been any time at all to give thought to the question of what place men of science and technology would occupy in the building of a revolutionary society. Nevertheless it was precisely in those days that Lenin wrote in his work *Can the Bol-*

sheviks Retain State Power?, ". . . In contrast to the past, we need ever more engineers, agronomists, technicians and scientifically trained specialists of every kind."

The victory of the Socialist Revolution posed the practical problem of the utilization of science and technology for the recovery and further advance of Russia's economy. On November 4, 1917, as soon as the detachments of the Red Guard ended the White Guard offensive of Krasnov against Petrograd, and routed the counterrevolution in Moscow, Lenin, speaking at a session of the Petrograd Soviet, declared: "In order to be able to produce, we must have engineers and we greatly value their labor. We will be very happy to compensate them." On November 9, in a Decree of the Soviet of Peoples' Commissars on the establishment of a State Commission on Education, signed by Lenin, a scientific department was also added to the Commission.

Academician Ivan Pavlov, a holder of the Nobel Prize, received support, material aid, fuel and whatever was necessary in those days of hunger and cold. Every possible assistance was given to the founder of theoretical, experimental and applied aerodynamics, N. E. Zhukovsky, whom Lenin referred to as "the father of Russian aviation," so that he might be able to go on with his work. Recognition and understanding were accorded to the works of the remarkable self-taught scientist Konstantin Tsiolkovsky, who first developed the theory of jet propulsion, who also formulated the principles of the jet-propelled aircraft, and who laid the foundations of cosmonautics.

On December 1, 1918, the largest scientific and research center for aviation was established—The Central Aero-Hydrodynamic Institute (TsAGI). Immediately after the end of the civil war, notwithstanding the difficult economic position of the country, the Soviet government allotted three million gold rubles to be used in aircraft production. At the end of 1922, a three-year program for the development of aircraft plants was ratified.

The country witnessed a proliferation not only of works in the aircraft industry, but also of scientific and research centers as well as educational institutes. On September 26, 1920, The Institute of Engineers of the Red Air Force was organized, and in 1922 it was reorganized to constitute The Air Force Academy (now The Zhukovsky Military Air Force Engineering Academy). I should mention in this connection that my teacher, Academician I. I. Mints, was appointed Military Commissar of this academy at the end of the civil war, from which he had come out with the rank of Commissar of the First Calvary Corps of the Red Cossacks. He recalls the kind attention the academy and aviation as a whole received from Mikhail Frunze who headed the Revolutionary Soviet of the Republic from 1925 on. Serious attention was also paid to aviation by Marshal Tukhachevsky. Vladimir Bekauri and Leonid Kurchevsky, who headed special technical bureaus, enjoyed his support and favor.

". . . I have faith in Tsiolkovsky's ideas," said Tukhachevsky, "and it is my opinion that there is before him a brilliant future." Like many others, he too made every effort to bring this future closer to our days. In the twenties and thirties, the Designing Bureaus, headed by A. N. Tupolev, N. N. Polikarpov, D. P. Grigorovich and other designers in aircraft engineering, carried on very fruitful work. When the earliest Soviet-built aircraft made its appearance it in no way took second rank to the foreign models.

It was precisely those years that brought to public notice the brilliant talents of the then young Sergei Korolyov, whose name will be forever associated with the manifold achievements of Soviet cosmonautics.

This is what *Pravda* wrote in January 1967 in commemoration of the anniversary of Korolyov's death:

Sergei Korolyov grew up and developed to become an outstanding specialist during the Soviet period. His principal traits were those of a progressive human being and scientist, and a zealous patriot of his native land.

Korolyov's childhood was by no means easy. He was born on December 30, 1906, in Zhitomir into the family of a teacher. At an early age, Sergei was left alone with his mother. He first studied in secondary school and in 1924 he entered the Kiev Polytechnical Institute. To gain the means for an education, he began earning his own livelihood as a worker in the building industry, laying roof tiles. On completion of his second year at the Polytechnical Institute, he transferred to the Moscow Higher Technical School in the Department of Aeromechanics, which was the training center for aircraft engineers during the first development stage of the Soviet Air Force. The course of studies embracing the disciplines in the field of aircraft engineering had been founded here by Zhukovsky, and the students received instruction from Chaplygin and Vetchinkin. Many outstanding designers, among them Korolyov, received their initial training at the Moscow Higher Technical School. There he absorbed the finest traditions of the country's first aviators and even during his terminal courses, and particularly when working on his graduation project (under A. N. Tupolev), which concerned a light engine aircraft, he displayed originality and boldness of conception as a designer.

Sergei Korolyov combined his studies at the Higher Technical School with work as a designer in the aircraft industry. On graduating from the school in 1929, he continued to work in his beloved specialty.

The young designer's first sphere of interest centered on light engine units and engineless craft (gliders). As far back as 1929, Sergei Korolyov had a hand in the production of the Koktebel glider, also participating during that year in the All-Union Competitions. What took place at this point follows logically from the character of the young Korolyov, from his attitudes toward work and the tasks which belong to the designer of flying craft. He next decided to become a flier so that he might arrive at an opinion concerning his machine not only from what others had to say about it, but also to test in flight the correctness of his ideas and to find new means for the improvement of the technology.

In 1930, Korolyov received his pilot's license on completion of his studies at the Moscow Flight School. It was the same year that he designed the Krasnaya Zvezda (Red Star) glider, which he flew himself, training himself at the same time to execute the Nesterov loop for the first time in the history of gliding. Pilot Stepanchenok was the first to perform the Nesterov loop in this glider during the regular glider contests.

Sergei Korolyov accomplished a great deal in 1930. That year can be regarded as decisive in his life, since it was in 1930 that he became acquainted with the works of Konstantin Tsiolkovsky. The boldness of judgment and conclusions of the scientist stirred Korolyov's imagination. Subsequently, he gave the following appraisal of the work of his teacher: "The most remarkable products of the creative mind of Tsiolkovsky are his ideas and work in the sphere of rocket engineering. In this sphere, he has no predecessors, far outstripping the scientists of all countries, and his contemporary epoch."

Henceforth, Korolyov was devoted to the development of rocket engineering and realization of Tsiolkovsky's dreams concerning space flights. The excellent training he had obtained in engineering and the experience he had gained as a designer made it possible for a quick manifestation of the remarkable talent with which Korolyov was endowed in this sphere of science and technology.

Sergei Korolyov's inexhaustible sources of energy and his talent for organization speedily brought him into prominence among passionate devotees of rocketry. He made a vast creative contribution to the historic work of GIRD (Group for the Study of Jet Propulsion, established in Moscow in the early thirties) on the development and launching of the first liquid-fueled rockets and to the investigation of a series of theoretical problems. Korolyov gave his paramount attention to the creation of rocket units capable of lifting man to great heights. This subject was the leitmotiv of his addresses at scientific conferences and in the press. He subjected this problem to a thorough analysis in his book, *Rocket Flights in the Stratosphere*, published in 1934. Not only young workers in rocket engineering, but even the most experienced members greeted the publication of this book with great enthusiasm. Specifically, Konstantin Tsiolkovsky wrote in one of his letters as follows: ". . . Korolyov sent me his book *Rocket Flight*, but he did not include his address. I do not know how to convey to him my thanks for the kindness he has shown me. . . . The book is well thought out, rich in content and useful."

While still a member of GIRD, Korolyov took the first practical steps toward the achievement of man's rocket flight. His idea was to install a liquid-fueled jet engine on a glider. The first glider to be selected for that purpose was a tailless glider designed by B. I. Cheranovsky. The glider was personally tested in flight by Korolyov.

The next stage in the creative work of Korolyov was his research in the Scientific Research Institute on Jet Propulsion, established in 1933. Here again, he turned his primary attention to the design of winged guided rockets with a long flight range, and rocket gliders.

In the course of his work on the rocket glider, Korolyov used a glider of his own design, the SK-9, which had been designed in 1935, as the principal model. It was a two-seater free-floating monoplane which had proved its merit in long-range flights in tow, such as, for instance, the flight from Moscow to the Crimea. A special liquid-fueled jet engine, the RDA-I-50, with a maximum thrust of 140 kilograms, was built for mounting on the glider. The thrust was variable in flight. The outfitted glider had all of the component parts of an aircraft with a jet engine and was named the RP-318-I. V. P. Fedorov tested the first Soviet jet craft on February 28, 1940. It was in fact the first guided flight of the glider with the jet engine. The crew of the aircraft from which the flight of the jet glider was being observed reported as follows: "After the jet engine was switched on, we observed that object No. 318 rapidly gained in speed in horizontal flight and then disappeared as it gained elevation. . . . Notwithstanding the fact that the engine was boosted to its maximum speed, the P-6 aircraft lagged behind object 318."

The flight of the Soviet jet glider designed by Korolyov contributed greatly to the development of jet engines. It was apparent to all that the era of jet engines was quite near.

Korolyov's most creative forces soared to their fullest capacity during the years that were devoted to the solution of the cardinal problem of designing long-range guided rockets.

In the year that celebrated the Fortieth Anniversary of the Great October Revolution, the press throughout the world flashed a report to the effect that a multi-stage intercontinental rocket had been tested in the U.S.S.R.

October 1957 is written large in golden letters in the history of mankind. It was the year when, with the aid of a jet space system produced under the guidance of Korolyov, the first artificial earth satellite was launched into orbit.

The President of the Academy of Sciences of the U.S.S.R., Academician Mstislav Keldysh, correctly observed that the name of Korolyov "will forever be associated with one of the greatest triumphs of science and technology of all times, namely, the opening of an era of man's conquest of outer space."

The launching of the first artificial earth satellite illuminated like a flash of lightning the enormous achievements of the U.S.S.R. Many people throughout the world were unable to conceal their amazement at the enormous feat of the Soviet people that ushered in the space era. American historians wrote that the sputniks, the discussions concerning the Soviet system of education, the mighty sweep of the communist movement in Asia, the new phase of the communist foreign policy and foreign trade, all of this prompted one to strain every muscle to study Soviet Russia to every extent possible, gaining a knowledge of its past and its present.

Man and the Universe. Three and a half years after the launching of the first sputnik man himself also took his giant step into space. On April 12, 1961, the Soviet space ship Vostok, with pilot-cosmonaut Yuri Gagarin aboard, was placed in an orbit around the earth, and flying a full circle around the planet within a span of 108 minutes, successfully effected a landing in a pre-set region of the country.

The entire world followed this flight. The words "Vostok"

and "Gagarin" were on the tongues of people speaking all languages of the world. Then the newspapers went on to quote a figure which at first defied human grasp: "Engines with a capacity of 20 million horsepower. If so, then what sort of a rocket could it possibly be? What does it look like?" And so in May 1967, people from different countries of the world saw for the first time the rocket in which Yury Gagarin took his flight. A special correspondent of *Izvestia*, Tsyganov, who happened to be in Paris at the time in connection with the International Aircraft Exposition at Le Bourget airfield, wrote as follows:

The mighty ship beautifully loomed above Le Bourget. It looked like a Gulliver amongst the Lilliputians. And even the most perfect aircraft which flew here to participate in the international aircraft show gave the appearance of little envoys of the bygone past when compared with the Vostok.

From the very first minute, the rocket captured the minds and the hearts of those to whom the idea of outer space was entirely alien, as well as those who were interested professionally. The French newspapers christened the Vostok with the highest journalistic epithet, namely, "the hit of the 1967 show." In the meantime, thousands of Parisians who came daily to Le Bourget airfield spontaneously manifested their feelings about the Soviet marvel. One had to see with one's own eyes the stir and excitement with which the crowds eddied about the ship from morning to night, in order to believe it. Adults and children, both men and women left imprints of their palms on the ship. Reporters of different publications, and devotees of photography and motion pictures expended thousands of meters of film to immortalize the ship *en face*, in profile. . . .

The New York Times acknowledged the Soviet space exhibit as "the event of the show." The newspaper wrote that although ultimately the Americans had succeeded in producing powerful space ships, they were greatly impressed by the complexity of the jet system of the Vostok, in which twenty engines can be started simultaneously with a synchronous precision and develop the same thrust. A correspondent of the Associated Press reported that a three-stage Vostok rocket of the same type as the one in which the first Soviet cosmonaut soared into orbit had caught the center of attention. The principal surprise was the fact that the engine of this ship exhibited a very large number of nozzles. The first stage was made up of a bank of five jet engines, each engine being provided with four exhaust nozzles. In addition, the first stage had a total of twelve small engines intended for purposes of guidance and control.

These are present-day comments of the American press. Yet it will be worthwhile to recall what they wrote on April 12, 1961.

"The flight of the satellite ship Vostok marks man's crossing the threshold of the universe." (New York *Herald Tribune*.)

"A country that has produced an accelerator with the enormous power capable of launching a five-ton ship with a man aboard, and the technical know-how which would bring him back . . . has taken an enormous stride forward into a new era." (New York *Journal American*.)

The first flight of Soviet cosmonaut Yury Gagarin was not just any ordinary step into space, but signified the start of a new era in the mastery of outer space, also ushering in the beginning of a new epoch in the exploration of the Universe.

At one time, while engaged in working out the principles of cosmonautics, Konstantin Tsiolkovsky wrote as follows: "In many instances, I am compelled to conjecture and assume. I have no misgivings and know full well that not only do I fail to solve a problem in its entirety, but that there is a residual amount of work to be done which is a thousand-fold the work I have already put in. . . ."

Soviet scientists, engineers and cosmonauts continued pursuing this work and expanding it with the accomplishment of each successive flight. Every experiment in space introduces a new element in the exploration of the universe. As a matter of fact, from a single orbit around the earth to a twenty-four-hour flight (1962, German Titov), from a group flight over a period of several days (1962, Andrian Nikolayev and Pavel Popovich; 1963, Valentina Tereshkova and Valery Bykovsky) to the flight performed by the Voskhod (1964, Vladimir Komarov, Konstantin Feoktistov and Boris Egorov), and up to Aleksei Leonov's walk in space (1965), entire stages in the development of cosmonautics have been covered.

Of no less importance for the further mastery of space are the flights of the Soviet lunar stations. The scientists of the U.S.S.R. have succeeded in solving the problem of the soft landing of an apparatus on the surface of another celestial body, which is of paramount importance for future cosmic explorations and for orbiting artificial satellites around them. Ensuring a high degree of reliability and stability of performance in the equipment is of particularly great importance in this connection.

Two stations, Luna-9 and Luna-13, have made successful landings on the Moon, while Luna-10, Luna-11 and Luna-12 are orbiting the Moon as artificial satellites.

Soon scientists will be taking part in exploratory space flights, as was in fact the case in the flight of the Voskhod, in which Konstantin Feoktistov was the scientific specialist and Boris Egorov the physician. Conditions have now reached the stage where astronomers, physicists, biologists, medical personnel, and engineers will be able to participate in space flights, and where continuous and most diversified observations and explorations can be conducted under conditions of space travel.

The development of space flight leads to the expansion of the scope of man's activity in space. After the first walk in space, accomplished by Aleksei Leonov, and the performance of experiments outside of the ship by the American cosmonauts of the Gemini project, there will unquestionably be more complex and prolonged flights in which cosmonauts will have a goodly share of the work to perform. From experiments, they will go on to assembling and fitting together orbital stations and laboratories.

A pilot-cosmonaut of the U.S.S.R., Colonel Andrian Nikolayev, writes as follows on this subject:

". . . Even at this stage we can state with good reason that one of the first kindred professions which we, the cosmonauts, will have to master will be the profession of orbital fitter. Ours will be the job of splicing and bolting, of taking trips outside of the ship, to move in open space, of coupling ships, and beyond that, it will also be our job to erect large structures by combining individual sections."

An important stage in solving the problem of creating an orbital station, and its assembly in space, is the joining of two space ships directed to travel orbits in close proximity with the least possible capability of moving farther apart. A most complex system for achieving a rendezvous on command from the earth immediately after the second ship has been put into orbit was tested as far back as 1962 at the time of the group flight of Soviet cosmonauts Nikolayev and Popovich. Here is what Andrian Nikolayev himself had to say about it:

Still fresh in my memory are those minutes during the group flight of Vostok-3 when Vostok-4 was launched. At the time, I had already spent a 24-hour day in space. The path of the next revolution ran over the area of the Baikonur Cosmodrome. At that very instant, Vostok-4 started. It went into orbit in the immediate proximity of my ship. I observed a brilliant little star. It was moving slowly against the background of a black sky. That was in fact the ship of Pavel Popovich. The distance between the ships at that moment was no more than six and a half kilometers.

Thus, for the first time in history, space ships came close to each other. I recall that we did not make use at the time of the maneuvering devices. What we demonstrated at the time of our flight, was only the fact that there was a possibility of bringing the ships into orbits in close proximity to each other; but this was of great importance, since it was an absolutely requisite stage for the eventual rendezvous, inasmuch as the cosmic objects must be brought into close proximity to each other before a rendezvous is effected.

The problems of exploration and utilization of outer space have attracted the attention of many scientists throughout the world. At the Eighteenth Regular Congress of the International Astronautical Federation, which lasted from October 9 to October 15, 1966, in Madrid, more than a thousand delegates from thirty-three countries convened.

In the bio-astronautical section and in the section on space physiology, which was under the direction of a Soviet scientist, corresponding member of the Academy of Sciences of the U.S.S.R. O. G. Gazenko, an analysis of the results of physiological studies carried out as part of the Gemini program (address by H. Berry) aroused particular attention, along with a report concerning the results of biological research on an artificial earth satellite, Cosmos-110 (in addresses by V. Parin, B. Egorov and R. Baevsky). In a series of papers, considerable attention was given to methods of preventing disturbances of the human circulatory system under conditions of prolonged weightlessness.

A special meeting was devoted to the problems of life-support systems and the efficient performance of work by cosmonauts when they make excursions outside of the ship into open space, and in the event of a depressurization of the cabin. A representative of NASA (U.S.A.), P. Johnston, described and analyzed the space used by the Gemini astronauts for walks in space outside their ships.

Professor A. M. Genin (U.S.S.R.), Doctor of Biological Sciences, reported on the results of investigations conducted to determine the effects of a prolonged (up to seven full days) and continuous stay in the space suit under conditions simulating a flight in a depressurized cabin. The possibilities as well as the limits of utilization of the latent heat of vaporization of perspiration directly from the surface of the body, as the only means of heat dissipation, were demonstrated.

Several papers dealt with the problems encountered by cosmonauts in moving about in outer space with the aid of individual backpacks, and an analysis of man's capability of performing a whole series of operations outside of the space vehicle.

The development of outer space exploration and the increased number of measurements in space have brought about an overloading of the lines of communication between ground stations, unmanned scientific instruments and pilot-controlled spacecraft. A paper delivered by the Soviet scientist I. Akulinichev was devoted to the selection of the most important medical and biological information for transmission from outer space to the Earth. This problem will be solved by a special airborne computer which will become a sort of filter, relieving the ground stations of the task of processing an enormous quantity of telemetric data. The use of electronic computers aboard the space ships will increase the efficiency of scientific research.

The problems of the exploration of the Moon are becoming ever more significant. One of the previous Congresses of the International Astronautical Federation, dealt with the problems of organizing an international scientific station on the Moon. The Lunar Theme at this Congress was covered in a number of medical and biological papers. Scientific ideas, as a rule, precede technical progress and actual events. The Congress participants discussed such problems as the organization of work and rest for the lunar explorers, ways and means of moving across the Moon's surface, and how to preserve man's efficiency under conditions that are alien to him.

More than thirty papers delivered at the Congress dealt with the problem of using space instruments for the practical needs of mankind. Sputniks and manned space ships are capable of considerably improving meteorological services, of rendering forecasts more operative and accurate, and of warning in advance the populations of those regions of the earth threatened by typhoons, storms and other natural calamities. The Polish scientist Lunk proposed that a study be made of the possibilities of establishing a system of space communication for worldwide education. The satellites of such a system would serve only for the transmission of programs of general education. Appearing on radio and television channels, the leading scientists of the world would be able to carry knowledge to young people everywhere on the globe.

Ernst Kolman,* a noted Soviet scientist, Doctor of Philosophical Sciences and Professor of Mathematics, member of the Czechoslovak Academy of Science, and a man with an amazing personal history, has dedicated his work to the social aspects of the problem of outer space and society. Here is the reply he gave in answer to the questions posed to him by A. Romanov, a TASS correspondent.

"Why is it already necessary today to study and gain control of outer space?" was the question addressed to Kolman. "Is not mankind striving a bit too soon to get beyond the earth's boundaries?"

Kolman replied as follows:

It is a perfectly legitimate question. It is a known fact that two-thirds of the population of our planet do not eat their fill, and that about half of the people living in poorly developed countries die in childhood. Why then expend all of these enormous resources on space research, instead of expending them on the satisfaction of everyday needs here on earth?

The fact is that mankind has no right to concern itself only with the present day, leaving the future out of consideration. The earth's population is growing steadily and doubles approximately every fifty years. Along with it, the needs of each human being from the standpoint of material and cultural requirements grow steadily. The satisfaction of these needs demands ever greater expenditures of energy and raw materials.

It has been calculated that given the present state of science and technology, it would be possible to feed 13 billion people and that in the future when all of the resources of this earth have come under man's control, it would be possible to feed a population a hundred times greater than the numbers now living on earth. And yet, it seems to me, even on the most optimistic assumptions, one could not take it

---

* E. Kolman, of Czech nationality, one of the first fighters of the international brigades that fought in the ranks of the Red Army against the counterrevolution and the interventionists during the years of the civil war. In the trying year of 1918, he joined the Communist Party, remaining faithful to it throughout his life. On May 1, 1919, during a holiday celebration, Ernst Kolman was introduced to Lenin. Learning that the young man had a philosophical and mathematical education, Ilyich advised him to engage in science. After the end of the civil war Ernst Kolman followed this advice.

for granted that mankind will remain forever within the bounds of this earth, and that it will be able to provide for itself the necessary nurture and living space. It will be inescapably necessary for it to move out into outer space.

This is not only my personal viewpoint. However, there is also another viewpoint which contends that the population increment will be so regulated that there will be no need of transferring some part of the population to the other planets of our solar system.

Another problem is this: Sooner or later a time will come when the raw material resources and the energy available will become insufficient to satisfy the needs of this earth. I am convinced that sooner or later, we will find ourselves forced to exploit the Moon and other cosmic bodies.

There is also another reason which prompts us to take a look into the cosmos. To be sure, today it might appear somewhat theoretical and speculative, but be that as it may, we cannot permit ourselves to keep it entirely out of account. Sometime in the future, some hundreds of millions of years hence, the conditions of the solar system (the distance between the Earth and the Sun and solar radiation) will undergo a change. Conditions which are adverse to life on earth are apt to develop. However, mankind will not sit by passively awaiting its own extinction. It is likely that the problem of moving on to other cosmic bodies or of the building of artificial residential planets will take on concrete importance. And all of this is inconceivable without man's excursion into space.

For this reason, I am convinced that the first steps in the sphere of cosmonautics are by no means premature. This is only the beginning, and the initial steps that are now being taken are only the start of long preparation for mankind's cosmic era, and for man's conditioning so that he will be able to live under non-terrestrial conditions.

The mastery of outer space is of course associated with a great risk. But this in fact is true of man's entire history of struggle for mastery over the elements of nature. How many human sacrifices have been made toward achieving it! There is not a single sphere of science or technology wherein discovery and invention has not exacted an enormous price, namely, the lives of the finest of the finest.

"What effect did man's journey into space have on our scientific and technological progress?"

I have already partially answered this question. I only want to repeat that once science becomes free of its terrestrial limitations, it will also discard the notion that our "terrestrial" laws have universal validity. However, the effect on scientific and technological progress is already in evidence at this early stage of probing into outer space. Many of the materials, facilities and instruments which have been produced for space exploration have been found to be unusually useful on earth. Special satellites have already been used in establishing radio communication and telecasting from one end of the world to the other. In the future, these will be used to introduce a radical improvement in weather forecasting, and in providing a warning system in the event of natural catastrophes. Cosmonautics lends an impulse to the development of many branches of industry, such as electronics, radio engineering, telemechanics, the chemistry of refractory materials, rocket building, microelectronics, and the technology of quantum generators. Cosmonautics has accelerated the development of cybernetics (and it would have been entirely out of the question without cybernetic devices).

"What grounds does mankind have to hope for the realization of Tsiolkovsky's idea concerning the conquest of near-solar space?"

The coming of the cosmic era has not only been foretold by Tsiolkovsky, but also prepared for by the work he has accomplished. We reached its threshold on October 4, 1957, when the first artificial earth satellite was launched in the Soviet Union. The significance of our earliest cosmic steps could not possibly be overestimated. Man's excursion into outer space emancipates us from many terrestrial limitations that have hitherto set the limits of mankind's economic, technological and scientific development.

To begin with, our capabilities for transforming our own planet will become almost limitless, as we will be able to draw raw materials and energy from the natural resources of the cosmic bodies that are nearest to us. Moreover, advancement in the cosmic era calls for the concentration of not only all the scientific, technological and material means of our planet, but also for the collective efforts of people with higher physical and intellectual capabilities. And in fact, such people are apt to appear as a result of the new advance in the sphere of social consciousness under conditions of peace, true freedom and brotherhood of nations.

The carrying of astronomical instruments beyond the bounds of the terrestrial atmosphere, which is deleterious to them, will cause a manifold increase in the radius of the universe under observation. It will become possible to solve many hitherto unsolved problems of astronomy, physics, chemistry, geology and unquestionably also to discover new and unexpected phenomena. The biological sciences will receive a powerful stimulus.

The path from the plow to the space rocket is not only the path traversed by Russia; it is also the path of mankind as a whole towards the complete victory of brotherhood, equality and of all human ideals towards which mankind has been aspiring throughout its entire history.

Storming Heaven. In 1871, Karl Marx, speaking of the Paris Communards who sought to establish a government free of exploitation, referred to them as "those who stormed heaven." No one suspected at the time how much insight was contained in these words.

In the twenties of our century the Danish writer Martin Andersen-Nexo uttered these prophetic words: "The old world came to an end by virtue of the fact that its analysis went so far as to probe into the mystery of the Sun and the stars so that it was able to determine their weight with a precision within one pound. Yet it has done nothing to weigh out bread to the hungry. Revolution means a complete revaluation of the world. The proletariat has reshuffled in man's mind all phenomena, and it was the first to show man's problems in their true sequence. Its point of departure was the weighing out of bread. This is the way it began, but the day will come when it will reach the stars."

And the day has come.

To storm the heavens is not a simple matter. Mankind is paying with the lives of its finest, most courageous sons for its efforts to probe the mystery of the universe.

On April 24, 1967, as he was completing his test flight on the space ship Soyuz-1 Colonel Vladimir Komarov, an engineer, one of the first conquerors of outer space, twice-decorated hero of the Soviet Union, and a pilot-cosmonaut of the U.S.S.R., met his tragic death.

He was born on March 16, 1927, into the family of a worker. His childhood dream was to become a pilot on a fighter plane.

Having graduated from a specialized secondary school, Vladimir Komarov entered the Military Aviation School at Batai, graduating with good results in 1949, and serving thereafter in the fighter plane section of the Air Force.

Commencing in 1954, he studied at the Zhukovsky Military Aviation Engineering Academy, graduating in 1959.

As one of the gifted pilot engineers, he was assigned to the testing of new models of aircraft. On this job, his great capabilities as a competent organizer and engineer were discovered. The talents of Vladimir Komarov were manifested especially in the cosmonauts detachment, which he joined in 1960.

With an uncommon sense of responsibility, Vladimir Komarov persisted in his mastery of the most recent developments in space technology, fulfilling perfectly the program of flying, parachuting and special training.

In 1964 Komarov was entrusted with the responsible task of heading the crew of the first Soviet multiseater spacecraft Voskhod, and of carrying out an intricate program of scientific investigations and tests in outer space. This assignment was fulfilled with credit and honor.

On April 23, 1967, a new space ship, Soyuz-1, piloted by Vladimir Komarov, was put into orbit for the purpose of performing flying tests.

During the test flight, which continued for more than twenty-four hours, the cosmonaut carried out fully the scheduled program, which involved testing the various systems of the new ship, and all of the scientific experiments assigned to him. In flight he maneuvered the ship, testing its principal systems under various sets of conditions, and furnished a skilled evaluation of the technical features of the new spacecraft.

On April 24, when all of the test programs had been completed, Komarov was instructed to terminate his flight and effect a landing.

After he had performed all of the operations necessary for the purpose of landing, the ship successfully cleared all of the most difficult and crucial re-entry maneuvers in the dense strata of the atmosphere, and cancelled out completely the original cosmic speed.

However, on the opening of the primary parachute canopy at an elevation of seven kilometers, the ship failed to lose speed, owing to a snarling of the parachute's shroud line. This ended the life of an outstanding cosmonaut, a test engineer of space ships. He died having made a priceless contribution to the field of development and improvement of space technology. His memory, like the memory of the American cosmonauts who died in the tragic accident at Cape Kennedy, will eternally be cherished by the grateful inhabitants of this earth. The work of those who have laid down their lives is carried on by their friends and colleagues. The torch has been passed on to the younger generation as well.

The very first probe into space fired the hearts of many young men and women with a dream of taking part directly in the conquest of the Universe. The most impatient among them addressed themselves to the central institutions with an urgent plea to enroll them as candidate pilot-cosmonauts, or to be utilized in any work directly associated with the conquest of outer space. After the death of Vladimir Komarov, the flood of these letters swelled considerably. Many others decided to organize into circles, detachments, sections and schools of young cosmonauts for the purpose of studying the fundamentals of aviation and cosmonautics. And so, in many towns and workers' settlements, in numerous collective farms and state farms, clubs and schools of young cosmonauts sprang up.

The first club of this kind in the country appeared in Leningrad in April 1961 at the municipal children's park, immediately after the outer space flight of Yuri Gagarin. The organizers of the club, twelve young men and women, did not have any material means at their disposal, not even a separate room for the work they had set themselves to do. Nevertheless, with the aid of their elder friends, they were able to establish their club so that it became widely known. It attracted not only students in senior classes, but also students of technical schools and higher educational institutions. Articles appeared in newspapers and periodicals concerning the very interesting and useful activity of the club. From various towns and cities of the Soviet Union, and even from Bulgaria, Cuba, France, Canada and other countries, many letters poured into the club with requests for information concerning the work that was being done.

At present, this group, which calls itself the Y. A. Gagarin Club, has two hundred members. They are studying astronomy, aircraft and rockets, and radio engineering, as well as aviation and space medicine. They are going through preparatory physical and parachute training and preliminary training courses. For those who are interested, special courses have been organized for the study of physics and higher mathematics. The practical work is performed at the Military-Medical Academy, at a higher aviation school of Civil Aviation, at the Mechanical Institute, at the Aerosport Club of the Voluntary Society for Assisting Army, Air Force and Navy, and at the Planetarium. Classes are conducted on a voluntary basis without any remuneration by experienced instructors in given specialities as well as by scientific workers and university professors. The Chief Marshal of Aviation, Alexander Novikov, twice hero of the Soviet Union, is furnishing considerable aid to the club as regards the organization of the teaching system. The members of the club have a very cordial attitude towards their teachers and study diligently to master their two-year course. Some of them, under the guidance of scientists, take part in scientific experiments. Their study and work at the club enables young men and women graduating from secondary school to pick their profession conscientiously. Some of them enroll in aviation schools of the Air Force and Civil Aviation, or in civilian universities, or civil institutions of higher learning in their favorite subject, while still others, having mastered the skill of radio operator, take positions with Aeroflot.

The activities of the club also include lectures and discussions, contests and quizzes, as well as group attendance at movies and theater performances, chats with notable representatives of aviation and cosmonautics and with the heroes of the Great Patriotic War. During the summer vacation, members participate in walking tours, as well as sports competitions. All of these activities awaken a keen interest among the members of the club and weld them into one big family.

And so it goes on throughout the entire country. The storming of heaven continues. A Soviet Venus-4 spacecraft made a soft landing on Venus in October 1967 and transmitted the first data about this mysterious planet. Soon we shall learn about new achievements and new names will rise to our lips. However, none of us will ever forget the day on which the new era was inaugurated.

INDEX